Return code

The UPS Store

No Box No Label

Quantitative-Qualitative Friction Ridge Analysis: An Introduction to Basic and Advanced Ridgeology

Acquiring Editor:	(insert name)
Project Editor:	(insert name)
Marketing Manager:	(insert name)
Page design:	(Optional, only if new interior design)
Cover design:	(insert name)
PrePress:	(insert technician's name)
Manufacturing:	Carol Royal

Library of Congress Cataloging-in-Publication Data

McLachlan, Alan
    Molecular biology of the hepatitis B virus / Alan McLachlan
        p. cm.
    Includes bibliographical references and index.
    ISBN 0-8493-7007-?
    1. Hepatitis B virus. 2. Biology—molecular. I. McLachlan, Alan. II. Title.
    [DNLM: 1. Hepatitis B virus. QW 710 G289h]
    QR749.H64G78 1998
    616'.0149—dc20
    DNLM/DLC
    for Library of Congress   9?-?????
                                                           CIP

No claim to original U.S. Government works
International Standard Book Number 0-8493-7007-?
Library of Congress Card Number 9?-?????
Printed in the United States of America 1 2 3 4 5 6 7 8 9 0
Printed on acid-free paper

*This book is dedicated
to my wife
Linda Anne*

About the Author

David R. Ashbaugh, a Staff Sergeant in the Royal Canadian Mounted Police, is the Detachment Commander in Hope, British Columbia, Canada. He is also the Director of Ridgeology Consulting Services, a company that specializes in friction ridge identification training for accredited police organizations, and sits on the Fellowship Board of the Canadian Identification Society, the Editorial Board of the Journal of Forensic Identification, and the Forensic Identification Standards Committee for the International Association for Identification.

Staff Sergeant Ashbaugh has been a sworn police officer for 32 years and has served the last 24 years as a Certified Forensic Identification Specialist. He is a Life Member of the Michigan-Ontario Identification Association, a Life Member of the Canadian Identification Society, a Distinguished Member of the International Association for Identification, a Fellow of the Fingerprint Society of the United Kingdom, a member of the Forensic Science Society of the United Kingdom, and a member of the Pacific Northwest Division of the International Association for Identification. He has presented expert evidence at various levels of court in the provinces of Ontario, Manitoba, and British Columbia in Canada, and in the U.S.

During the last 21 years, Staff Sergeant Ashbaugh has carried out extensive research into the scientific basis and methodology of the friction ridge identification discipline. In 1982 he coined the term "Ridgeology" to describe a modern evaluative friction ridge identification process based in science. He has published several papers on the subject, and has lectured extensively in North America, South America, and the U.K. His Ridgeology philosophy and methodology are taught at the Canadian Police College, the Ontario Police College, and other training facilities around the world. He is frequently called upon as a lecturer and as a consultant on friction ridge identification cases or training needs in both the national and international arenas.

Staff Sergeant Ashbaugh played a key role in bringing about changes to the Canadian Identification of Criminals Act. He has contributed to the Scientific Working Group on Friction Ridge Analysis, Study, and Technology chaired by the Federal Bureau of Investigation in the U.S.; the Province of British Columbia Criminal Justice Branch Database on Ridgeology; and the Training Branch of the Province of Alberta Attorney General's Office. He is a consultant to the Royal Canadian Mounted Police on Ridgeology, and is an ad hoc national and international consultant for friction ridge identification training and for operational cases. In 1999 Staff Sergeant Ashbaugh was a key witness for the U.S. Government during a Daubert Hearing when the friction ridge identification science was challenged in U.S. Federal Court in Philadelphia, Pennsylvania. He also played an active role in the Training the Trainers Program for the Association of Chiefs of Police Officers of the United Kingdom at New Scotland Yard in London, and the National Training Center for Scientific Support to Crime Investigation in Durham.

Acknowledgments

During the last 20 years there have been so many forensic identification specialists who have shared the vision of friction ridge identification evolving into a modern forensic science that I cannot list them all here. Those who have worked with me on the bench, forwarded problem prints, or have given a few words of encouragement will know inside who they are, that I often think of them, and that I am grateful for their assistance. Many are referenced in this book.

There are key people who have gone beyond the call of duty to assist and at times tolerate. My wife Linda is at the top of the list followed by my daughters Lisa and Rebecca. Without their support I would have given up on ridgeology years ago. David and Rhoda Grieve of Illinois have edited my scratchings for the *Journal of Forensic Identification* and have become dear friends. David, a world-ranking expert in his own right, has unselfishly given moral and technical support as needed during occasional dark periods over the years. Pat Wertheim of Forensic Identification Training Seminars in Oregon, a colleague, expert, friend, and dedicated instructor, has frequently shared his perspective on the science and is diligently working to pass on to others what he has learned.

Several organizations have contributed to the contents of this book directly or indirectly: Tulane Medical Center, Department of Anatomy, Tulane University, New Orleans, Louisiana; The Canadian Identification Society; The International Association for Identification; The Fingerprint Society; The Forensic Science Society; The Federal Bureau of Investigation; and especially the Royal Canadian Mounted Police, an organization I have served for the last 24 years of my 32-year police career. To all of these people and organizations, "Thank you."

x

Table of Contents

Preface   **xiii**

I   **Introduction**   **1**

The First Step toward Quantitative-Qualitative Analysis   1
The Ridgeology Revolution   7

II   **History of Friction Ridge Identification**   **11**

Primitive Knowledge   11
Early Pioneers   20
Fingerprinting in North America   34
Scientific Researchers   38

III   **The Friction Ridge Medium**   **61**

Structure of Friction Skin   61
Friction Skin Histology   67
The Growth of Friction Skin   74

IV   **The Identification Process**   **87**

Premises of Friction Ridge Identification   87
The Philosophy of Friction Ridge Identification   97
Human Sight   103
Methodology of Friction Ridge Identification   108
Friction Ridge Analysis   109
Friction Ridge Comparison   136
Friction Ridge Evaluation   144
Verification   148

V   **Poroscopy and Edgeoscopy**   **149**

Poroscopy   149
Edgeoscopy   158

VI   Friction Ridge Analysis Report   165

VII   Ridgeology Formula   171

VIII   An Introduction to Palmar Flexion Crease
        Identification   177

IX   The Beginning   203

Bibliography   205
Glossary   217
Index   227

Preface

The unique patterns of friction ridges may have been used as a method of personal identification for hundreds or even thousands of years. The true origin of friction ridge identification is shrouded in the history of the Orient and we may never learn exactly when the science began. In the West the science is now over 100 years old. It is therefore rather surprising to note that as an identification science it has matured more during the last 25 years than at any other time since its inception.

In 1973 the gradual evolution of the science surged dramatically into the future. That year, the identification community in North America embraced a new standard for friction ridge identification. The out-of-date static threshold identification ideology was unanimously rejected and replaced with a floating threshold philosophy where the worth of friction ridge formations is evaluated by an expert.

During the first few years this new philosophy caused some confusion. The relevance of the change in doctrine was not fully understood. Few could describe how the process was actually used during friction ridge comparison, other than the fact that there was no longer a specific minimum number of ridge characteristics required for individualization. As a result of this obvious lack of insight, the evaluative philosophy was likely adopted and readily accepted as a solution to an old and ambiguous question — How many points are enough? — rather than modernizing the friction ridge identification science in preparation for the future.

That position is supported by the literature of the day. Friction ridge identification journals do not contain sufficient investigation or scientific discussion on the topic to have justified such a major doctrine change. Had the discipline evolved naturally to the point where an identification could be based on a quantitative-qualitative analysis of friction ridge formations, the various identification and scientific journals would have reflected this. There would have been supporting articles and discussion papers published for several years prior to the evaluative process being accepted and used. Notwithstanding the absence of a practical protocol, from that time forward friction ridge identification was based on a quantitative-qualitative analysis of friction ridge formations. While the change in doctrine was in the best interests of the friction ridge identification science, it placed a great deal of responsibility on the shoulders of those who practice within the science.

For example, the responsibility of ensuring that one has adequate knowledge of friction skin formation and is aware of how that relates to the premises of friction ridge identification was left to the individual expert. Also left to the individual were developing an understanding of how the friction skin leaves latent or visible prints on substrates and the various distortions which may take place during that deposition, gaining an awareness of the current philosophy and methodology used to individualize friction ridge prints, and being cognizant of the morals and obligations demanded of those who pursue forensic science as a career.

Those issues are addressed in this book. My hope is that this information will assist you with fulfilling those responsibilities, and that it will play a role in your ability to pursue a career in the friction ridge identification science, a career based on knowledge, understanding, and integrity where you can master your craft with confidence and self-assurance.

Introduction

I

The First Step toward
Quantitative-Qualitative Analysis

Everyone the world over carries out the identification process mentally in exactly the same way. The ability to identify is a natural process inherent to the human brain. This process corresponds to the way in which we see and identify objects every day of our lives. Any identification process must mirror as closely as possible the brain's natural approach to this task. Such a process would be truthful and would accurately reflect what actually takes place during comparison and individualization. Philosophies that stray from this natural identification process will continually develop procedural flaws. The farther the doctrine is away from the natural process, the more difficult it will be to explain and defend, and the greater the opportunity to develop procedural flaws.

While the ability to identify is inherent, an understanding of the process and the ability to describe it is not. This has resulted in a hodgepodge of doctrine that is far removed from the truth. Generally, these doctrines require a certain leap of faith and many of the rules have no supporting rationale. Over the years, as flaws developed, new arbitrary doctrines were enacted to patch the defects. Eventually, hyperbole without substance exists and one must either modernize or put one's head in the sand. A few years ago a giant step was taken toward modernization of the friction ridge identification science.

During 1973, this major change in friction ridge identification doctrine took place in North America. After a three-year study by a committee formed by the International Association for Identification, referred to as the "Standardization Committee," the following statement was officially endorsed and readily adopted by all North American friction ridge identification specialists:

> The International Association for Identification assembled in its 58th annual conference in Jackson, Wyoming, this first day of August, 1973, based upon a three-year study by its Standardization Committee, hereby states that no valid basis exists at this time for requiring that a predetermined minimum

of friction ridge characteristics must be present in two impressions in order to establish positive identification. The foregoing reference to friction ridge characteristics applies equally to fingerprints, palmprints, toeprints, and soleprints of the human body.

This new philosophy immediately replaced the old static threshold process, or number of points philosophy. The number of points philosophy had been in use since the inception of the science just over 100 years ago. With this new doctrine, an opinion of identification could now be based on a varying number of points. A point or ridge characteristic is a location on a friction ridge path where something dramatic takes place. The ridge path may bifurcate, stop, start, or two ridge characteristics may combine to create another distinct formation. At the time, the change in doctrine appeared to be only a minor adjustment in identification philosophy but the consequences were far-reaching. In the beginning this new doctrine was not fully understood, leading to uncertainty and greater confusion as opposed to a solution.

Adding to the confusion, the original number of points philosophy was also not fully understood. Prior to the Standardization Committee an identification was based on a specific minimum number of ridge characteristics. In North America this threshold was set somewhere around the 10 or 12 characteristic marks. Originally, this number was arrived at through what can best be described as an educated conjecture, based on past observations, as to when there was thought to be enough detail in agreement to feel safe that an error could not be made.

While the threshold philosophy was thought to have been simplistic, that was not the case. There was more taking place during the comparison and counting of ridge characteristics than realized. For example, during a comparison based on a specific threshold, each ridge characteristic is compared as to its type and spatial location. These attributes were knowingly compared and counted by the examiner in an effort to meet the predetermined threshold. At the same time, however, the brain was observing and comparing the smaller intrinsic shapes found within the ridge characteristic configuration. The identification specialist was usually unaware of that aspect of the comparison. Further, as the surrounding ridge configuration was assessed as to its spatial interrelationship to the recognized ridge characteristics present, the brain also assessed the intrinsic shapes found on those neighboring ridges.

In past years this involuntary comparison of smaller ridge configuration was not recognized as part of the identification process. Most identification specialists believed that friction ridge identification was based on an agreement of ridge characteristic type and location only. There was little, if any, understanding of the value and interrelationship between intrinsic friction ridge details and ridge characteristics during comparison, but it is these small intrinsic shapes that permit us to differentiate between similar ridge characteristics of the same type, an issue that must be understood before evaluative friction ridge identification can be adopted.

Another factor added to the uncertainty. During most discussions of the identification process, many early authors referred to ridge characteristics as *points* or *points of comparison*. The use of the word *point* tended to remove the fact that there was a configuration or shape to the ridge characteristic being discussed. A ridge characteristic may at times be a single point of comparison, such as a bifurcation in a very poor quality print. There are also instances when one ridge characteristic has several points of comparison within its configuration. Such a case may arise when a ridge characteristic is in a very clear print and is found to have an unusual configuration. As the clarity of a print increases, the opportunity for the smaller details on the ridges to be visible also increases. These small details add complexity to the ridge characteristic configuration and are additional points of comparison the brain considers. Therefore, the clarity of the friction ridge print usually dictates the complexity of ridge formations available for comparison and their value or weight toward individualization.

Comprehending the interrelationship between clarity and the presence of small friction ridge details is another key aspect of quantitative-qualitative friction ridge analysis. Without a basic understanding of the clarity factor, a large void would be created in one's ability to understand and explain this new philosophy. This lack of understanding was reflected in the identification literature and pedagogy of the day. Most efforts to describe or defend the evaluative identification process were more an exercise in reciting rhetoric and dogma as opposed to describing a scientific process. Specific facts and logical interpretation were conspicuous by their absence.

On occasion, the failure to understand the relationship between clarity and intrinsic friction ridge details presented a dilemma that most experienced identification specialists will recognize. This dilemma can best be described with the phrase, "I know it is an identification, but I don't have enough points to take it to court." In hindsight it is not difficult to understand how this situation frequently arose. Considering our current understanding of clarity and the brain's role during comparison, the phrase should read, "My brain tells me it is an identification, but I do not have sufficient knowledge of how friction skin forms or an in-depth understanding of the identification process, therefore I cannot defend that opinion." In the years leading up to the Standardization Committee, many forensic identification specialists struggled with friction ridge comparisons involving prints of this nature. They knew in their own minds they were identifications, but the unknown print had so few ridge characteristics they were uncomfortable with taking the identification to court. Possibly the continual reoccurrence of this situation was another mitigating factor that smoothed the transition to the new identification philosophy without serious debate.

A fundamental circumstance that helped the new identification process gain acceptance was the fact that few identification specialists were challenged in court. Legal counsel shied away from dwelling on a science that was considered exact and infallible, a belief that was difficult to dispel without adequate and structured literature being available. Most challenges were haphazard at best, usually ill-prepared, and often confusing. The majority were doomed to fail. Each failure further entrenched the infallibility of the science.

It is difficult to comprehend that a complete scientific review of friction ridge identification has not taken place at some time during the last 100 years. A situation seems to have developed where this science grew by default. This is especially alarming in light of the magnitude of change contained in the new identification philosophy put forward in 1973. Had challenges periodically surfaced, not only of the new process but the whole basis of friction ridge identification, they would have benefited all. Challenges should be welcomed within a science as an opportunity to present the founding premises and demonstrate the strength of current methodologies. Challenges lead to open debate, published articles, and a platform of discussion from which all can learn.

In the past the friction ridge identification science has been akin to a divine following. Challenges were considered heresy and challengers frequently were accused of chipping at the foundation of the science unnecessarily. This cultish demeanor was fostered by a general deficiency of scientific knowledge, understanding, and self-confidence within the ranks of identification specialists. A pervading fear developed in which any negative aspect voiced that did not support the concept of an exact and infallible science could lead to its destruction and the destruction of the credibility of those supporting it.

The failure of the identification community to challenge or hold meaningful debate can also be partly attributed to the fact that the friction ridge identification science has been basically under the control of the police community rather than the scientific community. In the eyes of many police administrators, friction ridge identification is a tool for solving crime, a technical function, as opposed to a forensic science.

Friction ridge identification had become commonplace within the police universe. It was a weapon to be used as needed, similar to other gadgets attached to an officer's Sam Browne belt, used as required and then stored away awaiting the next call. While this approach was appropriate when addressing the role of a scenes of crime officer, it was not acceptable for governing the behavior of those engaged in a scientific role. Friction ridge identification is a forensic science. As such, those who carry out comparisons are in need of adequate training, continual maintenance, and structured practice.

Many police agencies completely overlook the fact that there are actually two separate roles with separate training needs involved in the duties of most identification specialists. One role is the scenes of crime officer fulfilling the police function of collecting evidence. The second is that of a forensic scientist comparing the evidence. The expert in the forensic scientist role must also have an in-depth knowledge of scenes of crime procedures and development methodology to carry out accurate analysis on friction ridge prints. The failure to recognize this need can produce a general passive attitude within the police community toward meeting the needs required to fulfill the scientific mandate. The most blatant example is the movement of personnel into identification services for very short tours of duty as fingerprint *experts*. As with other sciences, it takes considerable training and years of practice to become an expert.

This attitude has been reinforced by the friction ridge identification science itself. The role of the scenes of crime officer is continually emphasized in literature. Over the last few years most advancements that have taken place within the science are related to how friction ridge prints are developed, stored, or searched by computers. As a result, most available funding is allotted to furthering those developments. Little, if anything, has been reported on the importance and need for scientific knowledge, understanding the evaluative identification process, or the training necessary to be able to analyze, compare, and evaluate friction ridge prints. Apparently, it is assumed that anyone has the ability to compare friction ridge prints and form an unbiased opinion of individualization.

The duality of the identification specialist role can put experts in a rather awkward position. They are, in effect, serving two masters with, at times, differing agendas. The scenes of crime officer performs technical duties that are consistent with the police environment. Once a physical task is mastered it can be efficiently repeated. Basic training may last a few weeks. However, the identification specialist fulfills a role consistent with other forensic sciences. There is a need to remain abreast of current knowledge by reading various identification journals, and possibly by playing an active role in an identification association. While an identification technician may possibly be trained in months, training a friction ridge identification expert may take years.

Few police organizations have developed an infrastructure or have implemented the processes necessary to ensure their experts receive adequate scientific training. There is also a need for some form of national certification process as well as periodic quality review. Such a review should include performance testing, blind case testing, and a vehicle to disperse pertinent research material. Employers should be mandated to encourage active participation in identification and scientific associations and support that position with some manner of funding. Most of these considerations are a prerequisite in other forensic disciplines. Friction ridge identification is the most positive method of personal identification. It is also the most cost effective of the police forensic sciences. Unfortunately, it has been basically ignored or overshadowed by the scenes of crime function.

It is only during the last few years that some training institutions have begun to consider how to incorporate the basic rudiments of friction ridge quantitative-qualitative analysis into their courses of study. It has been more than 20 years since the Standardization Committee published its report. It is becoming more apparent as time passes that the friction ridge identification science is more vulnerable now than at any time in its history. It may be said that an old science is finally maturing, but while the movement is forward, the effort appears rudderless.

Due to current social trends and the financial challenges faced by all areas of law enforcement, it is important to be effective and focused with any changes made in the training and management of personnel. However, today citizens are demanding rightful process or they seek civil redress. It is becoming incumbent on the administrators of justice to ensure all those who purport to be forensic experts are truly experts. It is unfortunate that these issues are surfacing at a time when budget restraint is the norm in our society. One can only speculate that future costs, for continued non-action may far outweigh current savings.

The friction ridge identification science was recently challenged in the United Kingdom. During 1980 the Home Office commissioned a study of the then current 16-point fingerprint identification standard. Dr. Ray Williams, a forensic scientist, and Ian Evett, a statistician, were tasked to conduct the review. A working group was formed and various forensic identification specialists from several countries were interviewed and requested to carry out a few comparisons and report on their findings. An unflattering report entitled, "A Review of the Sixteen Points Fingerprint Standard in England and Wales," was presented to the Chief Constables Council in 1989 but was not accepted. The authors of the report recognized there was a need to modernize the identification process in the United Kingdom by developing a clear and structured identification doctrine, as well as ensuring that adequate training was made available and that there was some form of quality review.

In 1994 the 16-point standard was again reviewed by Deputy Chief Constable Reynolds of the Thames Valley Police. The recommendation from that review was similar to the first, that the police forces in England and Wales drop the static threshold identification philosophy and adopt a process based on quantitative-qualitative friction ridge analysis. The Chief Constables Council endorsed that recommendation and set a target date of April 3, 2000 for the change.

Challenges to the friction ridge identification science in North America have been informal, infrequent, and usually very subtle. The absence of a jurisdictional mandate within the science has permitted either easy deflection or dismissal of any concern as the musings of overly cautious lawyers or scientists. The challenges in the U.K. were officially sanctioned by the Home Office and cannot be dismissed. The challenge in the U.K. was the greatest provocation to the science since its inception at the turn of the century. Another court challenge, the Daubert hearing in the U.S. federal court in Philadelphia, PA, will continue to unfold over the next few years. The future will harbor many similar challenges.

While the review of the 16-point identification standard report was originally completed in 1989, it was not released until June, 1995 during a meeting in Israel. As a result of its release and the subsequent dialogue, the original International Association for Identification Standardization Committee resolution was reaffirmed with a slight variation.

The friction ridge identification specialists attending the international symposium on fingerprint detection and identification in Ne'urim, Israel held from June 26 through June 30, 1995, agreed upon the following resolution: "No scientific basis exists for requiring that a predetermined minimum number of friction ridge features must be present in two impressions in order to establish positive identification."

This resolution was unanimously approved and later signed by 28 identification specialists from Australia, Canada, France, Hungary, Israel, the Netherlands, New Zealand, Sweden, Switzerland, United Kingdom, and the United States. Unfortunately, the views expressed in many cases were the opinions of the scientists and forensic specialists present and were not binding or intended to represent their individual agencies or governments.

There is little doubt that there is a need for the forensic scientific community to become more involved with scrutinizing the scientific rationale behind friction ridge identification protocol and training. The release of the Home Office report at the Ne'urim symposium may be that first important step toward global agreement on friction ridge identification philosophy, methodology, professional standards, training, and quality control.

The Ridgeology Revolution

The years following the Standardization Committee report were somewhat confusing to those working within the friction ridge identification science.

Independently there were several individuals in North America carrying out research in an effort to identify the scientific basis of the new evaluative identification process and to understand its protocol. For some the research was for no reason other than to clarify the process in their own minds. Some researchers published their findings in forensic and identification journals while others did not. A few authors who presented their material at various identification conferences were at times met with some degree of suspicion from their peers.

During this time the friction ridge identification science continued to evolve slowly in other countries. The debate taking place in the U. K. is an example of healthy evolution. In North America, however, the sudden change in identification philosophy was like jumping out of an airplane to solve a weight problem; shortly after solving the weight problem a second problem surfaced involving a safe landing. The act of suddenly removing the static number of points required to form the opinion of identification, without thought of what process was to take its place, meant that immediate research, ideologies, philosophies, and methodologies had to be developed in a very short time to meet the growing need. This rapid progression is more akin to a revolution than normal evolution.

The term *ridgeology* was coined by the author in an article published in 1983. The rationale was that a new word would draw rapid attention to new ideas, new ideas that involved a more scientific approach required to meet the needs of the floating threshold protocol laid out by the Standardization Committee. While most -*ology* words tend to drop the *e*, here the *e* was intentionally left in place to attract more attention and initiate debate. While the word *ridgeology* was originally an attention-getting device it was also intended to focus on the fact that this information was based on empirical study and related scientific research. It was also meant to underscore that this new evaluative identification process was not business as usual. Over the years ridgeology has gained acceptance as a word describing a friction ridge identification process based on a quantitative-qualitative analysis as opposed to the old static threshed method.

Ridgeology can be defined as "The study of the uniqueness of friction ridge structures and their use for personal identification." Today, evaluative friction ridge identification or ridgeology has a strong scientific basis. The scientific knowledge supporting ridgeology has been extracted from various related sciences such as embryology, genetics, and anatomy. A clear identification process has also been developed consisting of a philosophy and methodology of identification.

The first part of this book reviews the history of friction ridge identification. The balance addresses the scientific basis and the various steps of the identification process. While discussing the scientific basis, the formation of friction skin is covered in some detail. That knowledge is required to understand the premises of friction ridge identification and how various ridge formations are applied and evaluated during the identification process.

The identification of manufactured and biological media is also discussed and related to friction ridge formations. A clear philosophy of friction ridge identification is established and the issue of probability identifications is briefly discussed. The methodology of friction ridge identification is broken down into segments and each segment is addressed. That is followed by the historical and practical aspects of *poroscopy* and *edgeoscopy*. A chapter is devoted to a new branch of forensic science, *Palmar Flexion Crease Identification*. The original paper on the subject was published in 1990 by the author. Since that time several important cases have been solved using palmar flexion crease identification. A method of preparing a written report of a friction ridge analysis, comparison, and evaluation is presented, and an example is included.

The level of knowledge required to function as a forensic identification specialist today is far greater than only a few years ago. This book will lay out the basic information one must understand and the various processes one must use. It cannot, however, supply the balance of the formula required to be an expert — *experience*, which can only be gained through years of practice. The number of years of practice required to make an expert depends on one's ability. It should be remembered that practice only counts as experience when it is carried out from a position of knowledge, and gaining knowledge is the purpose of this book.

The History of Friction Ridge Identification

Primitive Knowledge

The historical aspect of a forensic science, especially one as old as friction ridge identification, has limited value in the day-to-day operations of a forensic identification section. However, having a general knowledge of where the science originated and how it arrived at where it is today can only enhance the overall enlightenment of forensic identification specialists. Having background historical knowledge of a science underscores one's interest in that science. Also, knowledge of the historical aspect of a science is one area frequently addressed when testifying in court. An expert is expected to be conversant to some degree.

The history of a science is a record of discovery, research, verification, and practical application. The record usually stretches from inception to the present. Friction ridge identification has a hazy past. Its origin is buried deep in the past of the Orient. It is uncertain if those early people understood the individualizing aspect of friction ridges. Evidence from various parts of the ancient world has been used by some to imply that the people of those early times understood the significance and uniqueness of friction ridges. Today we can only review the evidence and, from the threads of information that are available, draw our own conclusions.

Kejimkujik Lake Petroglyph

Prior to written records we have only archaeological fragments to ponder and reflect on. One such archaeological fragment is an etching which leaves little doubt as to what the author wished it to represent. An outline of a hand was scratched into slate rock beside Kejimkujik Lake in Nova Scotia by an aboriginal Indian (Figure 2.1). The carving is an outline of a hand and fingers. Within the outline the flexion creases of the palm and fingers are depicted.

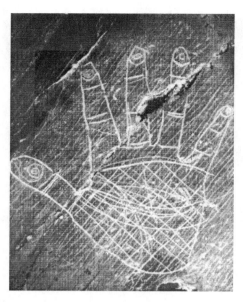

Figure 2.1 This petroglyph was found at Kejimkujik Lake. It can be dated before 1873, but it is considered to be at least several hundred years old.

Circular etchings on the finger tips are representative of friction ridge patterns and on the thumb a spiral whorl has been carved.

The original tracing of the petroglyph can only be dated to sometime before 1873, but the carving is considered to be at least several hundred years old. It is believed to be the first documented anthropological illustration depicting the friction ridges and flexion creases of the hand.

The Kejimkujik Lake carving has considerable historical significance. Although it does not demonstrate knowledge of the individuality of friction ridges or palmar flexion creases, it clearly illustrates an early awareness of the presence of those formations. It should be noted that without the hand outline the significance of the petroglyph may have been lost. Carvings of flexion creases or friction ridges on their own could easily have been interpreted as simply isolated scratchings or attributed to other designs found in nature.

L'ille de Gavrinis Stone Carvings

The significance of other ancient stone carvings has become suspect due to the lack of anatomical reference. The most famous example is a stone carving found on the L'ille de Gavrinis off the coast of France. Here a burial chamber, or dolmen, was discovered dating back to Neolithic times. The stone age chamber is embedded in a mound of earth and is constructed of one meter

Figure 2.2 This Neolithic carving was one of many similar stones adorning the wall of a burial chamber. Some interpret these marks as friction ridge patterns; others dismiss them as shapes found in nature.

size stone slabs. The stone slabs lining the inside of the passage way are adorned with various carvings. The carvings appear to be friction ridge formations depicting various patterns such as arches, whorls, looping formations, straight lines and other configurations (Figure 2.2).

Many anthropologists interpret these lines as representing finger or palm print patterns. There are just as many other experts who see ocean waves, wind blown grass, or a multitude of other natural shapes. The lack of an anatomical reference, as in the case of the Kejimkujik Lake carving, has left these carvings open to speculation.

Middle East Clay Pottery

Over the years archaeological excavations in the Middle East have recovered numerous specimens of ancient clay pottery. An example is shown in Figure 2.3. Some of this pottery dates back to before the first century A.D. Many specimens were found to have identifiable fingerprints impressed into their surfaces. Archaeologists have become familiar with the fingerprints of many of these early potters and have established when they were active by cross-referencing their fingerprints with other archaeological data. Many new specimens found at archaeological digs are immediately dated to a specific time frame by identifying the potter's fingerprints. Dating pottery in this manner is a bonus for archaeologists. Many ancient villages were often built on top of the ruins of earlier villages. The basements, wells, and other pits from a previous village were frequently filled in with available debris, including pottery shards, during the construction of the new village.

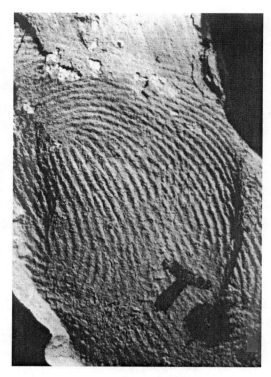

Figure 2.3 Potters' trademarks are used by archaeologists to date pottery shards found during excavations. Some potters' fingerprints are found on each piece of pottery.

Unlike stone carvings, fingerprints in pottery have an innate anatomical connection. The question arises as to their intent and purpose. Many fingerprints would have been deposited during the manufacturing process, but some fingerprints were placed in such a manner that it is obvious they were used as potters' trademarks. It is unknown whether the location of the fingerprint on the piece or the actual friction ridge pattern was used by the potter to identify his work. In either case the trademarks were used to prevent forgeries.

Fingerprint Trademarks in Clay

With the development of writing, historical events, contracts, laws, and day-to-day life were inscribed on clay tablets, buildings, pillars, and later on scrolls. Ancient scribes are reported to have used fingerprints to identify the author of a specific cuneiform manuscript. Archaeologists interpreting those ancient writings have found references describing that practice. Also, references by ancient historians have been found describing how finger seals were used on legal contracts in Babylon from 1855-1913 B.C. The finger impressions of the parties involved in a contract or agreement were apparently pressed into the clay surface along with the script. This practice identified the author and protected against forgery.

References dating from the rule of Hammurabi (1792-1750 B.C.) indicate that law officers were authorized to secure the fingerprints of arrested persons. Also, fingerprints were found on 3000-year-old clay slabs in King Tue-En-Khamin's tomb in Egypt. The fingerprints were pressed into the walls of the tomb creating intricate designs. Recently, during an excavation in northwest China, archaeologists recovered earthenware estimated to be 6000 years old. Several pieces were found to have identifiable fingerprints on them. Those fingerprints are considered to be the oldest found to date. While these references tend to be vague, they indicate that early civilizations were aware of the designs on their fingers.

Chinese Clay Finger Seals

Emperor Ts-In-She (246-210 B.C.) is reported as being the first Chinese Emperor to use clay finger seals for sealing documents. The documents of the time were wooden tablets or whittled pieces of bamboo bound together with string. The seal itself was a small dollop of clay. A carved stamp with a name or personal symbol was stamped on one side and a fingerprint was embossed on the other to prove authenticity (Figures 2.4, 2.5). Clay was used as seal material up to the Wei and Jin Dynasties (220-420 A.D.) Clay was abandoned as silk and paper began to be used as writing media.

Chinese Hand Prints

With the advent of silk and paper "Hand Prints" became the most common method of ensuring the genuineness of a contract. The right hand was simply traced or stamped onto a document. Figure 2.6 is a deed for the sale of land. The anthropometric values of hand size and shape, along with a signature, were often enough to ensure authenticity.

During 1975 in Yuen Meng County in China, bamboo slips were found describing a trial reported to have taken place during the Qin dynasty (300 B.C.). During a theft trial handprints were entered as evidence. A reference was also made to knee marks being found at several locations inside and outside the scene.

Deed of Hand Mark

Another anthropometric method used in early China was the "Deed of Hand Mark." This method involved marking the flexion crease location of each phalangeal joint of the right hand onto a document. In some cases the whole

Figures 2.4 and 2.5 The Chinese clay finger seal had a personal stamp on one side and a fingerprint on the other.

Figure 2.6 A Chinese hand print on a deed.

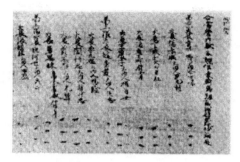

Figure 2.7 A Chinese Deed of Hand mark. The position of the phalangeal joints are at the bottom of the page.

hand was traced and the flexion creases of the fingers added to the tracing. Figure 2.7 is an army membership roster from 715 A.D. The names are above and the finger flexion creases are below.

Other Identification Methods

Other methods of identification used in ancient times are still used today. The Egyptians used detailed descriptions of a subject's physical features written out in longhand. The Chinese put notches randomly along the sides of writing tablets of duplicate contracts. The notches could be physically matched by holding the tablets together at some future time to ensure authenticity.

Fingerprint Identification Reference (650 A.D.)

The practice of notching wooden tablets was described by the Chinese historian Kia Kung-Yen in 650 A.D. While writing about an earlier time he said: "Wooden tablets were inscribed with the terms of the contract and notches were cut into the sides at the identical places so that the tablets could later be matched; thus proving them genuine; the significance of the notches was the same as that of the fingerprints of the present time."

In the last sentence of the quote Kia Kung-Yen clearly states that fingerprints are physically matched, just as the notches on the sides of the tablets were matched, to establish the authenticity of the documents involved. The comparison of the use of notches on tablets to the use of fingerprints establishes that fingerprints were used to identify people in 650 A.D.

Japanese Customs Adopted from China

Many of the laws and practices of China spread to surrounding nations through commerce, immigration, litigation, or conflict. It is reasonable to assume that the knowledge and use of finger and hand marks would also spread through these associations.

In 1894 Sir William Herschel, whose efforts while serving in India made him a prominent figure in the history of the fingerprint science, suggested that fingerprinting spread through the Orient due to his travel through neighboring countries. There is ample evidence, however, that the Chinese used their fingerprints in lieu of signatures prior to Herschel's time in India (Figure 2.8). Herschel's achievements are discussed later in this chapter.

Figure 2.8 This script is part of a Chinese land contract. The contract is signed with a fingerprint below a name.

A Japanese historian, Kamagusu Minakata, responded to Herschel's statement by drawing attention to the old Japanese custom of nail stamping. Legal papers were marked in ink using the top of the thumb and nail. While nail stamping cannot be considered a method of friction ridge identification, Minakata further comments about blood stamping. Apparently contracts were accompanied by a written oath confirmed with a blood stamp. The blood stamp was a print of the ring finger in blood drawn from that digit.

Minakata further quotes another historian from pre-Herschel days. He states that Churyo Katsurakwawa, a Japanese historian (1754-1808), wrote, "According to the 'Domestic Law' (Enacted in 702 A.D.), to divorce a wife the husband must give her a document stating which of the Seven Reasons was assigned for action. All letters must be in the husband's handwriting, but in case he does not understand how to write, he should sign with a fingerprint." An ancient commentary on this passage says, "In case a husband cannot write, let him hire another man to write the document...and after the husband's name, sign with his own index finger." Katsurakwawa felt that was perhaps the earliest reference of fingerprinting in Japanese literature.

The main points of the Japanese Domestic Laws were borrowed and transplanted from the Chinese Laws of Yung Hui (650-655 A.D.). This fact illustrates how Chinese customs, laws, and practices spread to other countries. Katsurakawa also stated that the Chinese apply the ends of the thumb and the four fingers on divorce papers, which they call "Shau-Mu-Ying" (hand pattern stamp).

Early Knowledge of Friction Ridge Individuality

Prior to the Tang dynasty (618-906 A.D.), the significance scholars placed on finger and hand prints is unknown. Our understanding and knowledge of the friction ridge science make it easy for us to accept the plausibility of Hammurabi's police fingerprinting criminals or Babylonian scribes signing their work with fingerprints to prevent forgery. The marking of pottery for decorative, symbolic, or trademark purposes obviously took place, as did accidental marking. It could be that most of the fingerprint signatures on documents from these early times were simply a token to express personal involvement with the creation of an item or the participation in an act. Similar symbolic gestures are still used today, such as swearing on a Bible prior to testimony in a court of law.

The ancient scholars prior to the first century understood the need for an independent method of personal identification. This is evident through the efforts taken to prevent forgeries and to ensure contracts were honored by using various methods such as anthropometric tracing, flexion crease marking, friction ridge signatures, or notches on the sides of writing tablets. The records are not clear as to exactly when it was realized that friction ridges were unique and could satisfy the personal identification need, but we can rest assured that the realization took place long before Herschel arrived in the Orient.

Early Pioneers

The early pioneers of the friction ridge identification science were generally government workers, police officers, or people who dabbled in friction ridge identification while employed in related scientific fields. They advanced our knowledge of friction ridges, applied the friction ridge identification system to various uses, devised a coherent classification system, and generally introduced the science to the West. Many of these people worked in environments very similar to our own.

Thomas Bewick (1753-1828)

One of the earliest and somewhat novel uses of fingerprints was in the form of a vignette or stamp. A fingerprint stamp was made by Thomas Bewick, a British author, naturalist, and engraver (Figure 2.9). Bewick made wooden engravings of fingerprints and published their images in his books. In two of the books he added "Thomas Bewick, his mark" under the impressions. Whether the prints were actually Bewick's is unknown, but considering the availability of the original models they likely were.

Bewick's carvings demonstrated extreme knowledge of friction ridge structure and overall pattern shape. Even pore openings were engraved along the ridge summits. Bewick may have understood the principle of individuality of fingerprints but his use of the finger marks in itself does not prove that.

Figure 2.9   A fingerprint stamp carved in wood by Thomas Bewick.

Sir William J. Herschel (1833-1917)

Sir William J. Herschel

Sir William J. Herschel is credited with being the first European to recognize the value of friction ridge prints and to actually use them for identification purposes. Herschel went to India in 1853 as a British administrator for the East India Company in Bengal. In 1858 he left the East India Company to become a member of the Civil Service of India. He was put in charge of a subdivision at Jungipoor on the Upper Hooghly River.

During his first year at Jungipoor he entered into a contract on behalf of the civil service with a local native, Radyadhar Konai, to supply road building material. Herschel had observed a local practice of putting a friction ridge print of the hand or finger beside a signature or mark on contracts. Contracts having signatures accompanied by a friction ridge print appeared to command more respect from the locals and disputes were less frequent.

On the back of the road contract Herschel asked Konai to apply his right palm print in ink (Figure 2.10). Later, Herschel claimed to have been the first to use friction ridge prints for personal identification purposes. His claim was based on the use of the palm print on the Konai contract. That claim was of course attacked almost from the beginning by historians. Indian authors and others have cited the use of palm prints and "Tip Sahib" (signature by impressions) as a practice and custom in India for hundreds of years.

Herschel refused to believe that the Chinese or anyone else used friction ridge printing for anything other than ceremonial purposes. In a letter published in *Nature* in 1894 he went so far as to describe how he used fingerprinting on a ship in the Indian Ocean in 1877 and that the Chinese may have caught on to the practice from that demonstration. Herschel described the "Tip Sahib" as a mere formality by illiterate persons who could not sign even a cross or caste mark.

In many cases Herschel was likely correct in assessing the average person's knowledge of the uniqueness of friction ridge prints. It is very hard to believe, however, that all people, including the various scholars of India at that time and of previous years, had blindly been using finger and palm prints for hundreds of years without some understanding of the basic principle of individuality. There is no evidence at the time of the Konai Contract that even Herschel himself understood individuality. He may have been simply

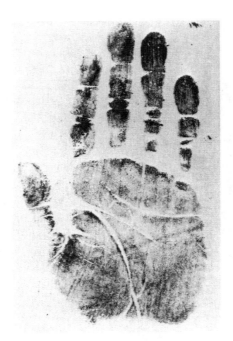

Figure 2.10   The palm print of Konai, a native of India, made by Sir W.J. Herschel in 1858. It is on the back of a contract between Herschel and Konai for road work.

following a custom of India that apparently caused locals to honor their contracts more faithfully.

With time, Herschel recognized the identification possibilities of friction ridges, especially fingerprints. In 1860 he was sent to Nuddea as Magistrate. In that capacity he expanded and promoted the use of fingerprinting to prevent various frauds. False impersonation and contract disputes were common. Some Caucasians had difficulty differentiating workers of Indian descent who had similar anatomical features. That ineptness only promoted the practice of false impersonation. One such plot used during that time was to feign the death of a prisoner or of someone under contract and replace him with a purchased corpse. Another was for some prisoners or their families to hire substitutes to serve prison sentences. On several occasions pension cheques were received and cashed long after the intended recipient was dead. Herschel realized that fingerprinting could eliminate most such fraudulent practices.

In 1877 Herschel was appointed Magistrate and Collector at Hooghly. He controlled the criminal courts, the prison, registration of deeds, and payment of government pensions. He implemented the use of fingerprinting in any area under his control. The system proved to be successful. On August 15, 1877 Herschel wrote what is referred to as the "Hooghly Letter" to the

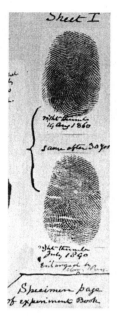

Figure 2.11(A)

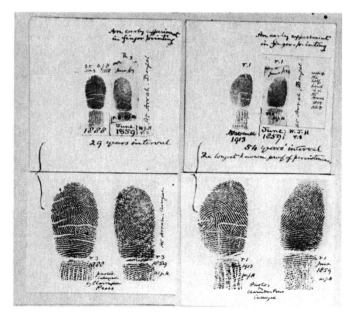

Figure 2.11(B)

Inspector of Jails and the Registrar General. Herschel described his ideas and suggested that the fingerprinting system be expanded to other areas. His request was denied. In 1879, in poor health, Herschel returned to England.

Herschel's experiments with friction ridge prints resulted in the first demonstration of friction ridge persistency. He first fingerprinted himself in 1859. Over the following years he reprinted himself and compared those prints with previously taken prints to ascertain if they had changed. Some examples of these experiments are shown inFigures 2.11A and 2.11B. These fingerprints were taken at 29-, 30-, and 54-year intervals. Herschel's left palm print can also be viewed in Figures 8.10A and 8.10B, taken first in 1860 and again in 1890.

Dr. J.C.A. Mayer (1788)

Although Herschel is usually credited as being the first fingerprint pioneer to realize the uniqueness of friction ridges, the facts do not support that. In 1788 Dr. J.C.A. Mayer of Germany, who will be mentioned again later in this chapter, published the following statement in his anatomical atlas: "Although the arrangement of skin ridges is never duplicated in two persons, nevertheless the similarities are closer among some individuals. In others the differences are marked, yet in spite of their peculiarities of arrangement all have a certain likeness." This deduction was published 100 years before the Konai contract. Also, the hundreds of years of use in China and other Oriental countries would lead one to believe that individuality was already understood before Herschel's claim. A truer statement may be that Herschel was likely the first man in the British Empire to understand the value of friction ridges for personal identification.

Dr. Henry Faulds (1843-1930)

Another prominent pioneer of the time was Dr. Henry Faulds. Faulds volunteered as a medical missionary to the Foreign Mission Committee of the Church of Scotland in 1871 and was appointed to the Darjeeling Station in India. He left India the following year and went to Tsikiji, Japan with the Foreign Mission Board of the United Presbyterian Church of Scotland. By 1875 Faulds had opened a missionary hospital and a year later started a medical school. Faulds may have been exposed to fingerprints during his year in India or through his medical work in Japan, for by 1879 he had begun to study the subject in depth. In February 1880 Faulds sent a letter to Charles Darwin telling him of his studies and requesting assistance. Darwin, who was rather ill at the time, forwarded the letter to his cousin Francis Galton.

In a letter a few months after sending his letter to Darwin, Faulds commented that his studies were only one year old. When examined in this light, Faulds's letter to Darwin contains some profound information. Faulds mentions in the third sentence that fingerprints can be classified easily and that ridge detail is unique. He points out the value of fingerprinting as being in "medico legal studies" and comments that photographs of people change over the years but rugae (friction ridges) never change. Faulds also

Dr. Henry Faulds

mentions apprehending criminals by locating fingerprints at crime scenes. Further references also mention how the Chinese fingerprint criminals and the Japanese and Egyptians use fingernail stamps for the same purpose. It appears as though Faulds had tapped into a source of information that gave him considerable knowledge in a very short period of time.

On October 28, 1880, prior to Darwin's return letter reaching him, Faulds, published a letter to the editor of *Nature* entitled, "On the Skin — Furrows of the Hand." He suggests that all his conclusions were original ideas. In the last paragraph of his letter he states, "I have heard, since coming to these general conclusions by original and patient experiment, that the Chinese criminals from early times have been made to give the impressions of their fingers, just as we make ours yield their photographs." He further says, "It need not surprise us to find that the Chinese have been here before us in this as in other matters." Past authors have found it very difficult to believe that Faulds did not receive information from the native scientists with whom he worked in India or Japan.

Both Herschel and Faulds published letters in *Nature*. Herschel claimed he had used fingerprints for years in India and offered the "Hooghly Letter" as documented proof. Faulds claimed *careful study* in Japan and to be the first person to publish notice on the subject in English literature.

Both men have contributed to the science of friction ridge identification. Herschel used and experimented with fingerprints for years beginning in 1860, possibly not realizing the impact his knowledge would have outside of India until Faulds published his letter in *Nature*. Faulds did publish his findings first and was the first of the two to comment on the use of fingerprints to solve crime. Both men are true pioneers and their main contribution was in the passing on of an ancient Oriental science. Their basic ideas have been augmented over the years with more recent anatomical information from the West. From their early contributions a massive amount of study and literature has been created.

Thomas Taylor (1877)

Although Faulds is given credit for being the first fingerprint pioneer to suggest that fingerprints could be used to solve crime, he was not the only one of that opinion. The July 1877 issue of *The American Journal of Microscopy and Popular Science* contained the text from part of a lecture by Thomas Taylor, a microscopist with the Department Agriculture, Washington, D.C. The note stated:

> Hand Marks Under the Microscope, — In a recent lecture, Mr. Thomas Taylor, microscopist to the Department of Agriculture, Washington, D.C., exhibited on a screen a view of the markings on the palms of the hands and the tips of the fingers, and called attention to the possibility of identifying criminals, especially murderers, by comparing the marks of the hands left upon any object with impressions in wax taken from the hands of suspected persons. In the case of murderers, the marks of bloody hands would present a very favorable opportunity. This is a new system of palmistry.

No further information has surfaced on Mr. Thomas. It would be interesting to ascertain if he had any exposure to the events taking place in the orient or if he independently came to the same conclusion.

Alphonse Bertillon (1853-1914)

Alphonse Bertillon

The first truly scientific method of criminal identification of which we are aware was devised by Alphonse Bertillon in Paris France. His system was called *anthropometry* or *Bertillonage*. Bertillon came from a family of scientific background. His father, Dr. Louis Adolphe Bertillon, was a distinguished physician, statistician, and Vice President of the Anthropological Society of Paris. His grandfather, Archille Guillard, was a well known naturalist and mathematician. Alphonse, however, was a poor student and apparently lacked the talent or drive needed to be successful in the scientific arena.

In 1879, through his father's good connections, Bertillon was appointed to a clerk position in the

Prefecture of Police. His job consisted of filling out and filing criminal information cards. Bertillon is described as being a sarcastic and bad-tempered individual and most of his colleagues avoided him. Bertillon had a great deal of time to himself as a clerk and came to the conclusion that the current method of establishing the identity of criminals was a tremendous waste of money and human energy. Furthermore, most criminals escaped detection by simply changing their names each time they were arrested.

As a young boy Bertillon had heard his grandfather, father, and other scientists discuss statistics and the hypothesis that no two people have identical physical measurements. From this Bertillon conceived the idea of using anatomical measurements to distinguish one criminal from another. He decided to use various body measurements such as head length, head breadth, length of left middle finger, length of left cubit (forearm), length of left foot, body height, face breadth, face height, and other descriptors including features such as scars and hair and eye color to distinguish criminals. This system would be capable of compiling data on a subject that could be used to identify individuals despite disguises, name changes, or mutilation.

Bertillon asked for permission to measure the criminals who were brought to him for registration. Even though his superiors and fellow clerks felt he was eccentric, and most doubted his idea, he was given the authority to take the necessary measurements and to compile a data bank on the criminals he registered. He sent several reports to the Prefect of Police requesting that anthropometry be adopted throughout the department. After several requests had been turned down, a new Prefect of Police who was a friend of Bertillon's father took office. As a result, the new Prefect finally allowed Bertillon to introduce anthropometry on an experimental basis for three months.

On February 20, 1883, less than two weeks before the experiment was over, Bertillon made his first identification. He discovered that a man named Martin was attempting to pass himself off as Dupont. That identification vindicated Bertillon and more identifications followed. The success of anthropometry spread to other countries; many even set up anthropometry laboratories. However, most would soon replace anthropometry with a new identification method called fingerprinting.

In 1888 Bertillon invited the British scientist Sir Francis Galton to Paris. The purpose of Galton's visit was to prepare for a presentation he had been requested to give on Bertillonage at the Royal Institution. The meeting also served to allow Bertillon to increase his knowledge of fingerprints. Galton examined and evaluated both systems. He eventually came to the realization of the superiority of fingerprints. That was the beginning of the end for anthropometry.

In the beginning Bertillon felt that fingerprints were not very practical due to the lack of a classification system for large collections. As time went on, he eventually included fingerprints on the rear of his anthropometric cards as a final check of identification. Upon Bertillon's death in 1914, Bertillonage was discarded in France and replaced by fingerprint identification.

Sir Francis Galton (1822-1911)

Sir Francis Galton

Sir Francis Galton has been described as one of the greatest scientists of the 19th century. Galton's early schooling included medicine, mathematics, and chemistry. The passing of his father, a wealthy banker, left Galton independently wealthy at a young age. He had an insatiable desire for travel in his early years. His travels, some into unexplored areas of South-West Africa, were recognized by the Royal Geographical Society for their scientific contribution. In 1853 Galton was elected a fellow of the Royal Geographical Society and later the Royal Society for his achievements.

Galton wrote articles designed to popularize the subjects that attracted his diverse interests. He published over 200 papers and nine books. Above all, he was an anthropologist. Eventually his keen interest in anthropology would be aroused by the possibilities for fingerprints, leading to several published articles and a book on the subject.

Galton first encountered fingerprinting sometime before 1880. In a letter responding to his cousin Charles Darwin, discussing Faulds' idea about fingerprinting, he describes how he looked into a Chinese plan of fingerprinting criminals. During that study he had obtained several thumbprints for examination but had failed to follow up after the initial interest. He had sent a letter to the Anthropological Institute outlining Faulds' ideas, but the Anthropological Institute had filed the letter and did not investigate Faulds' claims. Years later that letter was found still on file in the institute archives.

While Darwin's letter failed to interest Galton in fingerprints, he did carry on with his anthropologic studies. In 1884 he set up a laboratory at the International Health Exhibition held in London. He recorded various anthropologic data and took measurements recording such things as keenness of sight and hearing, color sense, visual judgment, breathing power, reaction time, strength of pull and squeeze, and force of blow. Galton was very encouraged with his results and requested authority to set up a laboratory at the Science Museum in South Kensington to further his studies. His request was granted and he maintained a laboratory at that location for the next six years.

Galton's interest in measuring human strength and the limitations of the various senses was likely the reason why the Royal Institute in 1888 asked him to give a Friday evening lecture on Bertillonage. After Galton had visited Bertillon and observed his staff measuring criminals, he came away impressed with the efficiency of the staff but not very impressed with the system.

Galton was of the opinion that fingerprinting might be a better method of identification. To facilitate this idea he expanded his lecture to the Royal Institute. He added fingerprinting to his presentation of Bertillonage and entitled the lecture "Personal Identification and Description." To prepare for the presentation he drew on all available sources including the publication *Nature*. The editor of *Nature* gave him Herschel's address and he corresponded with Herschel. Herschel was so happy that his work would finally be recognized he turned over all of his material on fingerprinting for study. Galton studied Herschel's material and fully realized its value over Bertillon's anthropometry.

After the presentation to the Royal Institute, Galton embarked on an indepth study of fingerprinting. In 1892 he published a book entitled *Fingerprints* in which he reported his studies up to that time. In his book he felt, as Herschel had before, that all previous uses of fingerprints in the Orient were by illiterate people living in semi-civilized nations. That position, of course, could only enhance their accomplishments in the eyes of the scientific community; a pioneer of a new science commands more prestige than one researching and improving an existing science.

Troup Committee

On October 21, 1893 the Home Secretary in England appointed a committee under Charles Troup of the Home Office. The Troup Committee was charged with enquiring into:

1. The method of registering and identifying habitual criminals now in use in England;
2. The Anthropometric system;
3. The suggested system of identification by means of a record of finger marks and to report which system should be used and how it would be implemented.

After extensive inquiries, including testimony and demonstration by Galton, the committee decided that fingerprints should be added to the files at Scotland Yard but Anthropometry would remain as the primary method of identification. The practicality and success of fingerprints soon overshadowed anthropometry. In 1901, as the result of another committee called the

Belper Committee, Anthropometry was abandoned and fingerprinting was established as the primary means of personal identification.

Juan Vucetich (1855-1925)

Juan Vucetich

Fingerprinting spread to South America and advanced at an even faster pace than in England due to the ingenuity of one Juan Vucetich, who was employed as a statistician with the Central Police Department at La Plata, Argentina. In July 1891 the Chief of Police assigned Vucetich to set up a bureau of Anthropometric Identification. While giving Vucetich his instructions the chief also gave him a copy of the May 1891 *Revue Scientifique*, which contained an article by Henry de Varigny describing the contents of one of Galton's lectures, "Patterns in Thumbs and Finger Marks." The article also included a chart of fingerprint patterns and mentioned Galton's efforts to find a viable classification method.

Vucetich had the anthropometry laboratory functioning in a few days, but he was also intrigued with the article on fingerprinting. He started experimenting with fingerprints and set up his own equipment for taking criminals' prints. By September 1891 he had independently worked out a fingerprint classification system and was filing criminal fingerprints using his new system. As the collection grew, Vucetich used his own funds to purchase cabinets and equipment. In spite of his efforts, his superiors would not allow fingerprinting to be officially added to the anthropometric system.

The Rojas Murders

On June 19, 1892 an incident took place that would change the attitude of Vucetich's superiors about fingerprints. Two children were murdered on the outskirts of the town of Necochea on the coast of Argentina. The victims were the illegitimate children of a 26-year-old woman named Francisca Rojas.

Upon investigation, local police learned that late in the evening of the murder, Rojas had run into a neighbor's hut wild-eyed and screaming. She blurted out, "My children...He killed my children... Velasquez...!" The neighbors immediately went to the Rojas hut and found the children, their skulls smashed, lying in a considerable amount of blood.

Upon interviewing Rojas, local investigators learned that a man named Velasquez wanted to marry her. She had refused Velasquez's proposals several times as she was in love with another man. Early on the day of the murder Velasquez had visited Rojas again and had been very insistent. Rojas had told him she would never marry him and that she loved someone else. Velasquez had flown into a rage and threatened the children before rushing away. Rojas alleged that when she came home later she found the children dead.

Velasquez was an older man who worked at a nearby ranch. He was arrested later that night by the local police. Even under intense interrogation he claimed his innocence. He finally admitted to making the threats, but even after being bound and left beside the children's corpses for several hours he would not admit to the murders.

The report of the murder did not reach La Plata, the provincial capital, until July 8. Police Inspector Alvarez of the Central Police was sent to Necochea to assist the local police with the investigation. When he arrived he found that the local police had no leads. Alvarez quickly ascertained that Velasquez had an alibi. He had been out with several friends at the time of the murders. Alvarez also learned that Rojas' other boyfriend had been overheard saying that he would marry her, "except for the two brats."

Alvarez examined the scene even though it was several days old. After some time at the scene he noticed a brown stain on the bedroom door. Careful examination revealed that it was a fingerprint. Alvarez had received basic training in fingerprint identification from Vucetich. Remembering what he had been taught, he cut out the piece of the door with the fingerprint on it. He returned to Necochea and requested that Rojas be fingerprinted.

Alvarez compared the fingerprints under a magnifying glass. Even though he had minimal instruction in fingerprinting, he could plainly see that the print was Rojas' right thumb. When this evidence was presented to her she broke down and admitted that she had killed her children. The children had stood in the way of her marriage to the other man. She had killed them with a stone and then dropped the stone into a well. After the murders she had cleaned her hands and clothes but failed to notice the fingerprint on the door.

When Alvarez returned to La Plata with the piece of door with Rojas' fingerprint, Vucetich's faith in fingerprints was proven. This case is reported as the first murder solved by fingerprints. Many identifications were to follow, and as more crimes were solved with fingerprints its superiority to anthropometry became obvious.

In 1894 Vucetich published a book at his own expense entitled *General Introduction to the Procedures of Anthropometry and Fingerprinting*. In 1896 Argentina became the first country in the world to abolish anthropometry and file criminal records solely by fingerprint classification. Vucetich's classification methods are still used today in some South American countries.

The success of Vucetich should have sparked worldwide interest and acceptance of fingerprints as a sound method of personal identification. It may have been that Argentina was not in the mainstream of scientific study or commerce at that time. Whatever the reason, the world either did not know or chose to ignore Vucetich's accomplishments.

Sir Edward Henry (1850-1931)

Sir Edward Richard Henry

At the same time that Vucetich was experimenting with fingerprinting in Argentina, another classification system was being developed in India. This new system was called the *Henry Classification System*. A very important concept would again be conceived in the Orient and a new era in the friction ridge identification science would begin.

In 1873 Edward Richard Henry left England and entered the Indian Civil Service as an assistant Magistrate Collector. He was assigned to Bengal Province in India. Over the next 17 years he held several positions of ever-increasing responsibility and importance. In 1891 he was appointed Inspector General of Police for Bengal Province. Upon taking his new post, Henry found that the anthropometric system was being used to identify criminals. The old standbys such as the location of scars, tattoos, and deformities were the mainstays of the system.

Henry developed some doubts about the accuracy of the anthropometric measurements that were being stored in the files. He also found that close supervision during the collection of the data was very difficult. At the time, Henry was working in the area of India where Herschel had experimented with fingerprints years before. The same influences that Herschel was subjected to were now influencing Henry. He added the taking of a left thumbprint to each anthropometric file card. In 1893 he obtained a copy of Galton's book *Fingerprints*. To increase his working knowledge of fingerprinting, Henry began to correspond with Galton.

In the fall of 1894 he returned to England and paid Galton a personal visit at his laboratory in the Convict Supervision Office. Galton, now past 70, placed all he had learned at Henry's disposal, including the work of Herschel and Faulds. While in England Henry learned of the Troup Committee and that Galton had not solved the classification issue. Henry decided that when he returned to India he would attempt to solve the problem of finding a formula that would allow a fingerprint collection of several thousand to be filed and retrieved.

Henry returned to India and his first course of action was to instruct that all ten fingers of each prisoner be printed and added to the anthropometric cards. He assigned two Bengali police officers, Khan Bahadur Azizul Haque and Rai Bahaden Hem Chandra Bose, to study the classification problem. Henry's team was eventually successful in setting up a classification system with 1024 primary positions, and secondary breakdowns in each. In early 1897 Henry applied to the Indian government for an independent assessment of his classification system. As the result of this review, fingerprints were adopted as the official method for the identification of criminals in British India. The anthropometric cards were slowly phased out and replaced by fingerprint cards classified with the Henry system.

The British Association for the Advancement of Science heard of Henry's success in India. They were well aware of the disadvantages of the identification methods currently used in England. In 1899 Henry was invited by the association to present a paper at Dover. He returned to England and presented a paper entitled "Fingerprints and the Detection of Crime in India." In the paper he referred to the historical aspects of fingerprints and praised Galton's work and assistance. He also described the successes and uses of fingerprinting in India.

While in England, Henry was reassigned to South Africa, where he was to assist with organizing a civil police force. At about the same time a committee was sitting in England investigating "The workings of the methods of identification of criminals by measurements and fingerprints, and the administrative arrangements for carrying on the system." This committee was chaired by Lord Belper. Prior to leaving for South Africa, Henry gave evidence before the Belper Committee.

Shortly after Henry gave evidence to the Belper Committee, his book entitled *Classification and Uses of Fingerprints* was published. In December 1900 the Belper Committee recommended that the fingerprints of criminals be taken and classified by the Indian system. They decided that if the English anthropometry system did not prove to be superior to the Indian fingerprint system, the latter was to be adopted.

By 1901 the Belper Committee's recommendations were being implemented. In May of the same year Henry was called back to London. He took up the post of Assistant Commissioner of Police in Charge of Criminal Identification at New Scotland Yard. By this time the Indian system had prevailed and anthropometry was slowly being phased out.

In 1903 Henry became Commissioner of Police. Although he no longer worked with fingerprints, he still kept up his interest. In January 1912, while on tour of India with King George V, Henry was entertained at a formal dinner. During his address he introduced Haque to the diners and praised his efforts in perfecting the classification system. It is not known if Henry met with Bose during his visit, but both Haque and Bose received monetary awards and promotions for their efforts to develop the Henry system in the fingerprint bureau.

In 1918 Henry left his position as Commissioner of Police. The Henry Classification System started what is considered the modern era of fingerprint identification. Even though the system was named after Henry, he gave credit where credit was due by not claiming to have solved the classification problem by himself. Henry's status as a modern scholar cannot be denied. The fact that the Henry system is the basis for most of the classification systems presently used speaks for itself.

Anthropometry in North America, 1897-1898

During the late 1800s North American police forces were entangled in the same dilemma as the British were prior to anthropometry. Identification of repeat criminals was a hit-and-miss situation where police officers' memories were the mainstay of the system. Scars, deformities, and descriptions were recorded in criminal files, but retrieval of this information was not systematic. Anthropometry had gained a strong foothold in Europe and eventually spread to North America.

In 1897 the International Association of Chiefs of Police established a National Bureau of Criminal Investigation in Chicago, Illinois. The bureau was to be a central storage and retrieval depot for criminal records. The cost of the bureau was shared by the police organizations that used the service. The records were classified and stored under Bertillon's anthropometric system.

The successes of Bertillon's anthropometry were also recognized in Canada, which was also in need of a method to accurately identify criminals. On June 13, 1898 the Identification of Criminals Act was passed into law by the Parliament of Canada. The act sanctioned the use of the Bertillon Signaletic System by Canadian police forces.

Fingerprinting in North America, 1877-1900

The idea of using a fingerprint as a signature or for the identification of an individual was slowly filtering into society in North America. As previously mentioned, in 1877 Thomas Taylor had suggested that friction ridges could be used to identify murderers. Others were also using fingerprints in various ways.

I. West Taber (1880)

In 1880 a photographer in San Francisco named I. West Taber suggested that fingerprinting be adopted for the registration of Chinese immigrant laborers. Apparently, a problem of identification had developed similar to that which had developed in India. Some Caucasians had difficulty differentiating Orientals with similar anatomical features.

Gilbert Thompson (1882)

In 1882 Gilbert Thompson used his thumbprint to ensure that the amounts were not changed or altered on payroll cheques. Thompson was the head of a surveying party in New Mexico. When issuing a payroll cheque, he would put an inked thumbprint over the amount. Galton heard of this and asked Thompson for an example. Galton received a copy of a payroll cheque dated August 8, 1882, payable in the amount of $75.00 to one "Lying Bob." The fingerprint in this case was not used for identification purposes but to prevent fraudulent cheque alterations.

Mark Twain (1894)

In 1894 the American author and lecturer Mark Twain enhanced the position of fingerprints when he included their use in the plot of a novel entitled *Pudd'n'head Wilson*. In the novel, a bloody fingerprint is found on the murder weapon and "Pudd'n'head," the defense attorney, has the whole town fingerprinted. He lectures the court and jury on the basics of fingerprinting, how fingerprints are immutable, and that two fingerprints will never be found to be the same. He also comments on how identical twins can be indistinguishable in appearance, at times even by their parents, but their fingerprints will always be different. No one is sure of the source of Twain's information, but it has been speculated that he read Herschel's and Faulds' papers in *Nature*.

New York State (1903)

By 1903 the New York City Civil Service Commission was using fingerprints to prevent impersonations during examinations. During the same year fingerprinting was introduced into the New York State Prison System and at Leavenworth Penitentiary. By 1906 there were six police departments in the U.S. that were known to be taking fingerprints for identification purposes.

Fingerprinting in Canada (1904-1920)

In 1904 St. Louis, MO, was the site of a World's Fair. A chance meeting took place that was to bring fingerprinting to Canada and eventually spell the end of the Bertillon Signaletic System. Detective John Ferrier of Scotland Yard was at the fair to guard a display of British Crown Jewels. Ferrier and New York State both had displays illustrating fingerprint identification. During the Fair the International Association of Chiefs of Police also had a convention and invited Ferrier to present a paper on fingerprints.

Edward Foster (1863-1956)

A Canadian constable, Edward Foster of the Dominion Police, attended the World's Fair to guard a display of gold. He attended Ferrier's

John Kenneth Ferrier

presentation at the convention and likely visited the New York State exhibit. He was intrigued by the possibilities that fingerprinting had to offer. He felt that a fingerprint bureau would be more effective than an anthropometry bureau, which had been recommended in 1898. He also felt that a national organization in Canada, similar to the International Association of Chiefs of Police, would encourage cooperation among Canadian police departments and be an ideal body to promote a national interest in fingerprinting.

Upon returning to Canada, Foster approached Sir Percy Sherwood, the Commissioner of the Dominion Police for Canada, with his new-found knowledge and his idea of a national bureau. Sir Percy was not only encouraging but also a source of knowledge and assistance. He suggested that Deputy Chief Constable Stark of Toronto would be an ideal man to interest in the formation of a Canadian Chiefs of Police Association. Sherwood contacted Deputy Chief Stark and received an enthusiastic response. An organizational meeting of the newly proposed association was held in Toronto, Ontario on September 6, 1905.

Inspector Edward Foster,
Royal Canadian Mounted Police

With an association formed, the next step was to organize a national bureau.

At this first meeting a committee was formed to further the cause. The mandate of the committee was to meet with the Minister of Justice and recommend the establishment and maintenance of a national bureau. The Minister of Justice reacted favorably to the proposal and presented it to the government. With continued support from his Chief of Police, Foster's ideas were kept before government until July 21, 1908, when an Order-in-Council was passed sanctioning the use of the fingerprint system and sanctioning that the provisions of "The Identification of Criminal Act" were applicable.

The National Bureau itself did not open until February 1911. The offices for the bureau were in the Langevin Block on Wellington Street in Ottawa, directly across from the Parliament buildings. The staff was composed of Foster, three assistants, and a stenographer. The original files consisted of 2042 sets of fingerprints taken by Foster between 1906 and 1910. Once the National Bureau was operating, several police departments sent their complete fingerprint collections.

During 1911 the Chicago Police Department arrested a man named Thomas Jennings for murder. Jennings had murdered a man when he had been caught attacking the man's daughter. The evidence against Jennings was slim except for fingerprint evidence. The prosecution wanted to ensure the fingerprint evidence would be admitted before the Illinois Supreme Court, which had not previously ruled on the issue. To strengthen its case the prosecution called several recognized fingerprint experts as witnesses, including Edward Foster.

During cross-examination Foster was asked by the defense if he could raise fingerprints on various surfaces. When asked about a piece of paper the defense lawyer had in his hand, Foster said that he could. He took the paper and developed a fingerprint on it. The lawyer realized he had made a grave error and immediately spilled a glass of water on the paper to destroy the print. The Jennings trial is considered a landmark case in the courts as far as the science of fingerprints is concerned. Jennings was convicted and sentenced to hang on December 22, 1911.

The first conviction in Canada based on fingerprint evidence took place in 1914. Peter Caracatch and Gregory Parachique broke into the CPR station in Petawawa, Ontario. They left fingerprints on glass at the point of entry. Edward Foster gave expert evidence at their trial.

In 1920 the Dominion Police was absorbed by the Royal Canadian Mounted Police (RCMP). Foster was also absorbed into the RCMP with the rank of Inspector and continued to head the Fingerprint Bureau until his retirement in 1932.

Summary

The pioneers of friction ridge identification were people of vision. Many had careers similar to our own. They applied the science as they knew it. Many strived to increase their knowledge of the science in an effort to promote and improve its effectiveness. Due to their unselfish efforts, friction ridge identification has become what it is today, the most positive method of personal identification.

Scientific Researchers

The scientific basis of friction ridge identification has evolved over many years, or even centuries. Prior to the 20th century most research centered on observations of the anatomical aspects of the friction skin. As the 19th century ended, research studies and papers began to explore the evolution and genetic aspects of the friction skin.

Attempting to include the work of all the researchers involved with establishing the scientific basis of friction ridge identification would be a monumental task. Science fosters science through knowledge or simply the encouragement to keep going. Each research project, regardless of how insignificant it may appear, has contributed in its own way to the science of today.

An effort has been made here to document some of the more celebrated scientists and their research. The purpose is to create a paper trail through history touching the more important areas worthy of study, where interested students of the science can seek knowledge. This list does not even scratch the surface when one considers the number of scientists who could be documented.

Nehemiah Grew (1641-1712)

Nehemiah Grew, M.D. was an English botanist, physician, and microscopist. In 1684 he published a paper in the *Philosophical Transactions* of the Royal Society of London describing his observations of the "Innumerable little ridges of equal bigness on the ends of the first joints of the fingers." Grew described sweat pores, epidermal ridges, and their various arrangements. Included in his paper was a drawing of the

Dr. Nehemiah Grew

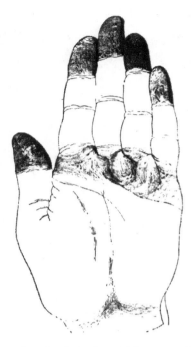

Figure 2.12 A sketch of the hand from Grew's paper, 1684.

configurations of the hand displaying the ridge flow on the fingers and palms (Figure 2.12). Grew did not refer to the uniqueness of friction skin or take that aspect into consideration.

Govard Bidloo (1685)

In 1685 Govard Bidloo, an anatomist in Amsterdam, Holland, published a book on human anatomy which illustrated friction ridges and pore structure on the underside of the fingers. The drawing of a thumb, illustrated in Figure 2.13, was described in great detail with reference to the pattern of the friction ridges. Bidloo exaggerated the breadth of the ridges in his drawing, possibly to emphasize their details. His comments were morphological in nature and he did not refer to or mention the individuality of friction ridges.

Figure 2.13

Marcello Malphighi (1628-1694)

In 1685 Marcello Malphighi, a professor at the University of Bologna, Italy, published the results of his examination of the friction skin with the newly invented microscope. He has been credited with being the first to use a microscope in medical studies. His work was received with such enthusiasm that one of the layers of the skin was named in his honor. Malphighi was a professor of anatomy, and that fact was reflected in his research. His paper dealt mainly with the function, form, and structure of the friction skin as a tactile organ, and its use in the enhancement of traction for walking and grasping.

Marcello Malpighi

J.C.A. Mayer (1788)

During the 1700s further research papers were published by anatomists, each contributing in its own way to furthering the scientific knowledge about the friction skin. One paper stands out from the others, mainly because the author clearly addresses the individuality of the friction ridges. J.C.A. Mayer was a German doctor and anatomist. He published a book in 1788 that has often been referred to as an atlas of anatomical illustrations. Each illustration in the book was accompanied by a detailed explanation. Under an illustration depicting the friction skin on the fingers, shown in Figure 2.14, his comments were: "Although the arrangements of skin ridges is never duplicated in two persons, nevertheless the similarities are closer among some individuals. In others the differences are marked, yet in spite of their peculiarities of arrangement all have a certain likeness."

Mayer was the first to describe the repetitiveness and similarities of friction ridge patterns in the same breath with the recognition that specific friction ridge arrangements are never duplicated. This is the first clear enunciation of two of the basic principles on which friction ridge identification was founded.

Johannes Evangelista Purkinje (1787-1869)

In 1823 Johannes Evangelista Purkinje, a professor at the University of Breslau, Germany, published a thesis that contained his studies on the eye, finger-prints, and other skin features entitled, "Commentatio de Examine Physio-logico Organi Visus et Systematis Cutanei." Purkinje classified nine principal configuration groups of fingerprints (Figure 2.14) and assigned each a name.

Joannes Evangelista Purkinje

Although some historians credit Purkinje with drawing attention to the individuality of the friction ridges, he did not mention personal identification or individuality of ridge structure in his thesis.

Arthur Kollmann (1883)

Arthur Kollmann of Hamburg, Germany published a paper on the primate hand entitled "Der Tastapparat der Hand der menschlichen Rassen und der Affen in seiner Entwickelung und Gliederung." (Hamburg, Leop. Voss) He published another paper about the foot two years later entitled "Der Tastapparat des Fusses von Affe und Mensch." (*Arch. f. Anat.u.Physiol., Anat. Abt.* pp. 56-101) Kollmann was the first researcher to address the formation of friction ridges in embryos and the topographical physical stressors that may have been part of their growth. He identified the presence and locations of the volar pads on the human hand and foot. While Kollmann has the distinction of being the first to address this topic, later scientists reported that his conclusions were errant.

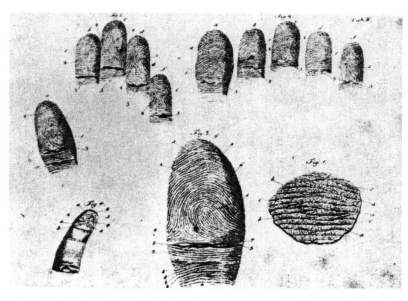

Figure 2.14 A sketch of the friction skin on fingers from J.C.A. Mayer's 1788 book of anatomical illustrations.

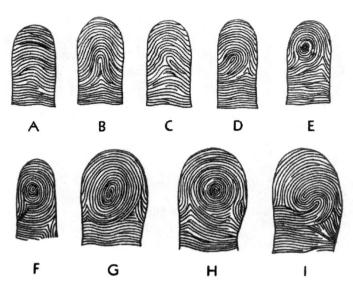

Figure 2.14 Purkinje's nine types of finger patterns taken from his paper. The patterns do not appear as above in the paper but are part of a sketch that includes the eyes and a hand.

H. Klaatsch (1888)

H. Klaatsch, also from Germany, published a paper entitled "Zur Morphologie der Tastballen der Saugetiere" (*Morph. Jahrb. Bd.* XIV pp. 407-435)in which he extended his research beyond primates to other mammals. He examined the walking pads and eminences of several pentadactylous or five-fingered mammals. Klaatsch is credited with being the first researcher to examine the walking surfaces of other mammals. He also refers to the arrangement of the fundamental units of the friction ridges as the reason why all ridge formations are different.

L. Reh (1894)

L. Reh of Germany published a paper entitled "Die Schuppen der Saugetiere." (*Jenaische Zeitschr. fur Naturwiss. Bd.* XXIX pp. 151-20), which describes the scales that appeared on early mammals. He did not associate scales to the epidermic wart (ridge unit) or rows of scales to ridges. Also, he felt that the scales, which had once covered the walking surfaces, had disappeared early and that the friction ridges had a separate origin.

David Hepburn (1895)

David Hepburn, of the University of Edinburgh, Scotland, published a paper on the similarity in appearance of the eminences or walking surfaces of primates entitled "The Papillary Ridges on the Hands and Feet of Monkeys and Men." (*Sci. Trans. of the Royal Dublin. Soc.* Vol. V (SeriesII) pp.525-537) He named two of the volar pads the *thenar* and *hypothenar*. He did not associate the primate volar pads with the more obvious walking pads of lower mammals; in fact, he made statements to the contrary. Hepburn felt that in the process of evolution, whenever an animal commences to use its hands and feet for purposes of grasping, it would then develop volar pads. That hypothesis is the reverse of what is believed to have taken place. Hepburn was the first, however, to recognize that ridges on these surfaces assisted grip by creating friction and that they had a function other than increasing tactile stimulus.

Inez Whipple (1871-1929)

Inez Whipple Wilder

Inez Whipple was a graduate of Brown University, Rhode Island, and held a Master of Arts degree from Smith College, Massachusetts. She taught high school biology from 1893 to 1897 in Northhampton, Massachusetts, before accepting a teaching position in the Zoology Department at Smith College. In 1902 Whipple became an Assistant Professor.

While employed in the Zoology Department she met Professor Harris Wilder, the founder of the Zoology Department at Smith College and its first professor. His interest in dermatoglyphics and identification was eventually shared by Whipple. Wilder was involved in several projects at the time and delegated some of this research to his associate, Miss Whipple. To say Inez Whipple met the challenge is an understatement.

In 1904 Whipple published her paper "The Ventral Surface of the Mammalian Chiridium — With Special Reference to the Conditions Found in Man." Whipple's paper was prefaced by Wilder and the two were to collaborate on various projects over the next few years, including getting married in 1906. Under the leadership of Mr. and Mrs. Wilder, the Zoology Department at Smith College encouraged research and produced several scholars. Whipple's survey into mammalian palm and sole configurations has formed an important part of the modern scientific knowledge on the subject and is considered a landmark in the fields of genetics and ridgeology.

A large part of Whipple's paper discusses the aspects of comparative dermatoglyphics of various mammals. Whipple qualifies the starting point for her research with references to earlier researchers and some of their conclusions. The paper also has an excellent bibliography that reflects the research leading up to her study.

Whipple's conclusions have caused some controversy over the years as she expressed an opinion as to the evolutionary process of the human species. However, whether we evolved from other mammals or have always been the animal we are today is not the issue here. What we can learn from Whipple is that the development of the surfaces of the hands and feet (chiridia) of all mammals are similar to some degree. This gives us an insight into the past and present development of the volar surfaces of the human species.

While earlier scientists contributed to the growing understanding of the evolutionary process of friction ridges on mammals, research now started to zero in on the evolution and development of friction skin on humans. Whipple's paper, more than any other, incorporates all of the available information from that era. It was prefaced by H. H. Wilder who discussed and referred to the conclusions of other researchers of the day. Whipple's conclusions are reproduced here in their entirety.

THE VENTRAL SURFACE OF THE MAMMALIAN CHIRIDIUM

CONCLUSIONS

I. In ancient mammals the larger part of the surface of the body was covered with imbricated scales. Each of these scales or scale elements possessed, associated with it, a hair (or hair-group) and a sweat gland, the position of each being constant with relation to the scale. In recent mammals the scales occasionally persist, especially on tails and paws, showing, however, more or less modification of the original type. The ventral surface of the chiridium is especially conservative in this respect, and exhibits scales or their modifications in species in which they have disappeared elsewhere.

II. Upon the ventral chiridial surface, there developed in the early mammals or in the pre-mammalian forms, a definite arrangement of walking pads in three rows (apical, inter-digital, proximal). In the accommodation of these pads to the movement of the chiridium, more or less definite folds of skin developed in connection with each pad. In typical walking mammals, these pads and folds persist in practically their original form and arrangement, while with the adaptation of the chiridium to other functions they undergo various modifications.

III. Over the pad surfaces which, because of their greater elevation, are brought in contact with external surfaces, a highly specialized friction skin is developed by the fusion into rows of modified scales, characterized by the loss of hair and by the hypertrophy of their sweat glands. The ridges form at right angles to the force which tends to cause a slipping of the

Figure 2.16 A sketch of the forefoot of a field mouse. The volar pads are in the typical arrangement. Folds between the volar form triradii.

surfaces, and therefore, in the case of pointed pads, are arranged in concentric circles about the summit of the pad.

IV. With the lowering of the pads due to the adaptation of the chiridium to prehension, the area of friction skin increased in proportion to the enlargement of the contact surface, until, in the majority of Primates, the entire chiridial surface has become covered by ridges, leaving separate scale units along the margin of the chiridium only.

V. The development of the friction skin upon intermediate as well as upon pad areas resulted in the formation of epidermic ridge patterns which followed the relief of the original pads and the folds of skin connected with them. The change of form and reduction in size of the pads are correlated, however, with pronounced modifications of the original typical patterns [Figure 2.16]. When these modifications cease to be of functional importance, the original pad regions become subject to a considerable range of individual variation by a comparative study of which the records of the past may be read. So far as studied, these records indicate:

(a) That all pentadactylous orders of mammals have descended from a primitive form possessing the typical primary walking pads upon both anterior and posterior chiridia.

(b) That in the evolution of the Prosimians and Primates, these pads developed friction skin while still practically in their primitive, elevated, walking form. Thus ridges upon these pads were originally concentrically arranged, a primitive condition from which two divergent lines of development lead respectively to the Prosimians and to the Primates.

(c) That in the line of development leading to the Prosimians there occurred very early, an almost complete substitution of the prehensile for the walking function, prehension being accomplished through the extreme opposability of the first digit. This resulted in (1) the flattening and broadening of the apical pads, (2) the reduction of all the remaining pads except the first interdigital, which from its position adds much to the width of the opposing digit, and (3) the development of secondary pads in such locations as to still farther increase the width of the opposing digit.

(d) That in the line of development leading to Primates the early acquirement of prehensile power was accompanied by a retention of the walking function. There was, however, a tendency to a digitigrade use of the chiridium in walking, while prehension was for the purpose of grasping relatively small branches involved, at most, only a slight opposability of the first digit. This combination of conditions resulted in (1) the longer retention of the interdigital pads in their typical form with a tendency in the posterior chiridium to fusion and to the lengthening of the proximal slope, (2) the broadening and flattening of the apical and proximal pads (especially the hypothenar), (3) the reduction of the thenar and first interdigital pads in those cases in which prehension involved an opposability of the first digit, and (4) the development of secondary pads upon the proximal and middle phalanges.

(e) That in the line of development leading to the Anthropoids and man, the increased weight of the body involved an adaptation to the power to grasp larger limbs, a condition accompanied by the loss of the walking function, especially of the anterior chiridium. As a result of these modifications there occurred (1) greater opposability of the first digit and (2) the gradual reduction of pads until the whole surface of the chiridium became nearly level, a great variety of ridge patterns being the only vestiges of the ancestral pads.

(f) That the ancestral line of man diverged from that of the other Anthropoids before the reduction of the interdigital pads of the foot had been accomplished. This divergence was characterized by the early assumption of an erect position and led to the following modifications of the foot: (1) shortening of the digits, (2) a loss of opposability of the hallux, (3) a fusion of the interdigital pads, especially the last three, (4) a reduction of the proximal pads, and (5) an extensive proximal development of the plantar surface, with a secondary pad formation over the os calcis, often designated by a secondary ridge pattern. In regard to the anterior chiridium (hand) the conditions in man are not very different from those of the Anthropoids, save in the types of modification of the ridge patterns.

In summary, the first part of Whipple's survey found that all mammals have the same morphological arrangement of volar pads on the hands and feet. The formation is referred to as the *typical arrangement* in these early papers. A volar pad appears on each of the five fingers, in the four interdigital areas, and one on each side of the palm.

Whipple reported that these primary mammalian walking pads are primitive organs that have a tendency to vary from the typical arrangement in response to external conditions. Examples of this can be found in both the cat and humans. The cat has three interdigital pads fused together to form one large walking pad. This is a specialized adaptation. On the feline embryo there are three separate pads. In the case of the human hand, the first interdigital pad does not appear as a separate pad, likely due to its proximity to the thenar pad. The lack of a distinct formation is believed to be either a case of the first pad fusing with the thenar pad or a total failure of the pad to form. In either case the change is believed to be due to the development of prehensile use between the thumb and index finger.

Whipple found that the mammals in which the majority of pads still develop in the typical arrangement are those slightly removed from the main line descent of primates. When volar pads cease to serve their original function they tend to persist and, if possible, adapt to new functions. Further explanation of this can be found by studying volar pad physiology or function. The human hand, for example, illustrates an extreme adaptation. The long discontinuance of use, both as a walking surface and a mode of locomotion by prehension, is obviously correlated with an almost complete degeneration of the pads as distinct elevations in the postembryonic human, simply a case of "use it or lose it." The presence of walking pads on postembryonic humans is only evident by examining the flow of the ridge patterns.

The second part of Whipple's paper deals with the origin of epidermal friction ridges on the volar surfaces. She describes the evolutionary steps that took place in the process of forming ridges. The ridges as we know them are constructed of individual units, each having a pore, fused together end to end in the early development stage to form a friction ridge. Early researchers referred to ridge units as epidermal warts. The mammalian scale is considered the ancestor of the wart. Primitive mammalian scales each had a hair and a sweat gland as part of its configuration.

Whipple describes the evolutionary process of friction ridge development in the following order. First mammals lost the hair from the scales on the volar surfaces. The loss of hair caused the sweat glands to become more active, which moistened the volar surface and improved grip. The volar scales began to fuse into rows which again enhanced grip. As the contact areas became specialized in function, such as for locomotion or grasping, the modification of the ridges evolved accordingly.

The third part of Whipple's paper deals with epidermic ridge patterns. The ridge patterns are affected by external forces and from pressure by neighboring developing ridges. Whipple found that friction ridges form at right angles to the possible direction of motion of a contact surface. This development was designed to prevent slippage. The prevention of slippage was found to be the single factor determining the evolution of the friction ridge pattern.

Friction ridges evolving on flat contact surfaces simply form at 90 degrees to the direction of possible motion. When ridges are forming on a contact surface that is not flat, such as a convex-shaped walking pad, the shape of the pad increases the number of possible directions in which slippage may occur. On an elevated pad slippage is possible in all 360 degrees. Therefore, the ridges forming at right angles to the possible direction of slippage will tend to form concentric patterns.

When some mammals began to use their volar areas for prehensive locomotion, the walking pads evolved a lower profile until they were at the level of the surrounding skin. The lowering of the pads caused the intermediate skin between the pads to become a contact surface and friction ridges also developed on them. The areas of contact skin increased until all of the volar surfaces were covered with friction ridges. Each volar pad remained the center of an area of disturbance and was surrounded by a ridge system. In areas where three of these ridge systems met, a triradius was formed (Figure 2.17). The triradius is often an area of considerable disturbance in ridge structure, caused by the forces from three ridge systems exerting pressure on one another during friction ridge development.

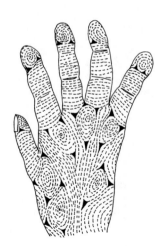

Figure 2.17 A sketch of the pattern flow on the forefoot of the East Indian Monkey. The volar pads are in their typical arrangement. Concentric patterns have formed on the raised surfaces. Triradii, formed where ridge systems meet, are marked in black.

Whipple's paper is still referenced in the bibliographies of many modern genetic and dermatoglyphic papers. Her research is not only the culmination of all the previous studies on the subject, but also the starting reference for a great deal of research that followed.

Harris Hawthorne Wilder (1864-1928)

Harris Hawthorne Wilder, Ph.D. was a graduate of Amherst College, Massachusetts. After graduation he began his career by teaching biology for three years at a high school in Chicago. As a young boy he had been interested in animals. In 1889 he decided to advance his study of zoology and specialize in anatomy. He went to study at the University of Freiburg in Germany. He received his Ph.D. after two years, returned to America, and taught high school in Chicago for another year.

In 1892 Wilder accepted the position of Professor of Zoology at Smith College, Massachusetts. His early studies caused a sensation when he reported in a paper that some salamanders have no lungs. In 1896, while Wilder was studying monkeys, he was struck by the resemblance of their volar friction ridges to man's. He became very interested in dermatoglyphics and in 1897 published his first paper on the subject entitled "On the Disposition of the Epidermic Folds Upon the Palms and Soles of Primates." (*Anat. Anzeiger. Bd.* XIII, pp. 250-256). This paper was the first of many, for over the next three decades he continued research in morphology, the methodology of plantar and palmar dermatoglyphics, genetics, and racial differences.

Harris Hawthorne Wilder

Wilder was the first to suggest that the centers of disturbance of primate friction ridge formations actually represented the locations of volar pads. Prior research had suggested that primate volar pads could only be located by examining the topology of the surface. It is now understood that this practice confuses the volar pads with present muscle structure. Wilder's hypothesis of a relationship between primate friction ridge patterns and volar pads has been confirmed through subsequent research. Wilder was also the first to supply embryological proof that the large pad of a cat's paw is composed of three interdigital pads fused together.

In 1918 Wilder joined with Bert Wentworth, the former Police Commissioner of Dover, New Hampshire, to publish a book entitled *Personal Identification*. The contents of the book consisted mainly of Wilder's research. He

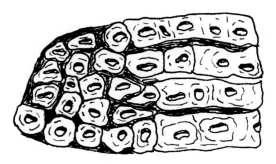

Figure 2.18 A sketch of ridge units, the building blocks of the friction ridge, as viewed in the transition area along the transitional edge of friction skin. The ridge unit is the successor of the epidermal wart. Ridge units fuse together during formation to construct friction ridges. When a small number fuse together they appear as short islands or short ridges. The smallest island has only one ridge unit.

did, however, include some of Whipple's research and Locard's findings on poroscopy. The basis for the quantitative-qualitative analysis of friction ridges can be found in this book. For example, in Chapter Two, p. 124, Wilder discusses the variability of friction ridges:

> However, quite aside from patterns, that concern whole systems of ridges, the Galton details, the ends, forks, island and so on, are so numerous and so variable that even in a small area a duplication is impossible. As the ridges are formed by the fusion of rows of units there is a possibility that during the formation a break might have occurred between any two of the units as marked by sweat pores, forming an end or an interruption. It is equally possible that islands or short ridges might have occurred at any point [Figure 2.18], or that a unit, instead of fusing lengthwise with its next neighbor, might happen to fuse across with the adjacent unit on one side and form a fork. Although it has been shown that the influence of heredity from parent to child is operative in the formation of similar patterns, viewed as a whole, yet there is absolutely no indication of such hereditary control of the details of the individual ridges, and so far as we know all the infinite possibilities in the formation of the ridges are widely open in each individual case, so that it is quite safe to say that no two people in the world can have, even over a small area, the same set of details, similarly related to the individual units.

In this passage Wilder describes the anatomical formation of the friction ridges. He further describes how ridge units are subjected to differential growth and, as a result, all areas of friction ridge are unique.

Wilder published seven books and 39 papers during his career. He was a respected member in good standing of many societies and academies including the International Association for Identification (I.A.I.). As an early member of the I.A.I., Harris Hawthorne Wilder was the epitome of that association's pioneering and scientific spirit. He was considered the leading American fingerprint expert of the day.

Harold Cummins (1893-1976)

Harold Cummins, Ph.D.

Harold Cummins, Ph.D. was a professor of anatomy and assistant dean of the School of Medicine at Tulane University, Louisiana. He spent a great deal of his life studying dermatoglyphics. In 1943 he coauthored a book entitled *Fingerprints, Palms, and Soles — An Introduction to Dermatoglyphics*, with Charles Midlo, M.D. Midlo was an emeritus associate professor of microscopic anatomy at Tulane. Cummins' book incorporates material from most of the recognized papers and surveys that were available on the subject at the time. The bibliography in *Fingerprints, Palms, and Soles* is extensive and includes many of Cummins' papers.

Fingerprints, Palms, and Soles was dedicated to Wilder. The author's dedication reads: "To the memory of Harris Hawthorne Wilder (1864-1928), Pioneer Investigator of Dermatoglyphics." The recognition of Wilder's work is testimony to Wilder's status and accomplishments as a scientist.

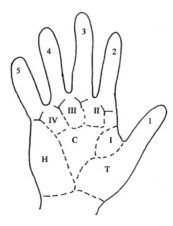

Figure 2.19   The human hand is divided into twelve areas: the five digits (1-5), the four interdigital areas (I-IV), the thenar side of the palm (T), the hypothenar side of the palm (H), and the central area of the palm (C).

One of Cummins' earlier papers followed Whipple's research. In 1929 Cummins published a paper entitled "The Topographic History of the Volar Pads in the Human Embryo." Cummins described the formation and development of volar pads on the human fetus. He found that volar pad regression took place during the same time frame as the beginning of friction ridge development. He concluded that the physical aspects of volar pads such as location, growth differential, and configuration variances affected friction ridge development and overall pattern configuration. The degree of influence is dependent on the stage of volar pad regression at the time the friction ridges begin to develop.

Cummins further describes how other factors such as disease or birth defects may interfere with volar pad development and may also affect the friction ridges. The content of Cummins's paper is not summarized in any one area in the paper itself, but in his book *Fingerprints, Palms, and Soles* his paper, reference 159, summarizes some of the material. The following quotes are taken from Chapter 10, entitled "Embryology":

Volar Pads — Hand. The volar pads (159) first to appear (second, third and fourth interdigitals) are evident at about the sixth week of development. At this time the hand is still paddle-like and, though the five digital rays are indicated, the free portions of digits are only broad scallops of the distal border. At the close of the second month, when the total length of the fetus is about 2.5 cm., the digits are elongated and separate. The pads of palm and fingers are evident as localized bulges, conforming in their placement to the morphologic plan which has been described. [Page 178] [*Morphologic Plan is the same as the typical arrangement — five pads on the fingers, four pads in the interdigital areas, and two pads on the palm in the thenar and hypothenar areas. Auth.*]

All fetuses develop pads in conformity to the morphologic plan (Figure 2.20). There is considerable variation in the time relations of the appearance and regression of pads. This variation is evident in corresponding pads of different fetuses and of right and left hands of the same fetus, as well as among the several pads of the same hand. There are variations also of contours, of the amount of elevation and shape of individual pads, and of definition of boundaries at their bases. [Page 179]

Factors Which Condition Alignment of Ridges — Epidermal ridges differentiate in their definitive character. That is to say, from the very first appearance of the ridges the minutiae and configurational arrangements are in their permanent form. The factors determining ridge alignments are identified with two major development circumstances, namely, variations in the histology of different regions and differential growth incident to the production of irregular reliefs of the volar surfaces. [Page 182]

The various configurations are not determined by self-limited mechanism within the skin. The skin possesses the capacity to form ridges, but

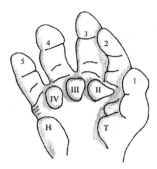

Figure 2.20 Cummins describes the volar pads as conforming in their placement to the morphologic plan. The first to appear are the second, third, and fourth interdigital pads at about the sixth week. At this time the hand is paddle-like. At about eight weeks, when the digits are elongated and separated, the pads of the palm and fingers are visible as localized bulges.

the alignments of these ridges are as responsive to stresses in growth as are the alignments of sand to sweeping by wind or wave.

Triradii, like any other alignments of ridges, are conditioned by growth factors. That their normal disposition is associated with conjunction points of three complexes of growth is demonstrated in developmental defects of the hands and feet.

Volar pads in the normal fetus are sites of differential growth, each being responsible for production of one of the local configurations comprised in the morphologic plan of dermatoglyphics. If a pad does not completely subside prior to the time of ridge formation, its presence determines a discrete configurational area. [Pages 184-185]

Alfred Hale (1952)

An associate of Cummins, Alfred Hale, Ph.D., also from Tulane University, published a thesis in 1952 entitled "Morphogenesis of the Volar Skin in the Human Fetus." Hale's paper not only describes the formation of friction ridges on the human fetus but also describes the development of friction ridges. His research involved the examination of thin slices of fetal skin, cut in cross section to the friction ridges, from the fingers of fetuses at different stages of development. The cross sections of skin, placed on microscope slides and stained for better viewing, revealed the various stages of ridge development. Hale's research explains differential growth of friction ridges, the major premise of friction ridge identification (Figure 2.21).

The importance of Hale's paper cannot be overstated. Some excerpts from his paper are reproduced below followed by his conclusions.

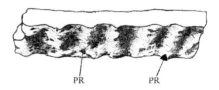

Figure 2.21   During the 12th or 13th week ledge-like formations begin to appear on the bottom of the epidermis. These ledges are *Primary Ridges* (PR), the substructure of the friction ridges. They are constructed of rows of ridge units fusing together as they begin to develop.

OBSERVATIONS

1. Initial phase (70-140 mm C.R.): During this period the primary ridges are established. Early primary ridges exhibit focal irregularities in contour that anticipate the development of the sweat glands [Figure 2.22]. These ridges penetrate deeper into the dermal substance, and at points of deepest penetration, the bulbous anlagen of sweat glands appear. Concomitant with sweat gland development; the primary ridges actively multiply. Such multiplications seem to occur primarily at the lateral surfaces of the primary ridge; they may occur, however, between adjacent primary ridges.

2. Secondary phase (140-220 C.R.): The secondary ridges appear between primary ridges [Figure 2.23]. These occur as irregularities of contour which extend parallel to the primary ridges. (page 159) The origin of these ridges reflects in every detail change described in the basal cell layer associated with the development of primary ridges except that sweat gland anlagen are confined to the latter.

3. Development of the dermal papillae (220 mm C.R.): The contour of the epidermis between primary and secondary ridges is essentially smooth during the growth of the secondary ridge. This growth continues until the depth of the dermal penetration of these ridges approximates that already attained by the primary ridges. As this stage is reached, irregularities appear in the contour of the zone between primary and secondary ridges which later are manifest as anastomoses between these ridges. The stratum papillare between the anastomotic epidermal trabeculae is therefore progressively molded into the peg-like structures characteristic of the dermal papillae of this region. [Pages 151 — 153]

   Branchings arise out of the lateral swellings described on the primary ridge [Figure 2.24]. During the period of ridge multiplication, relative increases in area are not suddenly relieved by the immediate cessation in growth of the curved surface of the volar pad, but are gradually diminished by differences in growth rate between a pad and its surroundings. Thus tangentially directed stretch on the epidermis pulls these new proliferations away from the original primary ridge. This is a

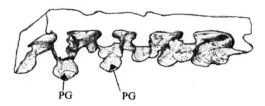

Figure 2.22   Primary ridges develop pores. The *Pore Glands* (PG) penetrate into the dermis. Primary ridges continue to proliferate until about the fifteenth or sixteenth week.

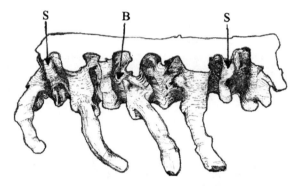

Figure 2.23   Around the sixteenth week *Secondary Ridges* (S) develop between the primary ridges. At this time the proliferation of primary ridges stops. This sketch also illustrates a *Branching* (B) and shows that the pores have developed deep into the dermis.

Figure 2.24   This is an area of a palm print. Islands and branches can be found throughout the print. Friction ridges are constructed of ridge units fused together during formation. Each ridge unit has one pore. The pores, therefore, appear evenly spaced along the ridge. The distances between the pores actually vary, which can be verified with comparative measurements.

dominant method of formation since a large proportion of minutiae are branchings and since there are more lateral ridge swellings than isolated ridges. [Page 167]

Islands arise as new proliferations of the basal cell layer immediately prior to the appearance of the secondary ridge. Their proximity in time to the appearance of the secondary ridge determines their ultimate length. Thus a new proliferation which occurs just prior to secondary ridge formation would be short, perhaps containing only one associated gland. Older islets would manifest themselves as longer structures being associated with several sweat glands, grading into dimensions meriting their designation as ridges. [Page 168]

Summary and Conclusions

A quantitative and qualitative description of the morphogenesis of volar skin is presented. This account is based upon 122 hands and feet selected from a graded series of human fetuses ranging in size from 40 mm C.R. length to 350 mm. The morphogenetic process has been described as occurring in three phases, the most important of which is the initial phase of ridge differentiation and multiplication.

1. During the initial phase, which begins at 70 mm C.R. and ends at 140 mm C.R., the primary ridges appear first as ledge-like penetrations of the stratum basalis into dermis, the alignment of these ledges being profoundly influenced by growth of the part. The nodular appearance of these early ridges anticipates the subsequent appearance of sweat glands, although their individuality is partially masked by fusion with adjacent proliferations.

    Increase in area of the volar surface is attended by multiplication of ridges which results in the appearance of an increased number of minutiae per standard area. The contribution of the basal cell layer to increase its area, supply cellular elements for the manufacture of new ridges, and to thickening of the stratum intermedium exhausts its potentialities such that the older primary ridges discontinue their dermal penetration. Sweat gland anlagen secondarily appear from the summits of primary ridge irregularities; these effect a firm attachment between epidermis and dermis.

2. Growth in area continues. At 140 mm C.R. the secondary ridges appear and the primary ridge systems cease their multiplications. Growth and proliferation of the secondary ridges continue until the depth of dermal penetration approximates that already attained by the primary ridges. Increase in area results in widening of the attached bases of primary ridges followed by a similar process involving secondary ridges.

3. Stress lines which are directed parallel to the skin surface are translated into forces directed perpendicular to the skin surface at the site of attachment of the secondary ridges. This results in folding of the surface at these points. Subsequent increase in the thickness of the stratum corneum, which initially appears at 115 mm C.R., reproduces this contour and the rugae appear upon the surface.

From the foregoing it is concluded that:

1. The primary ridge appears as a genetically controlled phenomenon, its early morphology reflecting its phylogenetic history; its unit of structure is the "epidermic wart" (Whipple).
2. Differential growth plays the major role in the establishment of the morphology of volar skin. Stresses arising out of differences in growth rate condition the alignment and fusion of the ridge units, thereby establishing the primary ridge. Increasing surface area demands the reproduction of ridges. This is manifest in the adult by the various minutiae.
3. The ability of the basal cell layer to proliferate, as established from measurements of the resulting structures, indicates that it has limitations; when that ability is saturated one structure propagated by its mitotic activity must cease to grow if a different structure is to arise.

During the last 25 years there have been numerous scientific papers published about friction skin. In many cases this subsequent research confirmed and enriched the results of earlier studies. Most of this information is found in research papers dealing with other sciences such as dermatoglyphics, anatomy, or genetics as opposed to friction ridge identification journals. While addressing various aspects of their science, researchers frequently cover anatomical topics that are of interest to the friction ridge identification science.

One such paper, published in 1976 by Dr. Michio Okajima, is entitled "Dermal and Epidermal Structures of the Volar Skin." (*Birth Defects: Original Article Series*, Vol. XV, No. 6, pp. 179-198, 1979) Okajima's paper contains photographs of the dermal and corresponding epidermal surfaces which have been dye stained for easy viewing. Some photographs clearly show where the sweat gland ducts penetrate the dermal surface.

Okajima's paper also has photographs illustrating that the original structure of the papillae are in double rows under the epidermal friction ridge. As the host ages, however, the structures may become more complex until the double rows are no longer discernable. In some cases the dermal papillae ridges are indistinguishable from the dermal furrows. As friction ridges form in the generating layer of the epidermis, the changing connective tissues on

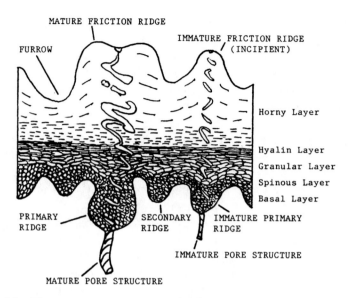

Figure 2.25   The immature incipient ridge has the same substructure as mature ridges. The double row of papillae pegs, which would lie beside the immature primary ridge, are smaller than those beside mature primary ridges. (See Figures 3-5 and 3-6)

the dermal surface are of little consequence to the immutability basis of the science.

Okajima also examined incipient ridges on both the epidermal and dermal surfaces. He found that incipient ridges have double rows of papillae under their structures in the same manner as mature ridges, except that they are smaller (Figure 2.25). While Okajima comments that he did not see pore ducts in either the epidermal surface or the dermal surface, research by the author revealed that some incipient ridges were found to have pore formations. (See Incipient Ridges and the Clarity Spectrum, *JFI* 42(2), 1992) Incipient ridges are believed to be normal forming ridges that were immature at the time of differentiation when primary ridge formation stopped. If this is the case, the pore duct and surrounding ridge formation would have been a natural part of the early growth of incipient ridges. This leads to the question of what criteria establish a ridge as an incipient ridge as opposed to a very thin mature ridge for the purpose of friction ridge comparison, or does it really matter?

Another interesting paper is entitled "Early Human Hand Morphology: An Estimation of Fetal Age," by Brigitte Lacroix, Marie-Josephe, Wolff-Quenot and Katy Haffen of Strasbourg, France (*Early Human Development*, 9 (1984) 127-136). This paper identifies three phases to fetal hand development — 6 to 10 weeks is related to the shape of the hand, 10 to 13 weeks to the appearance of the creases, and 13 weeks onward to the formation of friction ridges. The following is a quote from the paper:

> The external shape of the hand is entirely accomplished during the period from 6 to 10 weeks of gestation. As early as 6 weeks (the earliest stage studied) an asymmetry of the hand primordium, defined by the slot of the thumb, appears and represents the first organization of the hand. An opposed position of the thumb constitutes a characteristic of the human hand and distinguishes it from the hand of primates. The phenomenon of thumb opposition occurs progressively: at 8 weeks all the developing fingers are in the same spatial plane, whereas at 10 weeks thumb rotation is achieved.
>
> The configuration of digital and interdigital pads is acquired progressively: in a first phase of intense development extending from 9 to 10 weeks, the interdigital pads become very prominent whereas the same phenomenon occurs for the digital pads between 10 and 12 weeks. In a second phase of development, both types of pads regress. Although this regression is a well-known phenomenon, it is interesting to note that it starts much earlier than the 5 months proposed by Hirsch and Schweichel. Indeed, interdigital pads begin to regress as early as 11 weeks and digital pads from 13 weeks onwards.
>
> The present observations illustrate the complete development of pads precedes the appearance of the ridges, confirming the much older views of Bonnevie and the more recent ones of Hold, Blechschmidt, and Mulvihill and Smith. To validate our SEM observations on the configuration of pads, the following comments can be made. As far back as 1952 Hale was able to show that the pads correspond to mesenchymal condensations on the surface of which the ridges appear. Several other authors using combined histological and ultrastructural studies confirmed the mesenchymal origin of the pads and their structural arrangement; they further suggested the role of blood vessel nerve pairs in their appearance.
>
> The development of the creases is characterized at 10 weeks of gestation by opposition of the thumb which induces the first appearance of a crease demarcating the thenar pattern area. It is followed by the appearance of the palmar distal and proximal creases, which become evident at 11 and 12 weeks, respectively, the consequence of which being the delimitation of the hypothenar pattern area. The interphalangeal flexion creases are the latest to appear in a progressive manner from 11 weeks onwards.
>
> The ridges represent the first anlage of the fingerprints. In our study, the use of SEM shows that ridges are present as early as 13 weeks. This precocious appearance has also been suggested by Hale, but is at variance with the five months stage proposed more recently by Hirsch and Schweichel. The formation of ridges begins on the lateral part of the fingertips as seen with SEM and proceeds further from a lateral-distal to a medial-proximal position on the end phalanx. This description correlates very well with the histological pictures of Hale and Hirsch and Schweichel.

More recently, Dr. William J. Babler, currently of Marquette University School of Dentistry, Milwaukee, WI, published "Embryologic Development of Epidermal Ridges and Their Configurations" (*Birth Defects, Orig. Artic. Ser.,* 27(2), 112, 1991). This paper contains an excellent review of earlier research, and references Babler's and others' research into the prenatal relationship between epidermal ridge dimension and bone dimension of the hand.

In earlier research, Babler reported preparing several histologic sections of fingers from 81 human abortuses ranging in age from 11 to 25 weeks post-fertilization. Many sections were taken before friction ridges were visible on the surface. The sections were taken parallel to the finger bone starting at the finger pad surface, and progressed down through the finger until the primary ridges were revealed. At this point the pattern established by the primary ridges was evident.

The observations of Babler et al. confirm the findings of many other scientists also investigating friction ridge formation and development. If we add to this the many years of observation and comparison by forensic identification specialists, the picture is nearly complete. Years of scientific research supported by more than 100 years of observation cannot be discounted. The observations of friction ridge identification experts overwhelmingly support the facts as described by research scientists.

The Friction Ridge Medium

Friction ridge identification specialists are purported to have considerable knowledge about the friction skin. This knowledge is considered so great that they are permitted to offer expert opinion in court as to the clarity, uniqueness, and individuality of friction ridge prints. It is not possible to develop such an ability without first having extensive knowledge of the donor medium. The current identification system, which is based on a quantitative-qualitative analysis of friction ridge print formations, is only as genuine as the knowledge, experience, and ability of the identification specialist carrying out the comparison.

An understanding of friction skin structure and development is a prerequisite to developing the necessary skills required to become an expert in the science. Even a very basic decision, such as deciphering whether a ridge formation is a specific or nonspecific characteristic, depends on the identification specialist's level of knowledge about the friction skin. It is becoming more obvious as time passes that the courts are demanding more than a regurgitation of doctrine. The courts are expecting a rational understanding of the dynamics of the friction skin and an ability to explain the intricacies of the identification process. They depend on that ability to assist them with deciphering the value of the physical evidence presented before them.

This chapter introduces the reader to the structure and growth of friction skin. The nomenclature and the key histological aspects required to understand the premises of friction ridge identification are also presented. In the previous chapter there was discussion about the specific findings of some scientists' research and conclusions that involved considerable technical descriptions. After reading this chapter, it may be worthwhile to reread those conclusions.

The Structure of Friction Skin

Human skin is classified as an organ but is often incorrectly described as the largest organ of the body. The skin is the heaviest organ and is almost the

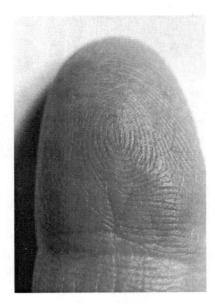

Figure 3.1   Friction skin on a finger.

largest, being approximately two yards square. The gastrointestinal tract and the 404 million alveoli in the lungs both have more total surface. The skin is extremely variable in that it has numerous functions and seemingly endless structural and topographical differences. The most striking difference in humans is between the volar skin, which is furrowed (Figure 3.1), and the skin on the rest of the body, which tends to be smooth.

Smooth skin contains hair, sebaceous glands, and sweat glands while volar skin contains only sweat glands. In the previous chapter Whipple's paper described a possible hypothesis for this difference. While volar skin does not secrete sebaceous oils, body oils are frequently found on volar skin, especially the hands, due to touching other parts of the body. The skin in the volar areas lacks pigmentation and is frequently lighter in color than the surrounding smooth skin. This phenomenon is more evident in dark-skinned races. There have been complete books published on human skin. This chapter will narrow its scope and address only the ridged volar skin.

Friction Ridges

The surface of volar skin has a special texturized surface in that it is continuously corrugated with narrow ridges. The purpose of the ridges is to increase friction between the volar surfaces and any other surface they contact. As a result they are commonly referred to as friction ridges. The friction ridges, described as islands by Hale, vary in length, from a section of ridge with one pore to a ridge with hundreds of pores.

Most texts state that between the ridges are furrows or sluci. To a degree, furrows are a misnomer when discussing friction skin. If the side of one friction ridge is followed into the furrow it meets the side of the ridge next to it. Furrows are more akin to friction ridge prints where they appear as blank spaces between the ridges. In the context of the friction skin the term *between the ridges* is irrelevant since physically the ridges meet and are fused together. This situation is similar to standing in a narrow mountain valley, which means one is standing on the side of one or the other mountains at its base. This rationale becomes important when attempting to understand the interactions of ridge units flowing in concert during friction ridge formation and during friction ridge analysis. The friction skin infrastructure below the surface is constructed of friction ridges, one beside the other, with no spaces between.

Friction Ridge Breadth

The width of friction ridges varies in different areas of friction skin as well as in different people (Figure 3.2). In general they are narrower in females and wider in males. The friction ridges naturally coarsen during their growth period from the fetus to adult. The ridges of the foot are noticeably coarser than those of the hand.

Figure 3.2 An illustration of the variability found along the friction ridges. Some ridges are fat and others are thin. The white arrow points to an area with several incipient ridges. This area has been enlarged in Figure 3.3.

The average ridge breadth of the hand is approximately 0.48 mm in young male adults, while on females they are slightly narrower and smaller. Ridge breadth can also be measured by the number of ridges per centimeter. Young adult males have an average of approximately 20.7 ridges per cm and females, approximately 23.4 ridges per cm. Differentiating between male and female friction ridges is not practical as some people are simply bigger than others. The difference in ridges per centimeter between an adult and a child is considerable, and young children's prints can be differentiated from adult prints by this measurement.

Ridge Units and Pores

Pore ducts open along the top of the friction ridges. They appear to be evenly spaced along the ridge. The appearance of even spacing is due to the fact that friction ridges are constructed of ridge units. Each ridge unit has one sweat gland and a pore opening randomly somewhere on its surface (Figure 3.3).

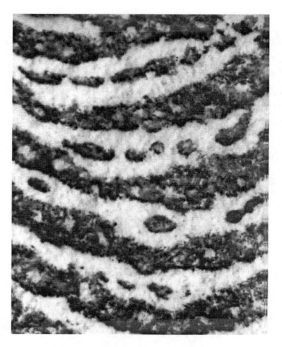

Figure 3.3 Incipient ridges are immature ridges that develop in the same manner as normal ridges. Some will have pore formations. Many larger incipient ridges are accepted as thin normal ridges. Can we differentiate one from the other? This area of friction ridges also illustrates the intrinsic shapes of the ridges. They fluctuate in thickness from fat ridge units to thin; some are misaligned while others flow smoothly.

As a result, the spatial distance between pores frequently appears to be in proportion to the breadth of the ridge. Ridge units will be addressed in depth in the next part of this chapter.

The pore opening is the duct of an eccrine or sweat gland which is buried deep in the dermal skin. Sweat glands found in the volar areas tend to be larger and more active than on other parts of the body. The sweat gland duct travels through the various layers of skin on a spiral course to the surface. The purpose of the sweat glands is to remove waste and to increase friction by depositing moisture onto the surface of the friction ridges. The increased friction retards slippage. The function of sweat glands in other parts of the body is to dispose of waste and to cool the skin surface through evaporation. The sweat glands in the volar areas tend to be triggered more when the person is nervous or during a "fight or flight" scenario.

Eccrine sweat contains approximately 99% water and 1% solids. The solids are half inorganic salts and half organic compounds. The salt is mostly sodium chloride while the organic compounds include urea, amino acids, and peptides.

Specific Ridge Path

The friction ridges have been compared to corduroy, but unlike corduroy they are not continuous in nature (Figure 3.4). The path taken by the ridges may branch, start or stop, turn, twist, or thicken and narrow independently,

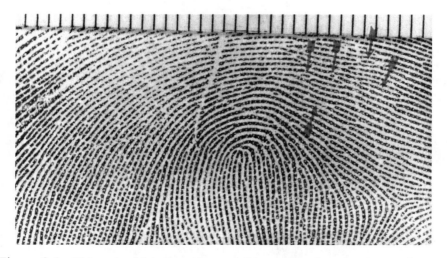

Figure 3.4 This area of friction ridges exhibits various lengths. Across the top, ridges of 2,1, 3, and 10 ridge units are marked by arrows (Left to Right). The bottom arrow points to a ridge of approximately 16 ridge units. The ridge unit is the building block of the friction ridge.

or as the pattern flow dictates. The ridge path can also appear segmented into its basic ridge units. This is often very noticeable along the edge of the pattern area where friction skin and normal skin meet. At times individual ridge units are not attached to any other structure. Some may appear to stand alone in a furrow while others appear to stand at the end of a ridge. When fully developed, the ridge unit is about as wide as it is long.

Incipient Friction Ridges

On occasion, narrow and often fragmented ridges may appear between normal friction ridges. These ridges are called incipient, rudimentary, subsidiary, or nascent ridges (Figures 3.5, 3.6). They differ from the typical ridge by being thinner and fragmented. Incipient ridges may or may not have fully developed pore formations. They develop in exactly the same manner as normal friction ridges except that they fail to reach maturity. Incipient ridges

Figure 3.5 A photograph of the surface friction ridges with incipient ridges in the furrows. Incipient ridges are immature ridges and have the same substructure as mature ridges.

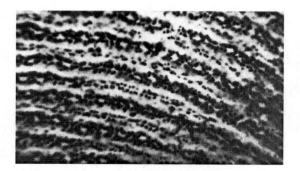

Figure 3.6 The dermal surface of the same area shown in Figure 3.5. Papillae pegs are found under mature friction ridges and under the incipient ridges. Pegs under incipient ridges are miniature.

are simply immature friction ridges and they will be discussed further during the next part of this chapter.

Friction Ridge Imbrication

In some areas of the volar surfaces the friction ridges all tend to lean in the same direction. This feature is referred to as *imbrication*. Imbricated ridges vary among individuals and even the regions of volar areas where they are found. The friction skin is very flexible. When an area of friction skin is pressured laterally it will resist slippage by rolling over slightly before releasing and slipping. This characteristic enhances the ability of the friction ridges to grip surfaces. When the ridges roll before slippage, that is also referred to as imbrication.

Overall Friction Ridge Pattern

The friction ridges form patterns on the volar surfaces. The most common are concentric, looping, or arching formations. Friction ridge patterns also enhance the ability of volar skin to resist slippage. The various patterns are believed to be the result of an evolutionary process as indicated in Chapter II (Whipple). Ridges flowing in patterns, especially if they are concentric in nature, will resist slippage regardless of the direction in which force is applied. The pattern also enhances tactile sensitivity due to the increased friction.

Friction Skin Histology

The friction skin is divided into two main layers. The inner layer is the *dermis* and the outer layer is the *epidermis*. All of the surface friction ridge formations described thus far are part of the epidermis except the pore glands, which develop in the epidermis but penetrate into the dermis.

Epidermis

The epidermis is the outer layer of the friction skin. In the volar areas the epidermis is made up of several layers of skin cells. These various layers are sometimes divided into two groups. The inner layer of cells is the stratum Malpighii (also stratum mucosum), and the outer layer is the stratum corneum. The Malpighii layer is made up of the basal layer, being the deepest (also called stratum basal or stratum germinativum), followed by the spinous layer (stratum spinosum), and then the granular layer (stratum granulosum). The outer or surface group of cells consists of the hyalin layer (stratum lucidum) and the horny layer (stratum corneum).

Generating Layer

The deepest layer of cells next to the dermis is called the basal layer. The basal layer is only one cell deep. A membrane, the basal lamina, separates the basal layer from the dermis. As the epidermis is basically nonvascular, the basal lamina is porous to allow a diffusion of nutrients to pass into the epidermis from dermal capillaries. This membrane also permits waste to leave the epidermis and be removed through the dermis. Due to the key role the basal layer plays in generating new skin cells, it is often referred to as the *generating layer.*

Epidermal Cells

Basal epidermal cells are columnar in shape (Figure 3.7). They stand with their long axes perpendicular to the skin surface. Basal cells divide in the generating layer and start a slow migration toward the surface as they are displaced by newly generated cells. On volar areas the trip to the surface takes approximately one month, but there are numerous variables that can alter that rate. The basal cells lying under the center of a friction ridge tend to proliferate at a greater rate than those to the side of the friction ridge or

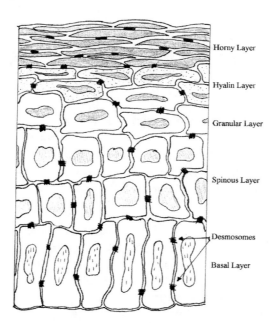

Figure 3.7 The shape of the epidermal cells are depicted in this sketch. The deepest cells of the basal layer are columnar. As cells move toward the surface they become cuboidal, and finally squamose as they reach the horny layer at the skin surface. "Desmosome" is a type of cell junction that binds the cells together. The junction releases and reforms as the cells change shape.

under the furrow. All cells are held together with a substance called *desmosome*, one of many types of cell junctions or cement.

As the cells migrate to the surface they become progressively flattened in a plane parallel to the skin surface. During this time the desmosome releases and reattaches as required when the cells change shape. Near the surface the horny layer cells are very flat or scale-like and firmly attached together with desmosome. Cells arriving at the surface are continually displacing surface cells which are shed when the cell junction points break down or through abrasion. The epidermis can be described as an automatic resurfacing mechanism of the skin.

Primary Epidermal Ridges

The bottom of the epidermis is covered with thousands of fibrous tufts of connective tissue. The topology of the epidermal underside is similar to the surface as it is covered with ridge-like formations. The ridge formations found directly under surface friction ridges are called primary epidermal ridges (Figure 3.8). Primary ridges mirror the surface ridge and contain pore structures.

Photographs or drawings of friction ridge substructure, viewed in normal cross section, tend to illustrate the primary ridge as a solid formation penetrating deep into the dermis, which is misleading. Areas of primary ridge between the pore ducts do not penetrate into the dermis as deeply as the area around the pore duct. For example, if a single ridge was cut along its length, the resulting cross section would clearly reveal that the primary ridge varies in its penetration of the dermis. The primary ridge pores penetrate very deep into the dermis and the areas between the pores do not penetrate as deeply.

Figure 3.8 This photograph is of an inked print made by friction ridges on the skin surface. The friction ridges appear as black. (Photo by Karen Anne Rice)

Figure 3.9 This print was made by the same piece of skin as in Figure 3.8 except that the bottom of the epidermis was inked and rolled. The secondary ridges are dark lines and the primary ridges are rows of dots. The dots are caused by the pore ducts and surrounding tissue. (Photo by Karen Anne Rice)

Secondary Epidermal Ridges

The secondary epidermal ridges are found between the primary ridges on the bottom of the epidermis (Figure 3.9). These ridges are found under the surface furrows or under the areas where adjacent friction ridges meet. The secondary ridges do not have pore structures. They tend to penetrate into the dermis to a depth about equal to the primary ridge formations found around the pore ducts.

Dermis

The inner layer of the friction skin is called the dermis. The dermis is a matrix of loose connective tissue composed of fibrous proteins. It is traversed by numerous blood vessels, lymphatics, various glands, and tactile nerves. The dermis serves the function of feeding nutrients to the outer layer of friction skin as well as giving physical protection to the internal body. Other than the sweat gland ducts, only very delicate nerves pass from the dermis into the deepest layers of the epidermis. The density and physical strength of the dermis may be appreciated by noting that leather is made from the dermis of animal hides. The dermis is often called the *true skin*.

Dermal Papillae

The surface of the dermis is covered with blunt peg-like formations called *dermal papillae*. The dermal papillae fit into pockets on the underside of the

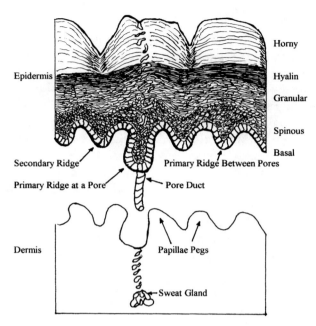

Figure 3.10 A cross section of a friction ridge where the epidermis and dermis have been slightly separated. The layers of the skin and the various formations on the epidermal and dermal surfaces have been labeled.

epidermis (Figure 3.10), filling voids between the primary and secondary epidermal ridges. The dermal surface therefore takes on the negative shape of the bottom of the epidermis. As the papillae pegs are filling voids on each side of the primary and secondary epidermal ridges, they appear to align in double rows. It is possible to establish the path of a primary ridge by following the double rows of dermal papillae. In this manner the path of the surface friction ridges can be established. Due to this relationship, friction ridges are sometimes referred to as *papillary ridges*.

Dermal papillae contain capillary loops to feed oxygen and food supplies to the generating layer of the epidermis and to remove waste. Nerve endings called *Meissner corpuscles* are also contained within the dermal papillae. Meissner corpuscles establish the sense of touch on the dermal surface. The volar skin contains more such nerve endings than other areas of the body. As one ages the dermal papillae tend to flatten and appear to increase in numbers. Papillae take on the appearance of a cauliflower floret in that they are basically the same overall size, but the surface of the papillae peg appears to be covered with several small peg-like bundles. These formations are more difficult to follow to establish the path of the primary ridges.

Effects of Injury or Disease

Injury or disease that penetrates the skin to the dermal papillae level can damage the epidermal basal layer infrastructure. This may destroy the ability of the basal layer to regenerate cells in the damaged area. Surrounding basal cells will repair the damage but the resulting deformation will appear at the surface in the form of a scar. Deep injuries are usually accompanied by bleeding. As the epidermis is nonvascular the damage must reach the basal lamina, the membrane at the junction of the dermis and epidermis, for blood to be let. Injury or disease that does not penetrate deeply enough to damage the basal layer will be repaired by the proliferating cells from deeper in the epidermis. In this case, the surface damage will eventually be erased and the surface ridges returned to their original shape.

The finger printed in Figure 3.11 was first printed in 1980. When the finger was printed again in 1981 (Figure 3.12) it had developed a wart running across the center of the pattern. By the time the same finger was printed again in 1982 (Figure 3.13) the wart had disappeared and the ridge formations had returned to their original configuration.

Figure 3.11

Figure 3.12

Figure 3.13

Friction Ridge Immutability

Other than injury, disease, or decomposition at death, the friction ridges are immutable. When the friction ridges form intrauterine on the fetus they are in their permanent configuration. The primary and secondary ridges are the blueprint or root system for the surface friction ridges. Once established it does not change. In the same manner, the location and size of pore ducts and pore openings along the friction ridge surface are also immutable.

Flexion Creases

Flexion creases are present in areas of volar skin where the skin is continually flexed through the movements of digits or the palms. The flexion creases are areas of firmer skin attachment to underlying structures. These areas remain relatively fixed during movement of the parts and are persistent within the friction ridge configuration. Almost all flexion creases appear on the fetus before the friction ridges. Flexion creases are devoid of ridge structures.

The path of the three large flexion creases (Major Creases) are genetically controlled through the location of the volar pads. The path of some of the medium sized creases (Minor Creases) are also controlled by the location of the volar pads but their structure is random. The smallest of flexion creases (Secondary Creases) appear at random in all areas of the palm and are very unique to the individual. Flexion creases will be covered in depth in Chapter VIII.

Other creases that appear on the volar surface are called *white lines*. The paths and structures of these other creases are influenced by the shape and flexibility of the hand. White lines are actually folds or a buckling of the skin surface, similar to a leather glove. They do not have the same firm subcutaneous attachments that flexion creases have. As with all creases, white line definition tends to increase with age or when subcutaneous fatty deposits change. Once established, white lines generally do not change. It is possible that they may be altered over time through a change in the flexion pattern of the part, possibly caused by serious injury or disease.

Summary

The accompanying diagrams in this part of the chapter have divided the various elements of the friction skin into neat segments. As with all biological formations, the friction skin is subject to numerous variables which may slightly or drastically alter its appearance. From the foregoing the reader should have established an understanding of the basic nomenclature required to describe the structure of the friction skin and the various formations found on its surface and subsurface. Also, the reader should have a basic understanding of how friction ridges remain persistent and the degree of trauma necessary to create a scar and cause bleeding.

The Growth of Friction Skin

In the first part of this chapter some nomenclature and the structure of the friction skin were established. The second part of the chapter describes the growth and development of volar friction ridge skin and the various influences it is subjected to during the process. This information becomes very important during the identification process. For example, the manner in which the various friction ridge formations develop and the influences they are subjected to dictate their role and value toward the individualization of friction ridge prints during comparison.

While the various stages of friction ridge development are expressed in a time frame of weeks for convenience, there are variations of development time with different fetuses. Some fetuses develop early and some develop late. The figures expressed here are from various respected texts and tend to reflect normal development. Many research papers do not use time to express fetal development. Crown to Rump, or C.R. length, is frequently used, as reported by Hale. In this chapter some C.R. measurements have been converted to an approximate age in weeks for the benefit of the reader.

The Epidermis

The epidermis is recognizable as an overall fetal covering at a very early stage. At three weeks the epidermis is approximately one cell thick. As the embryo grows the epidermal cells multiply to form a protective layer several cells thick. The epidermal resurfacing machine begins production as described in the first part of this chapter. Basal cells divide and for the first few months continue to add depth to the epidermal layer.

Volar Pads

The following describes the development of volar pads on the hands; the feet develop in generally the same fashion. The only qualification required is that the volar pads on the feet develop approximately two weeks later, regress two weeks later, and tend to be more expansive than on the hand.

The first noticeable development of friction skin on the volar surfaces takes place at about six weeks gestation (Figure 3.14). At this time the hand is paddle-like. The digits are present and indicated as broad scallops around its edge. The volar pads start to appear in their typical arrangement. The first to appear are the second, third, and fourth interdigital pads, as well as the thenar and hypothenar pads on the palm. These are followed by the five digital pads.

After eight weeks the fetus is about 2.5 cm long C.R. and the digits have separated and elongated. The volar pads appear as localized bulges. During the next two weeks the interdigital and palmar pads become very prominent

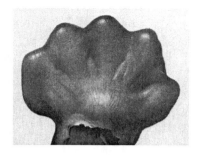

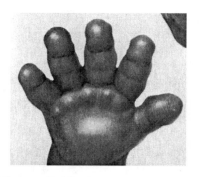

Figure 3.14 At six weeks the hand is paddle-like. The fingers are scallops around its edge. Some volar pads are starting to appear.

Figure 3.15 At ten weeks the interdigital pads are prominent and the thumb has rotated. The digital pads have also become prominent.

and the thumb rotates (Figure 3.15). The rotation of the thumb marks the appearance of the thenar flexion crease. By weeks 10 to 12 the digital pads have become distinct. The distal and proximal transverse flexion creases as well as the interdigital flexion creases appear.

The regression of the interdigital and palmar pads begins during the 10th or 11th week, followed by the digital pads from the 12th week onward. The flexion creases remain. At this time the fetus is approximately 7 cm long C.R. At about 12 weeks the friction ridges start to develop in the basal layer of the epidermis. At this time the interdigital and palmar pads have regressed more than the digital pads. Over the next few weeks the volar pads continue to reduce in size until their boundaries are indefinable from the surrounding skin.

Over the years there have been numerous studies investigating volar pad influence on friction ridge pattern formation. There is a correlation between the location, shape, and size of the volar pads and friction ridge pattern. The volar pads influence overall pattern flow, localized pattern configuration, and localized pattern trend of the friction ridges.

Overall Pattern Flow

The general consensus is that the varying topology of the volar surface creates surface stresses caused by the presence of the volar pads in their typical arrangement. Further stresses are created by friction ridge development and the growth of the part. These factors together influence the flow of overall friction ridge configuration. In normal and healthy fetuses, volar pads appear at specific locations and at approximately the same time during fetal development. As a result, all humans tend to have the same general friction ridge and flexion crease configuration.

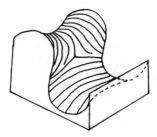

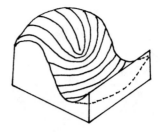

Figure 3.16 It is believed that a surface of this shape would cause friction ridges to create a triradius formation.

Figure 3.17 It is believed that a surface of this shape would cause the friction ridges to create a looping formation.

It is believed that friction ridge patterns are determined by the maximal curvature of the surface on which they develop. During studies of topology, it has been found that lines of curvature tend to follow the greatest convexity of a surface under stress. Under such conditions this influence naturally forms loops and triradii in surface patterns (Figures 3.16, 3.17). The same applies in an equivalent situation in areas of least concavity.

This topological rule would apply to friction ridges forming on volar pads. The friction ridges would tend to follow the paths of greatest convexity, such as ridges forming around the digital, interdigital, and palmar volar pads, or of least concavity such as the paths of ridges across the center of the palm which lie between volar pads (Figure 3.18).

The volar pads are areas of the greatest convexity on the volar surface and tend to be the centers of disturbance within ridge systems. The friction ridge patterns tend to expand outward from a central point situated on or near the volar pads. When three ridge systems meet a triradius is formed. A triradius is called a *delta* in most classification systems.

Localized Pattern Configuration

The size of the volar pad influences the localized pattern developing on its surface. Tensions within the surface layers of the skin are basically related to the curvature of the volar pad and the shape and growth of the part. If the volar pad is tall the friction ridges will form a concentric pattern (Figure 3.19). If the volar pad is flat the pattern will tend to be at the other end of the spectrum and form an arch (Figure 3.20). A pad of medium height will tend to have a concentric looping formation (Figure 3.21). The timing of the commencement of friction ridge development and volar pad regression therefore become factors in pattern design.

This theory is borne out by examining the resulting friction ridge formations on the hand. In a normal fetus the interdigital and palmar pads

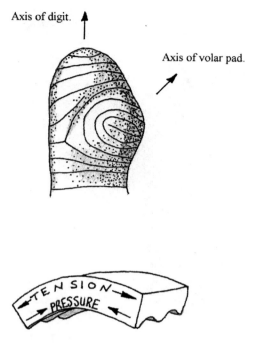

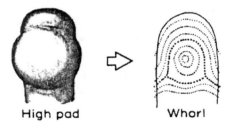

Figure 3.18 Tension and pressure created by the volar pads affect the friction ridge patterns. Also, external pressure may alter the volar pad shape and therefore alter a pattern.

Figure 3.19 High-centered pads are believed to form whorl-type patterns.

begin to regress before friction ridges develop. The resulting friction ridges on these volar pad sites are developing on shrinking pads and an expanding hand. Strong concentric formations are not often found in these areas. At 13 weeks when the friction ridges are starting to develop on the digital pads, the digital pads have just reached their largest state. Strong concentric formations are frequently found on the digits.

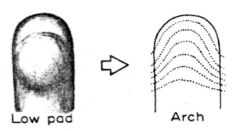

Figure 3.20   Low volar pads tend to form arch or low count loop patterns and can be the result of a disturbance during fetal formation.

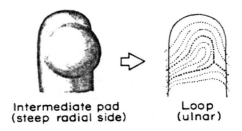

Figure 3.21   Intermediate pads with a trend are believed to form loop-type patterns.

Localized Pattern Trend

The shape of volar pads also affects the trend of localized pattern formations. Volar pads are not always perfectly spherical. At times they are offset or leaning to one side. The ridges follow the greatest convexity over the offset volar pad forming a pattern on a bias or displaying a trend.

Volar pad trend can be caused by genetic or external physical influences. The genetic relationship of volar pads has been established through numerous studies. There is an opportunity to pass overall pattern design from parent to sibling. This is believed to be manifested through the volar pads. The best example of this is in the case of identical twins, clones who develop in the same environment. Frequently they have very similar overall friction ridge patterns. However, some patterns are different at times. In these instances it is believed that external stresses and pressures, caused by any of a variety of factors, alter the volar pad shape or development during the time of critical friction ridge formation. This in turn alters the surface shape and stress, which in turn change the pattern design.

Some diseases or genetic aberrations may disrupt the development of volar pads and therefore alter overall or localized pattern. These afflictions tend to affect different fetuses in a similar manner. Fetuses suffering from

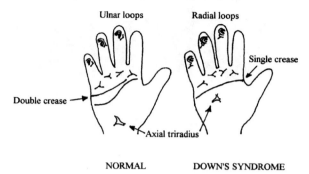

Figure 3.22 Aberrant formation of friction ridges and flexion creases. Disease or other physical factors may affect the type of pattern, structure of the ridge, or flexion crease formation and location.

the same disease frequently have similar deformities in friction ridge configuration. Many diseases or genetic aberrations can now be identified through the examination of friction ridge patterns on newborn babies. For example, Down's syndrome tends to appear in the friction ridge patterns as low count loops, possibly a simian crease. The palmar triradius, usually located near the wrist, is often higher on the palm than normal (Figure 3.22). The study of the effects of disease and genetic aberrations on the friction ridges is referred to as *dermatoglyphics*.

The primary basis for volar pad development is still unsubstantiated. Whipple's position of an evolutionary connection with the past is the only explanation that fits with all the other pieces of data. More recent research has established that the type of cells found in volar pads is the same type found in bone and cartilage.

Primary Ridges

At about 12 weeks, during the time of volar pad regression, bands of thickening tissue appear on the *bottom* of the epidermis. These bands are the first formations of primary ridges (See Figure 2.21). An average fetus would be approximately 10 cm long C.R. The epidermis has a fundamental biological factor encoded in it mandating it to produce ridge units and to have those units fuse into rows to form friction ridges. Each ridge unit will develop a sweat gland deep in the dermis with a pore opening on the ridge unit surface. Cells developing within the primary ridges immediately start their migration toward the surface of the epidermis fused together with desmosome plaques. Within three to four weeks the primary ridges cover the entire underside of the epidermis.

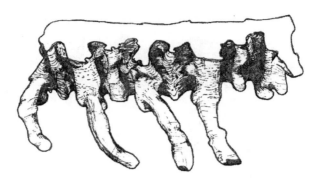

Figure 3.23   Primary ridges develop pores. They are the root system for the friction ridges. Secondary ridges develop between primary ridges under the surface furrows.

Secondary Ridges

By the 15th to 16th week the fetus is approximately 14 cm long C.R. At this time another ridge system starts to develop between the primary ridges. These ridges are called secondary ridges (Figure 3.23). When secondary ridges begin to develop the primary ridges cease their multiplications. While the primary ridges are now in their final or differentiated form, they continue to grow in size in relation to the development of the fetus. Secondary ridges do not develop sweat glands. They penetrate into the dermis about as deep as the primary ridges located between the pore ducts.

During growth the secondary ridges develop a stress between themselves and the surface. The stress lines are visible in cross sections of friction skin (Figure 3.25). The stress factor may be genetic in nature or may be the result of the stresses created between the various cells from different areas of the ridge unit. Cells developing in different areas of the ridge unit produce different types of keretin at different rates. This, in effect, causes cells in the center of the ridge unit to move toward the surface faster than those on the edges. This is believed to be the result of differing surface stimulation affecting keretin development. In either case this stress has the effect of strengthening the junction areas under the surface furrows. The arrangement of primary and secondary ridges continues to develop until about the fifth month of fetal life. At this time the surface friction ridges are visible. Friction ridge differentiation, the state when the final configuration of the ridges is established and will not change, can vary from between the fourth and fifth months of fetal development.

Figure 3.24 The pockets between the primary and secondary ridges are filled with dermal papillae pegs.

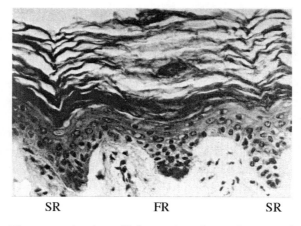

SR   FR   SR

Figure 3.25 The stress in the cell formation above the secondary ridges (SR) can be seen on each side of the friction ridge (FR). This cross section of friction skin also shows the depth of the primary ridge between the pore ducts (FR).

Blood Vessel-Nerve Pairs

Some researchers have published papers indicating that just prior to primary ridge formation there are blood vessel-nerve pairs under the surface where the glandular fold or primary ridge is about to develop. They theorize that the primary ridges are generated by the presence of the blood vessel-nerve pairs. When resin casts of interpapillary capillary networks are made they mirror the path of the friction ridges. Meissner corpuscles and other nerves are also found in the dermal papillae pegs. If a schematic of the nerves could be isolated they would also mirror the friction ridge paths. (Figure 3.24)

Even though a friction ridge appears to be one solid ridge, its early morphology reflects the fusion of individual units during initial development, resulting in friction ridge pore ducts spaced relatively evenly along the length of the ridge. In longitudinal friction ridge cross sections, transverse constrictions are often found between the pore ducts which mark the boundary of the next ridge unit. The stress lines above the secondary ridges mark the other boundary of the ridge units along each side. It may be possible that the presence of blood vessel-nerve endings is the first sign of ridge unit development as opposed to the blood vessel-nerve endings appearing in a support role to the ridge unit. In either case, once the ridge unit has started to develop the path of the friction ridges and their shapes are influenced by the physical aspects of differential growth.

Major Ridge Path Deviations

Hale reports that friction ridges develop two aspects, branches and islands (Figure 3.26). Branches are ridges that develop by diverging from other established friction ridges. Branches first appear as lateral swellings on the side of primary ridges. As the primary ridge and branch develop the friction ridge surface expands. This stretches the formation laterally. The expansion pulls the developing branch ridge away from the originating primary ridge. Branches tend to develop early in the ridge formation process. This major ridge path deviation is a *bifurcation*.

The other origin of a friction ridge is an island. Islands develop between existing primary ridges and may have from one ridge unit to several hundred ridge units in their paths or lengths. Islands that form early during primary ridge formation tend to be longer. The later formations are the shortest. Islands that do not fully develop prior to differentiation are incipient ridges. During comparison, if the ends of an island can be easily recognized as being from the same ridge, it is commonly referred to as a *short ridge*.

The major deviations in ridge path, when recorded in a print, are called *ridge characteristics* or *Galton details*. A major ridge path deviation does not develop in isolation (Figure 3.27). Other ridge formations must develop around it and in concert with it. Therefore, all major ridge path deviations display interaction with surrounding ridges.

The Uniqueness of Friction Ridge Configuration

The friction ridges are constructed of ridge units. The number of ridge units that make up a ridge is established at random. Where a ridge starts and stops, the factors that designate its length are completely dependent on differential

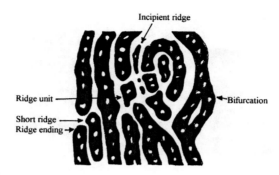

Figure 3.26 Hale's islands and branches. The ridge units align or misalign as they move in concert with surrounding ridges. Each ridge unit has a shape that is formed during differential growth. Pore location is at random on the unit.

growth. The location of the ridge unit where a branching develops is also established at random. Due to the plethora of genetic and physical variances the ridge units are subjected to during friction ridge formation and the numbers of units involved, the paths of friction ridges are unique to that area of friction skin.

The ridge units are not only subjected to differential growth factors while developing into rows and growing, they are also subjected to a random growth factor in relation to their shapes. Therefore, ridge units may vary in shape, size, alignment, and whether they fuse to the next ridge unit or not. For example, some units are thinner than others, some have bulges on one side, and some misalign with the next ridge unit or fail to develop to maturity. Friction ridges are three-dimensional and, due to the variables along the friction ridge surface, they are unique, even in a very small area. The location of the pore opening on a ridge unit is also established by random forces through differential growth. The random placement of pore openings on the friction ridges is another factor that enhances the uniqueness of friction skin. The comparison of relative pore locations is called *poroscopy* and is addressed in detail in Chapter V.

Aberrant Formation of Friction Ridges

Abnormalities occasionally appear on the volar surfaces. Disease of the skin such as eczema or injury such as frostbite will alter the skin surface and disrupt friction ridge formations. There are instances when ridge units are present but do not fuse together to form friction ridges. This aberration may affect all of the volar surfaces or just a small part. This condition, known to be inherited, is called dysplasia. It is believed that this aberration is caused by a genetic malfunction.

Figure 3.27 Major ridge path deviations do not form in isolation. When a ridge ends, the adjacent ridges converge to fill the vacant space. At times the actual location of a ridge characteristic can be found by examining the surrounding ridge formations. This ridge ending may taper at the end marked with the dotted line and, without extra deposition pressure, it will not reproduce completely in the print. The adjacent ridges indicate its true ending point.

A similar condition where small areas of the volar surface may be affected is called dissociated ridges (Figure 3.28). It is believed that external pressure

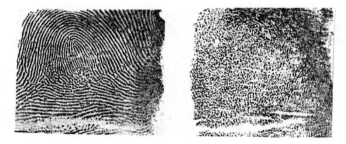

Figure 3.28 Dissociated ridges of dysplasia. In either case the ridge units have formed into several short ridges in part of the pattern or remained as single ridge units.

on an area of volar skin during ridge formation may modify the progress of epidermal differentiation and produce imperfect ridges. These defects often appear as patches of islands or short ridges in the final ridge configuration. Dissociated ridges are ridge units in their simplest form and have a configuration appearing similar to that of a dog's nose.

When ridge units are found in various stages of fusion as single units or in short ridges, these formations are persistent and are replenished by basal cells as previously described. The random formation of these units creates an extremely unique configuration (Figure 3.29).

Figure 3.29 Dysplasia or Dissociated Ridges?

Summary

Being aware of the growth process of friction ridges gives an understanding as to the origin of friction ridge path, intrinsic friction ridge shape, and relative pore location. These elements are the reasons why friction skin is considered unique. As with all scientific statements or hypotheses, there was a period where observation was part of the process. This is also the case with friction skin uniqueness. For over 100 years, thousands of friction ridge identification specialists and scientists have compared billions of friction ridge prints. No one has yet to find two areas of friction skin from different sources with the same friction ridge configuration. No other scientific hypothesis has been tested to this degree, other than possibly the hypothesis of gravity. Today it is accepted as a scientific fact that friction ridge skin is unique and can be differentiated using a very small area.

The Identification
Process

In the previous chapter the structure and formation of the friction skin was described. The first part of this chapter will capsulize that information in a discussion about the premises of friction ridge identification. Clarity will be defined and new terminology will be introduced. The identification process will then be presented and the information reported in the previous chapter will be applied to the friction ridge identification process.

The purpose of the identification process is to individualize. Individualization is the elimination of all similar items in the world, leaving only one possible source. The identification process is broken down into two main applications. The first application is the philosophy of friction ridge identification which basically answers the question, "How much is enough?" The second application is the methodology which describes the structured and systematic manner in which quantitative-qualitative analysis of friction ridges is carried out and an opinion reached.

A part of this chapter has also been devoted to human sight. The old saying, "You see what you want to see," can ring true if one is unaware of how the brain processes visual images. While human sight is extremely complex, our needs only require a general understanding of some of the shortcomings of the eye-brain combination.

Throughout this chapter there are references to palmar flexion crease identification, poroscopy, pressure distortion, and complex or problem print analysis. This book is designed and intended to introduce readers to these advanced topics. Once the basics of qualitative-quantitative friction ridge analysis are mastered, the established path of learning will naturally lead to proficiency in these advanced identification sciences, but further training and experience will be required to gain expertise in these areas.

The Premises of Friction Ridge Identification

The premises of friction ridge identification are not assumptions. Each premise is a statement of fact, a keynote representing a vast area of knowledge. The scientific information represented by each premise relates to specific factors of friction skin formation and development. In a way, the premises of identification is a summary of the previous chapter.

The physical and genetic influences associated with the development and growth of the various friction ridge formations establish the manner in which each formation is later applied to the identification process. For this reason memorizing the premises of identification is not enough. One must fully understand the meaning of each premise. An awareness of the knowledge capsulized behind each premise is a prerequisite to becoming an expert in the friction ridge identification science.

The premises of friction ridge identification are usually reported in a fashion similar to the following quote from the book *Scientific Evidence in Criminal Cases*, by Moenssens et al.

> The practical use in law enforcement of a system of fingerprint identification derives from three well established premises:
>
> 1. the friction ridge patterns that begin to develop during fetal life remain unchanged during life, and even after death, until decomposition destroys the ridged skin;
> 2. the patterns differ from individual to individual, and even from digit to digit, and are never duplicated in their minute details; and,
> 3. although all patterns are distinct in their ridge characteristics, their overall pattern appearances have similarities which permit a systematic classification of the impressions.

When the three premises are analyzed, taking into consideration our understanding of the structure of friction skin and friction ridge formation, there are actually four premises of friction ridge identification reported above. These are:

(1) Friction ridges develop on the fetus in their definitive form before birth.

(2) Friction ridges are persistent throughout life except for permanent scarring.

(3) Friction ridge patterns and the details in small areas of friction ridges are unique and never repeated.

(4) Overall friction ridge patterns vary within limits which allow for classification.

The fourth premise is not really a statement of fact relating to identification. Classification assists to narrow the search but is not a requirement for individualization. The mandate of classification is to remove all nonconforming aspects of the friction ridges so they can be placed into organized groups for retrieval. During classification, scars, incipient ridges, nonconforming appendages, and dissociated ridges are simply artificially and arbitrarily ignored. These aspects are often the most individualizing features present within friction ridge configurations.

While classification discards all the misfits found within the friction ridges, the identification process actually seeks them out. The more extraordinary or nonconforming the formation, the more individualizing power it has. Classification is not a prerequisite for identification. Searching unorganized piles of fingerprint forms could serve the same purpose, although obviously not nearly as efficiently as searching a classified collection.

Most friction ridge identification specialists understand the workings of one or two classification systems through necessity, either for convenience or for employment. For the purposes of this chapter no comment will be made about classification. The remaining three premises are worthy of further discussion.

The First Premises of Friction Ridge Identification

Friction Ridges Develop on the Fetus in Their Definitive Form before Birth

The factors underlying this premise are found in studies of human embryology. Embryonic studies of the friction skin describe the physical development of the friction ridges and the influences that affect their configuration. This information is necessary to establish the relevancy of the various ridge formations and the manner in which they can be used during the identification process.

There is a strong correlation between friction ridge patterns and the location, size, and shape of volar pads. The presence of volar pads alters the topology of the friction ridge surface and thereby alters surface stresses at the time friction ridges are forming. The volar pad configuration can be affected in two ways. The first is genetic or hereditary, and the second is through physical forces caused by disease or natural intrauterine pressures.

As the overall friction ridge pattern may be at least partially genetically controlled, other closely related individuals may have similar patterns. In the case of identical twins the similarity can be very close. Unrelated individuals may also have similar patterns through coincidence. Due to the limited possibilities of differing overall pattern flow on similarly shaped body parts and the fact that volar pads appear in a typical arrangement, overall patterns are frequently repeated. These factors diminish the individualizing value of overall patterns, which are therefore considered a class characteristic or a nonspecific detail when friction ridge prints are applied to the identification process.

A second example is the specific paths of the friction ridges which, while part of the overall pattern flow, have the freedom to form with varying lengths and to develop spatially. The specific pattern is constructed similar to that of a mosaic in that it is made up of hundreds of individual ridge units, each capable of randomness of configuration. Where the varying lengths of Hale's islands will start or stop and where the branchings (bifurcations) will take place are at random. Due to the numbers of units that make up the friction ridge paths and the immense number of genetic and physical variables involved in their development, specific friction ridge paths are unique when considered in the aggregate. Taking the second example a step farther would involve a description of the variables involved with the growth of the shape of the ridge units.

The random growth aspect of the friction ridge formation is referred to as *differential growth*. Heredity does not play a specific role. Similar ridge characteristics may appear in similar-shaped patterns, but this is due to the forces of pattern formation on the volar pad as opposed to a genetic connection. When the ridge characteristic is examined beyond the type, the smaller details such as relative pore location and ridge shape will always be different. The ridge formations formed by differential growth such as specific ridge paths, major ridge path deviations, obvious fluctuations in ridge width, alignment or misalignment of ridge units, and pore location are not repeated exactly in other areas of friction skin.

Summary of the First Premise

The key issue of the first premise is, by understanding how friction ridges develop before birth and the influences they are subjected to, we are able to understand their significance when applying them to the identification process. Without this information we are unaware of which ridge formations are class or nonspecific details, and which formations are unique or specific details. In the past this lack of knowledge has eliminated some of the most unique features of the friction ridges.

The Second Premise of Friction Ridge Identification

Friction Ridges Are Persistent throughout Life Except for Permanent Scarring

The information represented by this premise is found mainly within studies of the histology of friction skin. Having an understanding of the structure of friction skin is imperative to comprehend the manner in which friction ridges remain persistent as described in the previous chapter.

New epidermal ridge cells are generated in the basal layer of the epidermis. The basal layer is an immutable root system for the surface friction ridges. The cells from the basal layer slowly migrate toward the surface of the friction ridges and are held together with desmosome. As they migrate upward they change shape by becoming flatter. At the surface their appearance is flake-like. They slough off as the desmosome breaks down, or through abrasion. The continual proliferation of an immutable basal cell system and the constant migration to the surface to replenish sloughing cells achieves a persistent surface friction ridge system.

The knowledge required to understand this premise of friction ridge identification also contains other valuable information such as the manner in which scars are formed and how they may remain persistent due to damage to the basal layer of the epidermis. Also, in the previous chapter the epidermal-dermal surfaces were discussed. Understanding what these surfaces look like can be an asset in specific cases. For example, when the friction ridges are destroyed by putrefaction or fire, one may be required to examine a print taken from either the undersurface of the epidermis or the top surface of the dermis for identification purposes. Deciphering the relevancy of connective tissues in these areas is impossible without the appropriate knowledge.

Summary of the Second Premise

The key issue in this premise is, through knowledge of the structure of friction skin an understanding of friction ridge persistency is attained. Also, other side issues such as scars, flexion crease persistency, and the ability to use a print from the dermal-epidermal surfaces for identification purposes are gleaned from this area of knowledge.

The Third Premise of Friction Ridge Identification

Friction Ridge Patterns and the Details in Small Areas of Friction Ridges Are Unique and Never Repeated

This premise actually addresses two aspects. The first is that the specific pattern of the friction ridges or the friction ridge arrangement is never repeated and is unique. The second is that small areas of friction ridges are unique due to their innate formations.

The first part of this premise, dealing with the uniqueness of friction ridge pattern, was addressed when discussing the first premise. In this premise friction ridge pattern means specific friction ridge pattern, or the specific path of the friction ridges. As described earlier by Hale, where islands and branchings will appear are determined at random by differential growth.

Where the ridge characteristics are located is important, but due to the mosaic-like formation of the friction ridges, the path of the friction ridges can be compared to a maze. It is not only important where the island stops or where the branch is located, but the number of units that make up the ridge between these features also has value toward individualization and must be in agreement. During friction skin growth any one of the ridge units may or may not have fused to the next unit creating a ridge ending, or could have developed a bifurcation.

During comparison, ridge length is usually established through a visual measurement of relative ridge characteristic position, but this only has relevancy if the examiner is aware that the two ridge ends are on the same ridge. If the ridge ends are spatially removed from each other that fact may not be easily recognized. For this reason it is advantageous to follow along the ridge path between ridge characteristics during comparison to measure and evaluate the ridge length and to maintain continuity, as well as to examine adjacent ridge features. In complex or problem prints this type of comparative measurement may actually be a physical measurement carried out on enlarged photographs, or a comparison that moves from ridge unit to ridge unit.

The second issue of this premise is the uniqueness of details in small areas of a friction ridge. Formations, such as obvious fluctuations in ridge width, alignment or misalignment of ridge units, and relative pore location are also unique and never repeated. These small ridge shapes are created through differential growth factors between the developing ridge units. If one could remove all the furrows from a friction ridge print the friction ridges would generally fit together, a reflection of the fact that friction ridge growth actually takes place in the generating area where there are no furrows. These smaller shapes are persistent and have enormous individualizing value if clarity permits their comparison.

Summary of the Third Premise

The two key issues of the third premise are that specific ridge paths are unique due to the random length, specific path, and relative location of the ridge characteristics. Also, friction ridges are unique in a very small area due to the shape, alignment, and relative pore location of the connected ridge units.

As one can see, the premises of friction ridge identification are not simply statements to be arbitrarily recited whenever there is a need to establish credibility. They are keynotes representing vast pools of information about the friction skin. It is knowledge that must be understood before a friction ridge print can be applied to the identification process in a competent and systematic fashion. The basis of the friction ridge identification science is capsulized within the premises of identification. This knowledge is a requirement to be an expert.

Clarity

There is one more aspect of the premises of friction ridge identification that must be clearly understood. The premises of friction ridge identification represent scientific facts about the friction skin. The friction skin is a three-dimensional structure. During comparison, a forensic identification specialist is required to assess the quality of a friction skin print made by the friction skin. The print is only a two-dimensional impression. Many of the minute details that make small areas of friction skin unique do not survive the transition from ridge to print. How well the details from 3-D ridges that are reproduced in the 2-D print is referred to as the *clarity* of the print. When most of the detail found on the friction ridges is reproduced in the friction ridge print, the print is considered clear. If few of the details from the friction ridges are produced, the print is considered unclear.

The assessment of clarity is a formal part of the friction ridge identification process. Clarity is the key link between the premises of friction ridge identification, dealing with friction skin, and the scientific identification process, which deals with the comparison of friction ridge prints (See Ridgeology Formula, p. 172) . Statements about the two media are not necessarily interchangeable. Some of the following material may appear to be premature; however, the difference between the friction skin, and the issues that address that medium such as the premises, and friction ridge prints and the issues that address that medium, must be fully understood.

For example, when discussing the friction skin, it can be said that the friction skin is unique in a very small area. This statement, however, only applies to a friction skin print if clarity is present. When clarity is absent it may be an incorrect statement.

The Two Aspects of Clarity

The result of an assessment of the clarity of a friction ridge print indicates two main aspects. First, it dictates the level of detail available for comparison. If clarity is poor and only the ridge path is available for comparison, then mostly major ridge path deviations are used as focal points to ascertain if the ridge paths are in agreement. However, if clarity is excellent and the small details of the friction skin have been reproduced, these small details may also be compared to establish individuality.

Within physical evidence sciences it is generally understood that the smaller the detail found progressively in agreement, the more individualizing power it has. Small details are what differentiate like objects. To give you an idea how powerful small details can be, imagine an undistorted cyanoacrylate print with a bifurcation just below the delta. Each pore on the bifurcation is visible. The inked print has a similar bifurcation below the delta and each pore there is also visible. The flexibility of the friction skin in such a small area is very limited. If the relative pore locations in this one area are not in agreement in both prints, then these prints do not have a common origin. Should they be in agreement, the value of that one small area of the comparison is considerable. Small details on the friction ridges are a tremendous asset when used to individualize, if they are available for comparison. Usually a combination of ridge path, major ridge path deviations, and small innate features along the friction ridges are used in the aggregate.

Second, clarity dictates our level of tolerance for discrepancy. In the case of a very clear print where no signs of pressure distortion are present, the tolerance for discrepancy in ridge shape is very low. In this case, major ridge path deviations must appear in the correct locations and have the same ridge path configurations and ridge shapes. However, in a very poor print that has been subjected to pressure distortion, small discrepancies can be tolerated, but all discrepancies must be consistent with being caused by a common force. At times more than one force can cause more than one type of distortion in the same print, but friction skin cannot stretch in several directions at the same time without rational cause.

The idea of allowing more tolerance with poor prints appears to be the reverse of what it should be. There is a cost for this increase in tolerance with poorly recorded prints. The cost is that during the individualization process there usually must be more ridge characteristics present to individualize than would be required in a very clear print. This is due to the fact that each area found in agreement in the unclear print carries less evaluative weight than if their configuration was clearly reproduced. The very clear print would likely have more detail available for the brain to compare in a smaller area due to the clear reproduction of the ridge details.

Therefore, clarity may also affect the size of the area of friction ridges required to individualize. In a clear print a considerable amount of detail may be available in a very small area. Individualization may be possible with that small area of friction ridges, but if the print is poorly recorded the small ridge details will be absent. In this case, as the specific ridge path is all that is available for comparison and the major ridge path deviations (ridge characteristics) are usually more interspersed throughout the print than smaller details, the size of the area required to individualize will likely increase.

Clarity and Levels of Friction Ridge Detail

An understanding of friction skin development and structure is the first step in recognizing the intricacies of the friction ridges. The in-depth knowledge of how the friction ridges appear on the skin is a prerequisite to assessing how well they reproduce in a print. The premises of friction ridge identification must be fully understood before clarity is relevant. However, the degree of clarity found in a print is difficult to put into words or describe so that others can relate to one's observation. For example, stating that a print is very clear or sort of clear means different things to different people. During early research into the scientific basis of quantitative-qualitative friction ridge analysis, this issue surfaced during discussions where the clarity of a friction ridge print was being described to colleagues.

It became obvious that it was necessary to develop some nomenclature to define clarity, and that the new nomenclature must be tied to the various formations found on the friction skin and in the friction ridge print. This was accomplished by relating clarity directly to the friction ridge formations used during the identification process.

First Level Detail

Whenever one has an opportunity to observe something such as a fingerprint pattern or a passing vehicle for a short period of time, the details remembered usually are descriptive of the overall features of the item. For example, if a concentric friction ridge pattern is flashed on a screen for two seconds, most would recognize that the pattern was concentric in shape. If a blue, four-door, medium-sized vehicle flashed past a narrow opening in the field of view, most would recognize the vehicle as a medium-sized, blue car, and possibly with four doors.

The first details usually observed are the overall design or pattern of an object, and these features are class characteristics or nonspecific details, which do not have individualizing value. For our purposes it is convenient to describe the overall friction ridge pattern as *first level detail*, which guides the comparison toward like formations. It also allows us to narrow down the prospective group to be compared. For example, concentric patterns are compared to concentric patterns and areas of straight running ridges are compared to other areas of straight running ridges. At times, due to a lack of clarity, some prints only display first level detail.

First level detail describes patterns that may be repeated and therefore grouped. When discussing the value of groups of old cars or groups of old coins, it is appropriate to describe the frequency with which they are encountered with the word *rarity*. For example, some old coins are more rare than others. The same rationale is applicable to first level detail. The frequency with which first level details are encountered is described in *degrees of rarity*. Arch patterns are more rare than whorl patterns.

Second Level Detail

If the concentric friction ridge pattern mentioned earlier was flashed on a screen for approximately ten seconds, most observing the screen would initially recognize the concentric shape and then begin to explore its specific structure. The most obvious detail to explore would be the specific path of the friction ridges. The curious would begin to follow the route of the friction ridge paths throughout the pattern. Therefore, specific friction ridge path is designated as *second level detail.*

Second level detail, as discussed earlier, has individualizing power. Friction ridge path can have sufficient uniqueness to individualize but at times, due to a lack of clarity, only second level detail will be visible on a print. Due to the individualizing power of second level detail and the contribution that second level detail can have toward defining a unique formation, its value is described in *degrees of uniqueness,* which is descriptive of how out of the ordinary or removed from normal a specific formation is.

Third Level Detail

If the concentric pattern is left on the screen for an extended period of time, the brain will begin to examine the small intrinsic shapes of the friction ridges. Intrinsic ridge shapes and relative pore locations are the last level of detail that may appear in ridge formations. This level of detail is designated as *third level detail.*

In the past most friction ridge identification specialists described ridge characteristics as being unique or not unique. Uniqueness in this sense did not mean one but described the degree of being different from the normal or extraordinary in configuration. This evaluation of uniqueness was visual and was usually based on the number of intrinsic shapes observed within the configuration. For example, a clearly deposited print would exhibit more smaller details than a poorly deposited print, and would be described as being more unique. Smaller details differentiate like objects and, while the logic may not have been applied, there was recognition that clear ridge formations had more value. Therefore, third level detail is also described in *degrees of uniqueness.*

As the degree of clarity dictates the level of friction skin detail reproduced in the friction ridge print, and as those levels of detail have now been categorized, it is now possible to describe the clarity of a friction ridge print in words that have real descriptive meaning. For example, a fingerprint described as having only first level detail would indicate that only the overall pattern is visible and individualization is not possible. On the other hand, a friction ridge print described as having a large amount of third level detail would indicate that this is a very clear print that has recorded a lot of the small intrinsic friction ridge details and is likely capable of individualization.

Summary

Clarity describes the amount of detail from the three-dimensional friction ridges deposited in the two-dimensional print. The details found on the friction ridges are divided into three levels: first level detail, overall friction ridge pattern; second level detail, specific ridge path; and third level detail, intrinsic shapes of the friction ridges. The use of the descriptive terms first, second, and third level detail identify the clarity of the print and indicates to others its potential for individualization. The terms first, second, and third level details are used frequently in the balance of this chapter.

The Philosophy of Friction Ridge Identification

The chapter on the philosophy of identification is a guide or explanation of how friction ridge quantitative-qualitative analysis is transformed into an opinion of individuality. It describes the friction ridge formations used during analysis and generally establishes the parameters as to how much knowledge one must have to perform such an analysis. The philosophy of friction ridge identification can be paraphrased with the following statement: *Friction ridge identification is established through the agreement of friction ridge formations, in sequence, having sufficient uniqueness to individualize.* The purpose of this statement is not that it should be memorized, but understood. The philosophy statement should be examined in detail and can be broken down into four basic issues:

1. Friction ridge formations
2. In sequence
3. Having sufficient uniqueness
4. To individualize

Friction Ridge Formations

The friction ridge formations referred to in the philosophy of friction ridge identification are the formations found on the friction skin as discussed in earlier chapters. However, the friction skin has a third type of characteristic that usually is not addressed in friction ridge identification literature, *friction skin damage*. This type of characteristic is common in manufactured identification media. Manufactured media, such as footwear or vehicle tires, are individualized by comparing nonspecific details and specific details. The nonspecific details are created during the manufacturing process. In the case of tires and some footwear, the nonspecific details are mold shapes, which are not sufficient for individualization. The specific details of these media are caused by damage, such as cuts. In the case of vehicle tires, the mold shape would be considered first level detail, the path of a cut would be considered second level detail, and the shape along the edge of the cut would be considered third level detail.

Figure 4.1 The scar in the upper left pattern area of this print has a clear path but little third level detail, if any.

Other biological media also have three types of characteristics. For example, trees have nonspecific or class characteristics that are genetic in nature, such as the type of tree. Trees also have unique characteristics created through differential growth, such as growth rings. There are several possible sources of accidental characteristics caused by numerous types damage such as lightning strikes, axe blows, or saw cuts.

While the friction skin is a biological medium, it can also have characteristics caused by damage, which can be used in conjunction with naturally developed ridge formations to individualize. The details found in scars, if clearly recorded, are extremely unique. Permanent scars result from damage to the generating layer of the epidermis and there is often some type of puckering of the friction ridges (Figure 4.1). Temporary scars are superficial and will eventually disappear.

While most damage is the result of physical trauma to the friction skin, some damage can be caused by genetic, disease, or viral influences. Dysplasia and dissociated ridges are examples of genetic influences causing damage to the friction ridges. Warts are an example of viral influences (See Figure 3.12). In the past these various characteristics were not used during the identification process. This position is a throwback to the fact that they are historically not used during most classification methods. While these features are outside the bounds of classification, they are not outside the bounds of identification.

The same descriptive nomenclature can be applied to characteristics caused through damage to the friction skin. In the case of a scar, the path of the scar would be considered second level detail and the various abstract shapes caused by the puckering of the damaged friction ridges would be third level details. As most damage to friction skin, tires, or footwear is accidental in nature, the use of the phrase *accidental characteristic* is a common descriptive term used.

The numerous friction ridge formations developed through differential growth of the ridge units, such as major ridge path deviations, areas of open fields, intrinsic friction ridge shapes, and relative pore positions, are commonly referred to as *unique characteristics* due to their ability to establish a print as unique when considered in the aggregate. Accidental characteristics could also be considered to be unique characteristics or specific characteristics (Figures 4.2, 4.3).

Sequence

Sequence means the act or fact of coming one after the other. When relating this to the philosophy of friction ridge identification there are two important aspects to consider. The first is that sequence is synonymous with systematic or one after the other. When sequence is maintained during comparison the total available friction ridge area is analyzed and compared systematically; one area is compared after the other. When this progression is maintained the weight placed on each area of friction ridge structure is accumulative and contributes to the whole.

All friction ridge formations available should be examined, and not just enough to form an opinion of individualization. For example, various distortions such as double taps (Figure 4.4) are difficult to recognize under a fingerprint glass, but are very easy for the defense to see on an enlarged chart. Ignoring areas in a print where clarity is an issue may put the expert in a position of having disregarded a part of the print without a rational explanation.

Second, sequence means that all areas of the print must be joined directly or, if physically separated, undergo careful analysis where the opinion of the

Figure 4.2 Fingerprint taken before scarring. (Prints submitted by Csts S. Candie and F. NcNiven of the Edmonton Police Service)

expert is that sequence is maintained over the separation. When sequence is maintained, the weight placed on each area of the comparison is accumulative. Should the forensic identification specialist form the opinion that sequence was maintained between two separate areas of friction ridge print, the rationale must be such that it can be presented in court to defend that position by illustrating that the disjointed areas of the friction ridge pattern were deposited at the same time by the same donor. Pressure distortion causing a lateral shift, such as a double tap or possibly two-finger identifications, are examples of disjointed friction ridge formations. The techniques required to adequately address these types of disjoined prints are presented later in this book.

Having Sufficient Uniqueness

An identification specialist requires considerable knowledge about which details on the friction ridges may be used to individualize. The volume of details available depends on the amount of specific details present in the

Figure 4.3 The path of the scar runs diagonally through the pattern area. The path is second level detail The damage to the ridge units and the various curling and twisting shapes are third level. The fingerprint is a unique formation made even more so due to the addition of accidental characteristics.

donor friction ridge surface, the ability of the identification specialist to address those details that are present, and the clarity of the print. For example, a print may have numerous relative pore locations visible and available for comparison, but the identification specialist must have the training and expertise to carry out such a comparison.

How much friction ridge detail is considered sufficient depends on the capability of the expert of assessing the value of what is present and forming an opinion. When a print is analyzed by a different identification specialist the threshold of what is sufficient will fluctuate within parameters. These parameters have been set by the general population of forensic identification specialists through peer review. There must be sufficient specific detail, either

Figure 4.4 The line running through the pattern at the top of this print is a sign of a double tap. The left portion has been shifted one full ridge width, center to center. The ridge ending above the core actually joins the ridge above it in the exemplar as a simple recurving ridge. The two halves of this print are out of sequence unless the discrepancies can be explained through an appropriate analysis. (Submitted by Insp. M. Cassidy, RCMP.)

unique or accidental, to satisfy that specific identification specialist, based on his or her knowledge and experience, to form an opinion.

New forensic identification specialists usually begin their careers under supervision. Many begin under the restraint of a preset artificial administrative threshold for identification as a training parameter. While the current identification philosophy is based on quantitative-qualitative analysis, the static training threshold is an acceptable practice as a safeguard and permits one to gain experience and confidence with a reduced fear of committing an error. Should a trainee receive a print that is outside his or her ability it would be passed on to a senior, more experienced expert for analysis and comparison. The ability to use a quantitative-quantitative analysis during friction ridge formations usually starts to develop during the first year on the job if a trainee has received adequate training.

To Individualize

The opinion of individualization is the elimination of every other possible donor in the world except the one to whom the crime scene print is being compared in the opinion of the forensic identification specialist. The opinion of individualization is based on one's knowledge, understanding of the scientific basis of the friction ridge identification science, and ability. Knowledge and understanding of the identification process must be in combination with a certain amount of practical experience. As mentioned at the beginning of this book, practical experience is only relevant when it is acquired from a position of in-depth knowledge about the various aspects of the science.

How Much Is Enough?

A frequently asked question is, "How much is enough?" The opinion of individualization or identification is subjective. It is an opinion formed by the friction ridge identification specialist based on the friction ridge formations found in agreement during comparison. The validity of the opinion is coupled with an ability to defend that position, and both are founded in one's personal knowledge, ability, and experience. The types of opinions one can reach will be discussed under the methodology of friction ridge identification, but it must be clearly understood that if there is any doubt whether there is sufficient specific detail present to individualize, then an opinion of individualization cannot be formed.

How much is enough? Finding adequate friction ridge formations in sequence that one knows are specific details of the friction skin, and in *the opinion* of the friction ridge identification specialist that there is sufficient uniqueness within those details to eliminate all other possible donors in the world, is considered enough. At that point individualization has occurred and the print has been identified. The identification was established by the agreement of friction ridge formations in sequence having sufficient uniqueness to individualize.

Human Sight

The identification process is synonymous with sight. Even though friction ridge prints are physical evidence, the comparison of this evidence is a mental process. Physical data concerning friction ridge configuration is taken from the physical realm and through the eyes is relocated in the mental realm of the brain.

Many theories exist that attempt to explain the behavior of the human brain, but it is generally agreed that the human brain has some organizational qualities that assist us to see and to recognize various forms. However, some of these phenomena can work against the unbiased intent of friction ridge comparison. A basic understanding of how the brain sees is necessary to understand why certain scientific protocols and processes must be strictly adhered to during comparison.

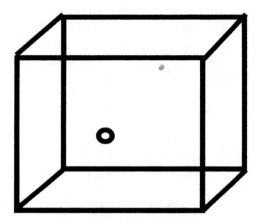

Figure 4.5   This figure alternates in depth. The face of the cube is marked by a small circle. Sometimes the circle appears on the front of the cube, sometimes on the back, and sometimes in the lower left corner. This is an example of perceptual hypothesis. The visual system entertains differing views and never settles on a solution.

The eyes are often incorrectly described as being camera-like. This is an extreme oversimplification of the visual system. The human eye is in fact an extension of the brain. When light is reflected from an object and strikes the retina of the eye, it does not create an image but is converted into a form of electrical impulse. The impulse is instantaneously transported to the brain as a neural coded message. When the brain receives the neural coded message it carries out a cerebral identification of what the coded message represents. This process is called sight.

While the functioning of the human brain is not fully understood, enough is known to recognize that how it sees is extremely complex. We can think of the brain as a storehouse of neural coded messages. New neural coded messages arriving in the brain are in the from of a hypothesis awaiting recognition or identification. Some hypotheses cannot be solved. Either this is construed as, "I don't know what that is," or the brain may continue to try to figure it out. The Necker cube in Figure 4.5 is an example of that phenomenon.

As we assimilate and take in new information, neural coded messages representing what we see are stored in memory. All newly arriving neural coded messages are basically compared with known data and identified.

There are many other faculties in the brain to support the sight process other than memory such as smell, touch, and sound. As they usually do not influence the friction ridge identification process we will not address them here.

The brain's ability to reason is a major faculty influencing the identification process and is worthy of discussion. Friction ridge comparisons must always be objective in nature. Nothing should be taken for granted. An expectancy of seeing something due to past knowledge or suggestion can cause errors to be made with recognition or identification. We often see what we expect to see. For example, the drawing in Figure 4.6 depicts a woman

Figure 4.6

washing a floor. She is on her hands and knees facing in the opposite direction with a bucket by her side. When this drawing comes to life, consider that it is only five lines plus subjective reasoning.

Subjective reasoning is also the culprit when attempting to greet a person believed to be a friend, only to have the person turn around and be a total stranger. The identification of familiar objects is often sanctioned by the brain with very little input of data, hence a jumping to conclusions. During forensic comparison one must maintain an objective state of mind to guard against seeing things that are not there. For example, during the comparison process, examining the clear inked known impression prior to carrying out an analysis of an unknown print could cause the brain to jump to a conclusion and see details in the murky unknown friction ridge structures that may not actually be there.

This phenomenon is commonly known as *set*. The brain has other inherent abilities to assist us with recognizing things with limited data. As an example, when viewing a few lines strategically place on a blank piece of paper the brain will attempt to organize the lines into recognizable shapes or objects, as with the washer woman cartoon. Cartoonists depend on this phenomenon when they construct whole scenes from a series of simple lines. Another example of this is is cloud-watching. Most of us have found all types of animals or other items in the configurations of cumulus clouds. It is always easier to see these forms come to life from lines or clouds when it is suggested that they are there.

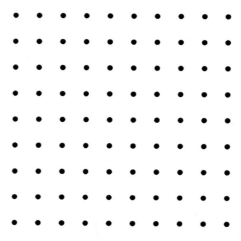

Figure 4.7

The brain is constantly surveying and does not concentrate on one spot for any length of time. It scans areas to fulfill its desire for organization and shape recognition. At times it can input a great deal of data in a single glance. The ability to compare shape and relative position of several shapes or objects very rapidly is a natural ability of the human brain. An example of this skill is when ascertaining which key will fit into a specific lock mechanism. This function involves several shapes and their relative position on the key and on the lock. Key size and shape on various different planes can be analyzed in a very short period time. During friction ridge comparison this ability has to be moderated and controlled until it becomes deliberate and objective.

The ability of attempting to organize or group things into simple units can be seen when we examine the rows of dots in Figure 4.7. The dots are equally spaced. When examined, the brain attempts to organize them into vertical and horizontal rows or into squares or triangles. Attempting to stare at just one dot is continually interrupted by the eye roving and including adjacent dots in an effort to form some type of configuration. Rows and squares of dots are continually flashed in and out of view as the brain attempts to include and organize the surrounding dots.

When fingerprints are examined a similar phenomenon of area vision occurs. The brain sees not only the friction ridge formation being examined, such as a ridge characteristic, but also the surrounding structures. The area of interest on the friction ridges is not viewed in isolation but is organized into a configuration unit or shape, which includes the surrounding ridges. The peripheral ridges and shapes cannot be ignored by the brain.

Friction ridge comparisons are frequently described as comparing the unknown or latent print to the known or exemplar print, even though latent really means hidden, concealed, or invisible. However, when the process the brain uses to see is considered, there is another step to the comparison. When an area of the latent print is viewed, the brain stores in memory the data representing that area. Then, when an area of the exemplar print is examined, this new data is forwarded to the brain and compared with the stored data of the latent print. Seldom is there a situation where the brain can see the areas in the latent and exemplar prints at the same time, even when under the same fingerprint glass. A mental picture is always part of the comparison.

An example of where the brain may possibly see both aspects at the same time is in the case of a physical match of a broken piece of glass or metal. Both sides of the break are visible at the same time when in juxtaposition. The impact on the brain in this type of case is immediate. Forensic identification specialists enjoy taking this type of identification to court as anyone examining the chart automatically forms his or her own opinion of a positive match.

A friction ridge comparison would therefore be comprised of an analysis of an area of the latent print, the storage of that data in memory, and then a viewing of the exemplar print, which would also cause that data to travel to the brain. When the data of the exemplar print arrives in the brain it causes an immediate comparison to the data from the latent print to take place. Even though the latent print was viewed a fraction of a second before the exemplar print, as soon as the eyes leave the latent print the brain is depending on its memory for the comparison.

Due to the fact that we see with brain waves, exterior stimuli may interfere with the efficiency of how the brain functions, which in turn can interfere with how well we see. Our perception of things cannot be separated from our thought process. Stimuli such as noise, fatigue, stress, or other interference can affect the thinking process. Realization that the brain has these inherent idiosyncrasies illustrates why a systematic and analytical methodology must be followed during comparison.

Comparisons should only be attempted when the brain is alert and not fatigued. A noisy or distracting work area is an inappropriate environment to carry out a friction ridge comparison and should be avoided. Also, allowing a pushy investigator to lean over your shoulder and scrutinize your comparison is not in the best interest of objectivity. An alert mind working in a quiet environment provides the greatest opportunity for a quality comparison and conclusion.

For these reasons a specific comparison sequence has been established within the friction ridge identification community. The latent print is always analyzed first, before comparison to the exemplar. This rule ensures an uncontaminated analysis of the unknown friction ridge detail. Comparisons conducted in this fashion ensure objectivity and prevent contamination through previous knowledge. At times, comparison and identification is as simple as recognizing one's own car. At other times it is not that easy and just the analysis may take hours. In either case, as much time is taken as needed to conduct a complete, unbiased, and objective comparison.

Commencing a comparison with expectations or with hope can be dangerous unless a very objective position is taken. The situation becomes more precarious as the knowledge of the expert decreases. Comparisons conducted with expectations and without adequate knowledge or regard for scientific process will eventually result in disaster. Even when carrying out the easiest of comparisons it is essential to have adequate knowledge, experience, and ability as required, and to follow the process in full as set forth in the remainder of this chapter.

Summary of Human Sight

The human brain is capable of carrying out comparisons and identifications of very complex objects. Its natural ability to decipher nonspecific and specific details in an instant and assess their level of agreement or disagreement is an extremely involved process. The sight process has been simplified to the extreme here; however, understanding even the few phenomena described will pave the way to a structured and objective friction ridge analysis and comparison. Analysis and comparison go beyond simply seeing to a higher level, which could be described as scrutinizing or observing. Seeing is a physical state. Observing, as that which takes place during analysis and comparison, is enhanced by experience, knowledge, understanding, moral values, and theoretical scientific commitments.

Methodology of Friction Ridge Identification

The following methodology is a structured and systematic guide for comparing friction ridge prints. There are four parts to friction ridge identification methodology: Analysis, Comparison, Evaluation, and Verification.

During each stage of the identification process the knowledge and understanding learned thus far is systematically applied. While it is impossible to describe every discrepancy that may be encountered during the analysis of friction ridge prints, some of the typical peculiarities will be addressed. The discussion of analysis, comparison, and evaluation will establish sufficient parameters to give guidance to the novice identification specialist and to reinforce the knowledge and skill of the seasoned veteran.

Friction Ridge Analysis

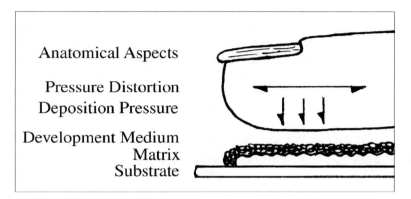

Anatomical Aspects

Pressure Distortion
Deposition Pressure

Development Medium
Matrix
Substrate

Figure 4.8

The first step of the methodology is an in-depth analysis of the latent friction ridge print. An analysis can be compared to intelligence gathering, a process where one learns as much about the latent print as possible. There are times when friction ridge comparison is simple and identification is easy, such as a situation where there is more than ample detail to individualize and clarity is not an issue. An analysis in this case is usually not time consuming. However, there are times when an analysis can be extremely difficult; for example, in situations where a latent print lacks clarity, when varying amounts of distortion are present, or when there are overlapping ridge formations. Generally, analysis increases in importance and value in proportion to the complexity of the print.

There are several factors to be considered during a complete analysis. Each has the potential to distort the latent print. The most common factors are: *substrate distortion, matrix distortion, development medium distortion, deposition pressure distortion,* and *pressure distortion*. The analysis would then establish the *clarity* of the print, *ridge path configuration* and, if present, *intrinsic ridge formations*. The last aspect to consider is *anatomical factors*. Each potential problem area should be analyzed independently. The analysis moves systematically from the substrate to the friction ridges, or from the bottom to the top. For example, the substrate is analyzed first, followed by the matrix and the development medium, and then up to the types of pressure applied during deposition and so on, ending with the anatomical aspects of the volar surface that were physically involved with the deposition of the print (Figure 4.8).

Distorted or convoluted prints require a more intimate analysis of ridge path than clearer prints. At times an analysis of a problem print may progress from ridge unit to ridge unit until all the paths of all the ridges have been examined and established. On occasion this type of analysis may take hours. In this situation it is best to spread the analysis over several days, analyzing the print an hour or two at a time. At the other end of the spectrum, an analysis of a well-defined print could take as little as 20 seconds. In both instances the same systematic procedure is applied.

A prerequisite to carrying out an analysis of a complex print is the ability to examine the friction ridge formations in detail. An inherent problem encountered during analysis is the size of the friction ridge formations. One ridge unit is approximately one-half millimeter square. There are approximately 2700 ridge units, on average, in one square inch of friction skin. The ridge unit is the smallest detail, other than pore location, available for comparison. The shape and alignment of ridge units and the relative position of their pores are difficult to analyze without some form of magnification. A standard fingerprint glass does not always provide suitable magnification for a complete examination of third level detail.

In other areas of forensic science such as tool mark or firearm projectile comparison, forensic identification specialists use comparison microscopes to examine small accidental details. Many of these formations are not a great deal smaller than the smallest friction ridge formations. While comparison microscopes can also be used for examining complex friction ridge prints, their cost is prohibitive. A stereo microscope is suitable for an analysis of an unknown friction ridge print but is somewhat cumbersome during the comparison of two prints. Lens/mirror-type comparators are excellent for examining problem prints and can also be used for comparison purposes. A marker can be used to trace ridge paths by placing acetate on the viewing surface.

When cost and convenience are considered, the most practical method of carrying out a detailed analysis of friction ridges is through photographic enlargement. While many police departments are moving away from photographing friction ridge prints at crime scenes, possibly in an effort to save money, it is likely only a matter of time before the courts insist that this type of initial evidence be collected.

Friction ridge prints should be collected in a manner consistent with other types of forensic evidence. In most cases forensic evidence is photographed showing the item or substrate location within the crime scene (Figure 4.9). Another closer photograph is then taken depicting the friction ridge evidence on the substrate (Figure 4.10). Finally, a close-up photograph

Figure 4.9 Overall photograph showing latent print in the scene. The black sheet enhances the contrast of the print. (Photo by W. Kuntz, RCMP)

Figure 4.10 Close-up photograph showing the latent prints developed. (Photo by W. Kuntz, RCMP)

of the evidential mark suitable for comparison purposes is taken at actual size or half size (Figure 4.11). When photographing friction ridge prints, the print should not be covered with lifting tape.

A fine-grain photograph of a friction ridge print is superior to a lift in most cases as long as there is contrast between the development medium and the background. At times filters may have to be used to enhance contrast. A photographic record of an unaltered print depicted in the crime scene

Figure 4.11 Actual size photograph of the evidential latent print. Shown larger here, this latent is a partial reversal. Half of the ridges are white and half are black. (Photo by W. Kuntz, RCMP)

removes almost all doubt as to its genuineness. Also, the close-up negatives can be enlarged for use during analysis and to prepare a chart for court if required.

The method of analysis is adjusted to meet the needs of the situation. For example, when analyzing less complicated friction ridge prints the analysis may consist of mental observations only. If the print has one or two simple distortions a brief note on the file will suffice. Some identification specialists use a check-off sheet (Figure 4.12) at the scene and record observations about the substrate, matrix, development medium used, deposition and pressure distortions, location on exhibit, and any anatomical issues that are relevant for each latent print collected. When the latent prints are submitted to the fingerprint bureau the first half of that form is used to inform the identification specialist making the comparison of the observations made at the crime scene. The examiner can then ascertain if the latent print is consistent with what the scene examiner described.

When the print is complex, involving more than two distortion issues, a written report should be prepared by the expert carrying out the analysis, describing the details of the distortions observed. Having an ability to prepare a systematic written analysis is especially an asset when working on major cases. In very serious cases a complete written analysis should always be completed. A written analysis has the same advantages as other police notes. Major trials are routinely delayed for a year or longer. When the case finally does come to trial the original analysis report is available to rapidly bring the intricate details of the print back into perspective. It has the ability to refresh memory or inform others of the details of the analysis.

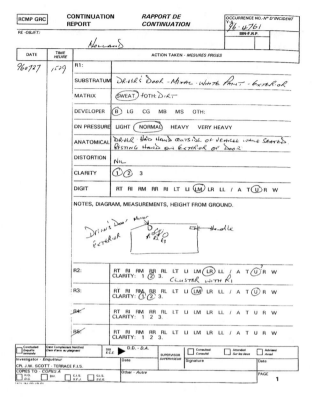

Figure 4.12 This check-off sheet is used at the crime scene to start gathering information for an analysis. The data sheet would be forwarded with the latent print to the fingerprint bureau. (Submitted by Sgt. John Scott, RCMP)

The number of factors included in the analysis is dictated by the properties of the print. At times some factors will not be present, will not influence the print, or will be unknown. Many of the necessary factors required for a complete analysis may only be known to the scenes of crime officer. This situation can be alleviated if most of the information gathered at the scene is passed on through scene photographs, pre-analysis reports, or in some cases verbally. While some factors may be obvious in the lift, a complete analysis cannot be carried out without all the data, but even a partial analysis has merit.

Preparing a detailed written analysis prior to comparison promotes objectivity and demonstrates professionalism. It also removes the opportunity for anyone to suggest that one is seeing friction ridge details where none exist. Tape recorders can also be used during an analysis and the narrative transcribed at a later time. This is not to suggest that a written analysis be prepared for every comparison. At times the print is uncomplicated and analysis is mainly a mental process. However, when the print has some distortions which may require an explanation at a later date or there is need for a detailed analysis to be submitted for the benefit of others such as the prosecuting attorney, then a written analysis should be used.

Substrate Distortion

The first consideration is to identify the type and condition of the substrate Various substrates can cause distortion or interfere with the deposition of a print, affecting its appearance and clarity. The following does not purport to be a complete list of substrates, but only a sampling of different types for demonstration purposes.

Flexible Substrates.   Flexible substrates, such as plastic bags, are capable of causing major distortion to prints. A fold in a bag under the area where a print is deposited can split the print in half and move the two pieces apart when the fold is unfolded (Figure 4.13). Small folds may leave marks that run through the print and appear as scars or flexion creases. Flexible substrates can wrap around a volar surface such as a finger and cause the print to have the appearance of a palm print or a finger-palm combination.

Double taps are a very common distortion with flexible substrates. A double tap happens when a single print is deposited with two distinct and separate applications of pressure. The time between the applications or touches of pressure can be as little as a split second. The most common result is two areas of friction ridge print separated by a smear or smudge. At times the two separate areas of ridge structure may overlap a few millimeters and, if the ridge ends align, the print will appear normal but will actually be distorted in size and/or shape. The telltale sign for this type of distortion is found where the two prints meet. All the ridges in the transition area usually do not join smoothly and thick areas of friction ridge will be evident, possibly with the occasional ridge end protruding from the side of a ridge. Another obvious indicator would be finding the relative position of the major ridge path deviations to be out of spatial sync or even missing when compared to a known exemplar print.

Double taps come in a variety of shapes, sizes, and causes. Some are obvious and some are extremely difficult to discern. When double taps are discovered it is at times possible to return the print to its natural configuration for comparison or for AFIS search. Crossovers, misaligned ridges, extra thick ridges, and protruding ridge ends are common features in double taps. These types of features are called *red flags* and are discussed later in this chapter.

Figure 4.13   This latent print is on a drug bag. It was treated with cyanoacrylate and dye stained. There was a fold in the bag when the latent was deposited. When the fold was opened the print split in two. Moving the two prints into juxtaposition will realign the ridges. An in-depth analysis will supply the rationale for such action. Unfortunately, the scenes of crime officer drew a line through one half. (Photo by Insp. A. Misner, RCMP)

Flexible substrates, such as plastic or shipping tape, are also notorious for transferring prints from one surface to another. For example, fingerprints deposited on one inside surface of a plastic bag may be transferred to the opposite inside surface if the two surfaces touch each other. When the transferred print is developed it is reversed laterally. Should an AFIS search be negative for a fingerprint found inside a plastic bag, it is worth considering searching the print a second time laterally reversed.

Substrate Shape.   The shape of a substrate can cause a distortion similar to a flexible substrate. For example, holding a round bottle in the hand allows the thumb and thenar palm area to wrap around the substrate. When lifted and put onto a flat surface the resulting print can appear as a little finger and palm. If the substrate is not identified as a round surface, the identification specialist may not consider this combination as coming from that part of the hand, reasoning that the thumb and palm do not normally lie flat. A hand wrapped around a shower curtain rod brings the fingers into juxtaposition with the interdigital areas. Again, a lift of the fingers and interdigital area of the palm in this configuration can be confusing. Friction ridge prints on all drinking containers such as beer bottles, glasses, and pop cans will have double taps of some nature within their ridge configurations due to the twisting motion used when bringing the container to the mouth.

Friction ridges also tend to dip into depressions on uneven surfaces such as rough window sills (Figure 4.14) or dents in wine bottles. When a print

Figure 4.14   This latent was lifted from a rough windowsill. A dip in the wood surface is visible in the latent by a void in the ridges and a line of powder that adhered to the edge of the depression. (Photo by E. Kramer, RCMP)

is deposited over an uneven area of the substrate the ridges flow over the edge of the depression, down one side, across the bottom of the depression, and up the other side returning to the surface. Viewed from above, as with a camera, the print will appear distorted in size or shape. Lifts of prints from this type of surface frequently fail or are distorted due to tape stretch. An inability to get the lifting tape into the corners of depressions often causes sections of the print to be missing.

Dirty Substrates.   Dirty substrates may not accept all of the matrix available during deposition. The resulting print can appear blotchy, have areas missing, or generally lack detail. The contaminants on some dirty substrates adhere to the friction ridges creating a takeaway print or a partial takeaway. This type of print appears to change ridge color halfway through the print when it is developed. These prints are sometimes referred to as *reversals* and can also be caused by pressure.

Soft Substrates.   Soft substrates permit the friction ridges to sink into their surfaces and create molded impressions. Seizing the substrate, taking a cast of the molded print, or using specific photographic techniques are the usual procedures followed when collecting this type of print.

Fingerprint Lifters.   When a developed friction ridge print is lifted with tape it is transferred to a new substrate. On occasion lifting tapes buckle or are improperly rolled onto the print. Improper procedures, and especially efforts to correct those improper procedures, can cause various alterations to the lifted print (Figure 4.15A). In one situation lifting tape had been

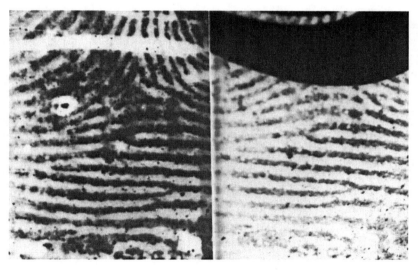

Figure 4.15   On the left is a lift that was inadvertently altered. On the right is a photograph of the latent on the exhibit. (Photos by Sgt. L. Palfy, RCMP)

partially applied to a print when it buckled. The tape was then lifted slightly to straighten the buckle and then laid down again. A portion along one side of the print was shifted laterally the exact distance as the distance between two ridges. This shifted part of the print exactly one ridge width, center to center, and realigned it with the other ridges within the print. The spatial sequences of several of the major ridge path deviations were altered by one ridge. The red flags in this print were very subtle. Fortunately, the print had been photographed prior to lifting and the error was discovered (Figure 4.15B).

Matrix Particulars

The matrix of a friction ridge print is the actual substance deposited by the friction ridges. This substance may be sweat, sebaceous oils from other parts of the body, foreign material, or a combination of any of the above. Different matrices have varying viscosities and adherence properties with differing attributes in their abilities to accurately record third level detail.

Sweat/Sebaceous Matrix.   Sweat is considered the most common matrix, but I doubt that is true. The friction ridges are continually touching other surfaces and picking up contaminants. The most common matrix is likely sweat mixed with sebaceous oils from other parts of the body, or sebaceous oils collected from a variety of surfaces such as doorknobs and countertops. The variety of foreign materials that may mix with sweat and sebaceous oils is endless. Many identification specialists feel they can recognize a sweat print matrix, but whether the matrix is sweat, a sweat/sebaceous combination, a sweat/motor oil combination, or a combination of several materials is really unknown without chemical analysis.

At times the volume and color of the matrix can be an indicator as to whether it is innate or from an external source. How the matrix reacted with the substrate can also be an indicator. For example, sweat tends to enhance grip and it takes considerable pressure to cause the ridges to slip. Motor oil and cooking oil tend to lubricate the ridges and slippage occurs with less pressure. In any case, the important aspect is whether the composition of the matrix caused a distortion in the print.

Wet Prints.   Prints deposited when the friction ridges are wet, usually with water or a fluid other than sweat, are commonly referred to as *wet prints*. The friction ridges tend to appear as a series of rounded units before and after development. This is believed to be caused by the pore openings acting as little containers for the liquid on the friction ridge. The water held in the concave pore openings is deposited when the ridges are in contact with the substrate. As the ridges are lifted from the substrate the water flows outward from the pore locations over the substrate until supine. See Figure 6.1 for an example of a wet print.

At times, water adhering to the friction ridges between the pores at the time of contact with the substrate tends to be pressed to the sides of the ridge next to the furrows. This can create thin matrix lines along each side of the ridge next to the furrows. The resulting print structure has ridge breaks between the pores giving the ridge a dot-like appearance.

While the friction ridges of a wet print appear broken, they are compared as if they were solid ridges or at second level detail. However, be prepared to defend this action in court if necessary by being able to describe the formation of a friction ridge and have some rationale as to why the print appears this way. In most cases third level detail cannot be trusted in prints of this nature. On rare occasions the pores will ball just enough water to mark only the pore locations. Relative pore location may then be a consideration as a method of identification.

Mud-Type Matrix.   A matrix deposited when it has the consistency of wet mud or plaster often only records second level detail. Due to the fragile nature of this matrix after drying, development is usually not recommended. Sometimes the same substance is picked up on the fingers in powder form and is deposited on a surface. Matrices such as mud, concrete, or drywall gypsum, when deposited in this manner, may record very clear ridge detail and should only be photographed and not physically developed. At times a powder matrix will cover a surface and the friction ridges will remove the matrix creating a takeaway impression. Photography is, again, the best nonphysical method of collecting these prints.

Paint/Blood Matrix.   Matrices of substances with heavier viscosity, such as blood or paint, may react similar to water but in a slower fashion due to the density of the fluid. Other factors may also come into play, such as gravity (Figure 4.16). A substrate, such as a vertical windowpane, will have different gravitational aspects than the forces applied to a print on a horizontal surface. The heavy viscosity of the matrix often causes a piling-up effect when the finger is lifted, similar to when taffy is pulled. When contact between the substrate and the matrix is broken, the resulting settling down of the matrix can create what appears to be strong third level detail. Many false artifacts can be created in this situation.

Corrosive Matrix.   Some foreign matrices are capable of removing part of the substrate. For example, some bug repellants will dissolve surfaces such as varnish, resulting in a takeaway print. In extreme cases the resulting print is molded into the surface. Also, amino acids from friction ridges can etch into some metals such as polished brass or galvanized ductwork.

Absent Matrix.   At times there is a general lack of matrix on the friction ridges, or the matrix present is overpowered by a substance on the substrate

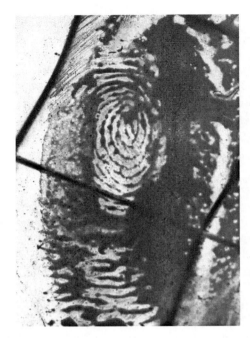

Figure 4.16 This print was deposited as the culprit ran out a door with blood on his hand. A blood matrix on a vertical substrate, due to its viscosity, will often be affected by gravity. (Submitted by Cpl. Alain Richard, RCMP)

surface. In these cases the ridges may remove part of the surface film from the surface of the substrate. Applying powder to this type of surface develops the background as opposed to where the print touched the substrate. Prints found on the sticky side of tape are another example of absent matrix. While this type of print is called a takeaway or a reversal print, it can be likened to a microscopic molded print.

Development Media

There are a plethora of development media available which are used to increase the contrast between latent friction ridge prints and the substrate. Each has its own *catalyst* and *signature*. The catalyst is the substance or lack of substance on which the development medium reacts. For example, ninhydrin reacts with amino acids, powder adheres to grease or sweat, and silver nitrate reacts to inorganic salts.

The signature of a development medium is the manner in which it appears after reacting to the catalyst. The signature is partly related to the location of the catalyst and partly to the physical makeup of the development medium. For example, powder is abrasive and tends to fill in small nooks and crannies along the ridge. Due to the characteristic of powder, it can fill in the area around a ridge ending causing it to appear as a bifurcation.

Other media such as ninhydrin tend to break a ridge into a series of units. The catalysts of ninhydrin, amino acids, are usually found around the pores and are frequently absent on the areas of the friction ridge between the pores. An understanding of this is very important when ascertaining which breaks constitute ridge endings and which breaks are simply a signature of the development medium. A knowledge of friction ridge structure and formation, coupled with a knowledge of the catalyst and signature of development media, are used to answer these questions. A few common development media are briefly discussed below to demonstrate why their properties should be considered as possible sources for distortion. One should be aware of the signature and catalyst of all the development media one uses.

Fingerprint Powder.   All powders are abrasive to some degree. Powder adheres to the matrix; it can pile up in nooks and crannies such as pore openings and fine ridge crevices in the matrix. While some powders adhere more than others, powder tends to fill in third level detail and may appear to alter second level detail. A careful analysis is required in areas where powder signatures may alter ridge path, especially when a generous matrix is treated with a generous amount of powder. In these cases the tendency of powder to fill in is increased to the maximum. Applying powder to a damp surface demonstrates fill in clearly as it may obliterate the whole print or leave sharp dark lines across the print. Also, the act of brushing powder damages the fragile matrix and can leave abrasion lines across the print.

Ninhydrin.   Ninhydrin reacts with amino acids in sweat. As the sweat flows over the friction ridges from the pores there is a concentration of amino acids on the friction ridge surface surrounding each pore. The result is that prints developed with ninhydrin are frequently spotty and to some degree similar to wet prints. When there is an understanding of the catalyst and signature of ninhydrin, an identification specialist can compare the broken ridges as a solid ridge path at second level detail.

On occasion ninhydrin prints are solid. This phenomenon is caused by excessive amino acid being evenly distributed over the whole ridge surface. A general knowledge of friction ridge development and formation will assist the examiner with an analysis as to which breaks in the ridge structures are second level details (ridge endings) and which are third level details (ridge breaks), possibly caused by ridge shape or exterior physical interference of the matrix.

Iodine Fumes.   Iodine fumes are absorbed into the matrix. The resulting print has a reddish tinge. Depending on the source of the matrix, the resulting ridge path is visible as a solid or broken ridge. Iodine fumes are nonabrasive and record third level detail well. Photographic techniques or the silver plate method are two ways of collecting iodine-fumed prints.

Cyanoacrylate.   Cyanoacrylate molecules polymerize with the matrix. The appearance of the resulting matrix is dependent on the process used. The heat and humidity method leaves a spaghetti-type matrix, while vacuum cyanoacrylate methods leave a flake-like matrix.

The spaghetti-type matrix has more reflective surfaces and is therefore more visible. The vacuum flake-like matrix does not reflect light as well. It is often recommended that the flake-type matrix be dyed and then made more visible by using various light sources. Cyanoacrylate is nonabrasive and at times reproduces friction ridge formations which have very fine detail (Figure 4.17).

Figure 4.17   This latent was treated with cyanoacrylate. The matrix tends to surround the pores. The ridges appear to be broken down into ridge units.

There are numerous other development media currently in use. It is not the purpose of this chapter to describe them all. However, when deciding to use any developer it is very important to understand how the method of application affects the matrix, the catalyst on which the developer reacts, and the signatures indicative of that specific developer. Any or all of these factors may alter friction ridge path or the ability to see friction ridge details.

Deposition Pressure

Deposition pressure generally changes the shape of the friction ridge by flattening or broadening each ridge (Figure 4.18). This increases the amount of

Figure 4.18 From left to right, a **Light Touch** records the top of the friction ridges. The furrows appear wider and third level detail is minimal. Clarity is good but not at its best. A **Medium Touch** flattens the friction ridge more than the light touch. It records the shape of the ridges as they are recorded when inked exemplars are taken. The medium touch reveals the most third level detail and clarity is at its maximum. A **Heavy Touch** flattens the friction ridges more than the medium touch. The furrows appear narrow and most of the third level detail is either filled in or altered. Clarity is poor. **Extreme Deposition Pressure** usually involves weight being applied through the digit from other parts of the body or by holding a very heavy object in the hand. At times extreme deposition pressure can obliterate most second and all third level detail. Clarity is absent in the center of the pattern. The outer edge of this print was not exposed to direct pressure from the digit bone and has recorded second level detail. Clarity in that area is fair.

friction ridge surface in contact with the substrate and narrows the appearance of the furrows. Also, the area of substrate covered by the matrix is increased.

The increase in pressure is visible when the matrix is developed. In situations where there is extreme pressure the ridges can be flattened against the substrate to such a degree that the matrix is pushed to each side of the ridge, resulting in a hollow ridge appearance upon development. At the opposite end of the spectrum a light touch will leave a thin line of matrix deposited from the very top edge of the ridges.

Light deposition pressure will also tend to not deposit the matrix from ridge areas that are lower in elevation in relation to surrounding ridges. For example, if the surface elevation of a friction ridge starts to taper down as it approaches a ridge ending, the matrix may not be deposited in that area. In the print the ridge would appear to end several ridge units before it actually does on the friction skin. The fact that the deposition pressure is light and the adjacent ridges converge at the real ridge ending location are factors that will permit a logical explanation for the ridge ending appearing slightly out of spatial sequence as discussed in Chapter 3 (See Figure 3.27).

While differing deposition pressures change the width of the friction ridges, they also change the perceived width of the furrow. During comparison one print may appear larger than the other due to differing furrow widths. This is a form of optical illusion which can be dispelled by comparative measurements from ridge center to ridge center. Should this type of comparison be presented as evidence in court, the inclusion of a small scale on each print on the chart will demonstrate the agreement of the ridge center to ridge center measurements and prevent unnecessary cross-examination.

Deposition pressure must also be consistent with the circumstances surrounding the deposition of the matrix. If a culprit hung from a window ledge to gain entry to a window, one would expect that this act would cause some visible distortion in the resulting ridge formations that would indicate heavy deposition pressure (Figure 4.19). However, if the culprit claims the prints

Figure 4.19 This print has crossover ridges in the furrows to the right of the core due to a minor double tap just to the lower right. Where the two prints meet, false bifurcations are created in the ridge path. The spreading "V" above the core is due to heavy deposition pressure being applied by the digit bone. Ridges on the edge of this heavy pressure area have smeared slightly causing the "V" to be visible. Matrix has piled up on one side of some ridges within this area due to pressure and some slippage, which develop as dark lines. This digit was used to push open a window.

were deposited during a visit three weeks before the entry, possibly while standing near the window, the presence of heavy deposition pressure would not support that hypothesis.

Another situation where deposition pressure becomes important is when there is confusion as to whether one or more prints is involved, possibly a double tap, in the overall makeup of the developed print. It is very difficult to deposit two prints with exactly the same deposition pressure. An analysis of deposition pressure along all the friction ridge paths of this type of print may assist an identification specialist in separating the two prints, even when they are from the same donor and were deposited a split second apart.

Pressure Distortion

Pressure distortion is different from deposition pressure. While deposition pressure describes vertical weight being placed on the friction ridges, pressure distortion takes place on the lateral or horizontal plane. Pressure distortion usually is accompanied by sideways sliding of the friction ridges resulting in a smearing of ridge matrix (Figure 4.20). An ability to read pressure distor-

Figure 4.20 This latent print was subjected to extreme pressure distortion as indicated by the smearing. Several ridges, near the center of the scale, have dark matrix lines on one side of the ridge where the matrix accumulated during a mini slide before the ridges released completely, causing the big smear.

tion indicators may permit the reconstruction of a double tap or otherwise altered print.

The friction skin is flexible within limits. Underlying bone structures may put lateral pressure on the surface ridges during some tasks. The purpose of friction ridges is to grip surfaces; however, when the pressure becomes too great the ridges will release and slide. Depending on whether the direction of pressure is along the longitudinal axis of a ridge system or perpendicular to the ridge system influences how the ridge will react to that pressure.

For example, during a double tap involving a small shift where pressure is applied lengthwise along the ridges, the ridges may be longitudinally stretched to their limit, or even if they slide just a little it is difficult to detect. The resulting matrix does not appear disturbed as the smear marks are along the matrix deposited by the friction ridges. This is evident in rolled prints. In a rolled print, ridges flowing in the same direction as the finger is being rolled, the direction of pressure, display little sign of distortion. However, ridges on a bias to the direction of pressure frequently show small amounts of smearing.

When the same pressure is applied laterally or across a ridge system, the ridges tend to imbricate or roll onto their sides before releasing. When they release the matrix is smeared into the furrows. In this situation the amount of slip can be calculated by the length of the smear. Sliding ridges often leave clear matrix indicators where they started to slide and where they stopped. For example, thin lines of matrix may be deposited where the ridge started to slide. This is caused when matrix is pushed to the sides of the friction ridge, which is placed under extreme pressure just before losing its grip and sliding. Also, in situations where the ridge is still under extreme pressure during the slide, a line of heavy matrix may be left where the ridge stops sliding.

If only some ridges slid, as in the case of some double taps, the original sequence of pressure distortion could be conveyed by following the indicators of the slide action. This process can be carried out mentally or in some cases by actually cutting up a photograph of the print to reconstruct the print's original configuration.

As with deposition pressure, the pressure distortion must also be consistent with the manner in which the matrix was deposited. For example, when a window is being forced open by pushing laterally along its surface, the ridges on a bias to the direction of pressure will tend to bunch up in the opposite direction to the force applied. This is not as evident in loop prints when the direction of pressure matches the longitudinal path of the ridges. If the pressure becomes greater than the ridges' ability to grip they will slide along the surface and the matrix will smear accordingly. Depending on the height of the window and the position of the culprit this may be accompanied by a twisting action of the fingers, which will be addressed further during the discussion on anatomical factors.

When lateral pressure is applied to a fingerprint pattern, the amount of pressure distortion can usually be seen to increase or decrease as one moves across the ridge paths. Also, the pressure distortion will usually be directional. It is seldom that pressure distortion will be found to travel in more than one direction in the same print. When one area is affected with pressure distortion the areas around it will also be affected to some degree. Therefore, the amount of distortion must be directionally consistent along the surface of the friction ridges unless a double tap has taken place along with a change in pressure distortion direction. If this is the case there will usually be an unnatural line artifact running through the pattern.

This knowledge has extreme value during comparison. When an area of ridge path is found in agreement but slightly out of spacial sequence, there may be pressure distortion indicators such as smears or directional distortion to explain this situation. However, when ridge formations are found out of spacial sequence in more than one direction or the pressure distortion is beyond the limits of the friction skin, the identification specialist is likely comparing two prints from two different donors. In other words, the skin cannot be distorted in more than one direction at once without leaving some indicators. When these pressure distortion indicators are analyzed, the direction, amount, and reason for the distortion will usually be consistent, rational, and tell a story as to what transpired.

Red Flags

There are several distortion indicators that can be described as *red flags* (Figure 4.21) of deposition and pressure distortion. These indicators are warnings and warrant careful analysis. Whenever a print has ridge disturbances, such as sudden differences in the appearance of the matrix or development medium (Figure 4.22), lines running though the pattern area, misaligned ridges running through the pattern area, extra thick ridges, hatch ridges, crossovers, angular joints, similar-shaped major ridge path deviations in close proximity, substrate artifacts, a lack of harmony in distortions, or each ridge formation compared having to be qualified before found in agreement, caution must be used and a complete analysis carried out. Matrix smears and double taps (Figure 4.23) are other obvious indicators. While techniques have been developed to address this type of print they are considered advanced analysis techniques. At this stage it is only important to realize that they are red flags and caution is warranted.

Figure 4.21 This print has more than one red flag. The ridges at the top of the print are thicker than below and the matrix appears different. This difference creates a line in the print from the core to 11 o'clock. The ridges in this transition area do not align as some run into the furrows.

Figure 4.22 This print has several red flags: overlapping ridges on the right, angular formations on the lower left and below the core, differing matrices between the core element and the area below the core, heavy ridges above the core due to increased deposition pressure, and smear striations running across the ridges just left of the core. The mini smears indicate how far the ridges actually slid.

Figure 4.23   This print has a line running into the top of the print, extra heavy ridges left of the core, and a smiliar ridge formation in the same area. This is a double tap.

Anatomical Aspects

The most obvious anatomical aspect is digit determination, or distinguishing what part of the palmar or plantar surface deposited the matrix. Digit determination is important for a follow-up AFIS or fingerprint collection search. Information describing the physical spatial aspects of where the print was located on the substrate is often an asset, if not necessary, for digit determination. This data is necessary to ascertain if it was anatomically possible for the matrix deposition to have taken place in the location described. If different personnel are performing the crime scene work than are carrying out the comparisons, this aspect of the analysis should not be overlooked. While falsifying evidence is a very unpleasant topic, there have been enough occurrences that an identification specialist must always be vigilant. Information about the scene should be forwarded with the print submission.

Anatomical aspects also play a part in recognizing double taps and similar distortions. For example, at the point of entry of a break-and-enter, when glass is picked out of a window and thrown away the action involves a shift

Figure 4.24 These two latents were developed on the inside edge of a pane of glass pushed open to gain entry. The window, five feet from the ground, had been nailed shut. The culprit had to reach overhead to push the window open using considerable force. When the arm is extended overhead and the wrist is bent, to deposit prints in this fashion the digits point downward in the direction of the arrows. After an analysis, including the anatomical aspects, these prints were found to be in sequence and their weight accumulative. The defense was that the prints were deposited during a lawful visit inside the building. Due to the anatomical aspects, the expert could describe how that was not possible without hanging out a window that was nailed shut. Also, the expert could describe how the latents were consistent with being deposited from the exterior.

in the weight-bearing surface on the digits. This action will be visible in the matrix deposited. Also, sliding a window open from the outside at a burglary (Figure 4.24) often starts with the palm nearly closed and the culprit's fingers pointing in a downward direction. As the window is opened the arm extends and the palm opens. The digits tend to arc away from the downward position toward a horizontal position. The smearing of the matrix as the fingers move from the downward position to the horizontal tell a story. The prints could not have been deposited in that fashion by a person casually standing inside the window.

Also, prints found in locations where it was impossible for deposition, except during or after the time an object was broken, establishes a time frame of likely deposition. For example, prints found in between double-pane glass broken at a point of entry during a break-and-enter, or on the inside surface of a broken bottle used during an assault, establish a time frame for deposition of the print. The prints were obviously deposited after the glass was broken.

Clarity

Clarity describes how well the small details of the three-dimensional friction ridges have been recorded in the two-dimensional print. As mentioned earlier in this chapter, clarity dictates the level of tolerance for discrepancies and can affect the area of friction ridge structure required for identification. During comparison, if the print is a cyanoacrylate print with no signs of deposition pressure or pressure distortion, the tolerance for differences is likely no greater than that of a properly inked print, which is very low. In other words, all friction ridge details compared should appear similar or there must be a very clear reason why.

When there is less clarity, there is room for some tolerance of discrepancies. However, discrepancies must be consistent with the factors found in the substrate, matrix, development medium, deposition pressure, pressure distortion, and anatomical factors. Also, due to these discrepancies each area in agreement will have less evaluative weight. Therefore, a greater volume of unique and accidental details in agreement will be required to satisfy an opinion of individualization.

Ridge Path Configuration

The analysis of ridge path configuration is simply to establish the route of each ridge path. While independent ridge paths should be discernable, their flow should be in concert. There are few places on the volar surfaces where ridge path configuration has sharp angular formations. One obvious exception would be palmar vestiges, which can form very sharp angular formations with surrounding ridges and obviously do not flow in concert. Should sharp angular formations be encountered in other areas of the volar surfaces during ridge path analysis, it is important to ascertain if this formation is consistent with the surrounding ridge system or was caused by a distortion.

An angular formation may be a red flag indicating where a double tap has joined. This type of junction is usually identified by finding a series of ridge ends projecting into the furrows, or a series of ridge units misaligned. If suspicious of a double tap, an easy identifying technique is to follow the furrows through the problem area. Some of the ridge ends from one of the prints will project into the furrow and will be obvious from the perspective in the furrow. In situations where ridges have overlapped or doubled up

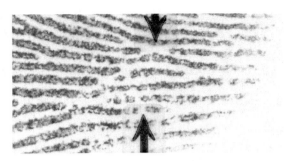

Figure 4.25 The top arrow points to two ridge endings. These ridge characteristics are second level detail. Ridges surrounding the ridge endings react to their pressure by pinching in to fill the void left between the ends. The arrow on the bottom points to an area where there are several breaks in the ridges. The surrounding ridges do not respond to their presence.

during a similar shift, this technique will cause the fat areas of the friction ridges to be more visible.

Establishing the locations of the major ridge path deviations is another aspect of this part of the analysis. At times, due to pressure, the end of a friction ridge island may not reproduce in exactly the same manner each time. However, the flow of adjacent ridges will assist in ascertaining the exact location of the major ridge path deviation, or even establish if the ridge formation is a major ridge path deviation. For example, there have been instances in court where defense counsel has had a disagreement with an identification specialist as to whether a friction ridge formation consisted of two ridge endings or if there was simply a break in the ridge. At this stage the reader should be able to describe the difference between a ridge ending and a ridge break. However, it is worth reviewing.

Major ridge path deviations are the result of differential growth during the fusion of the ridge units into islands of varying lengths and bifurcations. Adjacent ridges are affected in a similar manner and their ridge paths flow in concert around the ends of the islands or bifurcations. In the case of ridge endings, the ridges on either side will fill in any void left by the ending ridge and this directional change will be visible on the ridge path (Figure 4.25). There are no blank areas in friction formations. Major ridge path deviations are second level detail.

A ridge break may be caused by several factors including a failure in deposition of matrix, the signature of the development medium, dirt, or a dip in the ridge at a pore opening. The adjacent ridges flowing on each side of the ridge break will not be disturbed as with major ridge path deviations. This is due to the fact that there is a ridge system present under the ridge break and the adjacent ridge paths did not have a void to fill during development. Ridge breaks are third level detail. Unless third level detail is visible in both prints, ridge breaks should be treated as if the ridge is continual. This is the rationale used when comparing ninhydrin prints with broken ridges.

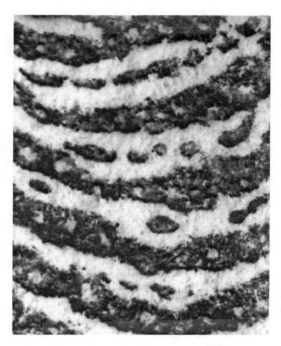

Figure 4.26 This area of friction ridges has an abundance of intrinsic ridge shapes. The ridges fluctuate in thickness, from fat ridge units to thin. Some are misaligned while others flow smoothly. Relative pore locations are visible and variable. The presence of incipient ridges may be a factor in developing such unique third level detail.

Intrinsic Ridge Formations

The intrinsic or innate ridge formations are all third level details (Figure 4.26). These include ridge unit alignment, shape, and relative pore position. Areas where the friction ridges have been recorded clearly and where relative pore position can be compared should be noted during the initial analysis. Some friction ridge surfaces will record pore locations readily in both the latent and inked prints while others will not. Even a small area of pore structure has considerable individualizing power when found progressively in agreement.

At times a section of friction ridge will have very unique shapes which are not considered major ridge path deviations. For example, an area of ridge may be naturally thin and therefore would not deposit matrix in the same manner as surrounding ridges. This formation may appear in the developed print as two ridge endings or a narrow section of friction ridge. The adjacent ridges may appear fatter, possibly due to developing into the space not occupied by the thin area of ridge, or simply by starting to develop first. While this type of friction ridge formation is third level detail, when all the aspects of the formation are considered in the aggregate these characteristics can carry a similar amount of individualizing power as a major ridge path deviation and, in some cases, more.

Cluster Identifications

When encountering friction ridge clusters, the anatomical aspects of the digits in the cluster assist with digit determination. The anatomical aspects of the cluster may also be one of many considerations which would come into play if more than one digit is used for individualization (Figure 4.27). In fact, most of the analysis factors described earlier in this chapter can be used to address this situation. The purpose of friction ridge comparison is personal identification of the donor and not the identification of a specific finger or palm print. This factor has been continually overlooked in the past.

Imagine two prints are located on opposite sides of a piece of glass that was removed from a window at the point of entry of a break-and-enter. Due to their shape and anatomical position they appear to be a thumb and index finger. Most identification specialists would attempt to identify one print or the other individually. Few would consider that this is one comparison to identify one culprit where the weight of both prints is accumulative. The problem encountered with this situation or any other type of multiple digit comparison, or even with separated parts of the same print as with a double tap, is with understanding and establishing sequence.

Let us suppose that in this situation the anatomical aspects are consistent with the digits being a thumb and index finger, including the shape and location of the prints. A thumb has a distinctive shape, and when thin objects such as glass are grasped, the side of the index digit is often used in opposition to the thumb recording that part of the pattern. In this case the thumbprint is full but slightly smudged. The index print on the other side of the glass is mainly the radial side of the finger, and individually neither print is complete enough for identification.

The pattern configuration is considered consistent with coming from the same hand that held the glass. Analysis reveals that the substrate received a similar type of matrix on both sides of the glass and that the deposition pressure is consistent with the piece of glass being held in one hand. The development medium adhering to the matrix left the same signatures in both prints. Both prints displayed slight and similar pressure distortion, possibly caused by the glass being thrown aside. The clarity of the prints was consistent considering the pressure distortion and displayed a similar level of detail along the ridge

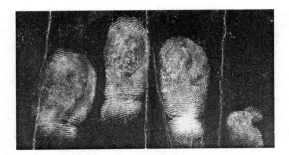

Figure 4.27 This cluster of prints is on the same substrate, the matrix has accepted the development medium similarly in each print, and the anatomical aspects are consistent with simultaneous deposition. The forensic identification specialist may form the opinion that sequence has been maintained and the weight from each print is accumulative.

paths. These factors would lead an identification specialist to form an opinion that these prints were deposited at the same time by the same donor.

Once this opinion is formed and the appropriate notations and rationale have been recorded, the ridge formations in both prints would be considered to be in sequence. When the prints are found to be in sequence in the opinion of the forensic identification specialist, the weight of unique details in both prints are accumulative in the aggregate toward individualization of the donor (Figure 4.28). The same rationale can be used when prints are found on two sides of small areas such as the zipper clasp on a sleeping bag. Also, when prints are found in a cluster on the same plane, an analysis may reveal that they are in sequence. This type of analysis must be recorded in a formal report which clearly lays out the rationale for the two prints to be considered in sequence.

An analysis of this nature is an advanced technique. The opposing prints on a piece of glass scenario may appear obvious, but it may not be as easy to defend in court without a clear rationale derived from a structured analysis. As this technique is considered an advanced technique, novices should seek advice from senior identification specialists before attempting a comparison where the sequence of two or more areas of friction ridge prints is an issue.

Analysis Summary

The ability to carry out a systematic analysis is a prerequisite of functioning as an expert within the friction ridge identification science as it is today. A thorough and systematic analysis insures that the forensic identification specialist is prepared to discuss any aspect of the latent print in court.

Figure 4.28 These two latents were developed with black powder on a cigarette package. The substrate, matrix, development medium, deposition pressure, pressure distortion, and anatomical aspects are in agreement. The weight of the unique friction ridge formations in these two prints will be accumulative if the expert forms the opinion that they are in sequence. One's rationale may have to be presented or defended in court, so thorough analysis notes are recommended.

Some experts start their analysis at the crime scene with a prepared check-off sheet while others simply make detailed notes. In either case, information collected at the crime scene must be passed on to the expert making the comparison.

Friction Ridge Comparison

The comparison is a process where visual comparative measurements, and sometimes physical comparative measurements, are made between the latent and exemplar prints. The measurements are sequential, spatial, and configurative in nature. These comparative measurements are mostly carried out by the brain in an almost automatic fashion. The comparison must be completely objective.

The identification specialist should not take any preconceived thoughts or expectations into the comparison. This is difficult if the identification specialist was also the crime scene examiner and took part in the investigation. Fulfilling both roles requires a mature psychological understanding of the mandate of each aspect of the science. It takes a special type of person with adequate training to be effective under this circumstance.

Others must be able to see what one sees. Most friction ridge prints can be compared visually using a fingerprint glass and fingerprint picks as ridge formation indicators. The picks not only keep track of the progression of the comparison, they also act as markers for the brain to carry out spatial measurements. If more advanced techniques are required such as in the case of a very complex print, an unclear print, or an identification that is mostly dependant on third level detail, a method of enlargement will be required. When comparing enlarged prints, some comparative measurements may be carried out with dividers or other measuring methods. As in the analysis stage, the ability to view the print in minute detail is paramount for the application of any advanced friction ridge identification technique.

Almost all descriptions of the comparison stage describe how the unknown or latent print is compared to the exemplar print. In most cases this is true. The exemplar print is usually taken under ideal conditions and should have more clarity than the latent print. Having said that, that is not always the case. On occasion the latent print has more clarity than the exemplar. In that situation an extensive analysis of the latent print may create an opportunity where one may see detail in the exemplar print which may not be there. Therefore, it may be more appropriate to describe comparison as a process where the poorest quality print is compared to the best quality print. However, for purposes of convenience the following narrative will describe the latent print as being compared to the exemplar print.

The comparison stage can be broken down into three basic levels of comparison. The first aspect compared is the overall pattern configuration or first level detail. The second is specific ridge path or second level detail. If the identification specialist is trained to address accidental formations such as scars or flexion creases, then those would also be compared at this time. Finally, third level detail, which includes intrinsic ridge formations such as ridge shapes or relative pore locations, is compared.

First Level Detail

First level detail or overall pattern design may be influenced by heredity through the volar pads, or be repeated by chance due to the limited possible pattern configurations that may appear on the volar surfaces. Therefore, first level detail does not have sufficient uniqueness to individualize. During the identification process the purpose of first level detail is to narrow the number of possible donors. The initial step may begin with an AFIS search, a search of a classified fingerprint collection, or simply a search of an unorganized file of finger or palm print forms.

The number of possible donors is narrowed down through elimination of all dissimilar overall pattern configurations. When a latent pattern is found to be very similar to the exemplar pattern the focus of the comparison changes from comparing nonspecific details to comparing specific details. Most identification specialists preselect an area of specific details or target group near a focal point that is easy to find, an enclosure under the left triradius, for example. If dissimilar shapes are found in the selected target area the print is eliminated. Eliminations proceed in this fashion until some second level detail is found to be similar.

When the preselected target area is found to be in agreement the comparison will start to move away from the target area. At this point the comparison moves to its next stage. The second stage is the comparison of specific friction ridge path or second level detail. While elimination of dissimilar overall patterns may take place after only a cursory comparison, the comparison of specific details is far more concentrated and specific. As the focus of the comparison moves from overall pattern configuration to the path of the friction ridges, the brain's focus also changes.

At this new level the brain will compare friction ridge paths but it will also continue to use its inherent ability to differentiate between various shapes. As the ridge paths are compared, the brain will also consider the smaller details such as the shape of the ridge or major ridge path deviations. While some of these shapes are third level details, this trait of the brain cannot be turned off, nor would we want to turn it off.

Second Level Detail

Second level detail consists of specific friction ridge paths, the specific path of accidental features such as scars, incipient ridges, and flexion creases. The specific friction ridge path is influenced by the volar pads; however, the location of ridge endings or bifurcations is random. Scars are accidental injuries that slice through the ridge formations, also at random. Incipient ridges are immature ridges that are subjected to the same forces as mature friction ridges. Some flexion creases form randomly before friction ridges form. All of these formations are products of differential growth or accidental damage and can be used to individualize if sufficient uniqueness is present.

During the comparison of second level detail, the specific ridge path of the latent print is compared to the specific ridge path of an exemplar. The purpose is to ascertain if the ridge path and major ridge path deviations, Hale's *islands and branchings,* are in agreement. That is established if each island starts and stops at the same spatial and relative location, follows the same intermediary path, and the locations and configurations of the various bifurcations along their lengths are also in agreement.

Figure 4.29 A ridge dot, one ridge unit, is the shortest of all islands and the building block of the friction ridge.

Figure 4.30 A short ridge has two or more ridge units with both ends easily recognized as being from the same island.

Figure 4.31 A ridge ending is one end of a long island. The island is long enough that the ends are not easily recognized as being from the same island.

Figure 4.32 A bifurcation is where the ridge path divides and continues on.

Basically, islands and bifurcations are the two major ridge path deviations found on the friction ridges at second level, but they may appear in various forms or combinations which take on different appearances and are called *ridge characteristics*. For example, a ridge dot (Figure 4.29) is one ridge unit, the shortest island possible. As the number of units within an island increases, yet both ends of the island can still be easily related to one another, they are called *short ridges* (Figure 4.30). When the ends of the islands are far enough apart within the pattern that it is difficult to recognize that they are the ends of the same ridge, they are just referred to as *ridges*, and each end a *ridge ending* (Figure 4.31).

A branching is called a *bifurcation* (Figure 4.32). When two bifurcations form on the same ridge facing each other and their branches join, the formation is called an *enclosure* (Figure 4.33). Sometimes one branch of a bifurcation terminates as only a short ridge and is called a *spur* (Figure 4.34). Should that short ridge join the ridge across the furrow, the ridge

Figure 4.33 An enclosure is where the ridge path divides and then comes together again.

Figure 4.34 A spur is where the ridge path divides and one branch comes to an end.

Figure 4.35 A crossover is where a short ridge crosses from one ridge to join the next.

Figure 4.36 A trifurcation is when two bifurcations develop next to each other on the same ridge, a unique formation.

characteristic would be referred to as a *crossover* (Figure 4.35). On occasion, two bifurcations will develop on the same ridge and flowing in the same direction. This ridge characteristic is called a *trifurcation* (Figure4.36). There are other ridge features that have been identified as ridge characteristics, such as *overlaps* (Figure 4.37) or pinches in ridges where the name of the ridge characteristic is self explanatory. While some authors list several ridge characteristics, they all break down to islands and branches.

Figure 4.37 An overlap is where two ridge ends meet and overlap on a bias.

Hale describes how the islands are constructed of varying numbers of ridge units connecting together during their initial formation. It is seldom that the number of ridge units within a ridge can be counted as the perimeter of each ridge unit is not usually visible. The number of ridge units could easily be established by counting the number of pores on a ridge; however, it is seldom that all the pores are recorded in both the latent and exemplar prints. The solution to this problem is a comparative measurement of the overall length of the ridges.

If we consider the structure Hale has described, the length of each island should be compared in sequence, one after the other. For example, the comparison would start at a ridge ending found in a common location in both prints and proceed along the ridge to the other end (Figure 4.38). Comparison of where the ridges started and stopped, the route of the intermediary ridge paths, and the spatial location of any bifurcations along the length of the ridges would be carried out. The next ridge over would then be compared in the same fashion.

The current method used to compare friction ridge paths follows Hale's description with a slight variation. As the brain begins to explore a ridge path it is drawn to the areas where something dramatic took place on the ridge, such as an ending or bifurcation. Ridge characteristics are natural focal points within friction ridge patterns. The brain easily measures the relative spatial distances between these focal points and other ridge features located in their vicinity. While moving from one focal point to the next, the intermediary ridge structures are also compared by the brain. The comparison continues until all the ridge structures available in the unknown print have been compared.

Agreement of ridge length is compared by visually collating the spatial relationship of the various ridge endings and bifurcations while moving between focal points. Moving across ridge systems from focal point to focal point by counting the intervening ridges is an accepted method of comparison. However, it is easier for the brain to maintain spatial sequence and measure the length of an island when the ridges are compared along the length of each ridge. It is also easier to find distortions in ridge path using this technique. Friction ridges should be compared as if one were comparing a maze. It is just as important to establish where the path goes as where it starts, stops, or bifurcates.

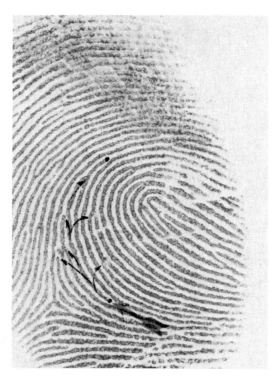

Figure 4.38 A comparison may start with any ridge feature common to both the latent and exemplar prints. For example, a comparison with this print may start in the center of the pattern. Each ridge path would be compared, one after the other, moving out from the center. The comparison systematically moves from one ridge path to the next, eventually working through the whole print in sequence. The ridge starting above the arrow illustrates how other formations are observed while following a ridge path from end to end. Following a single ridge path provides an opportunity to compare the route of the path, its intrinsic shapes, and the spatial relationship between that ridge and other ridge formations in the vicinity. Where a ridge goes is as important as where it starts, stops, and bifurcates. One should compare it as one would a maze.

As mentioned previously, major ridge path deviations are not independent formations. The friction ridges flow in concert (Figure 4.39). When a ridge ends the two adjacent ridges flow together to fill the void. Moving along the ridges increases an appreciation for these subtle formations. At times the location of poorly-recorded ridge characteristics can be established by examining the surrounding ridge flow. If ridges must be crossed during comparison, the crossing should be as short as is practical and the ridges carefully counted.

When a friction ridge print is clear and third level detail has been recorded, the brain will also observe and compare those shapes. Third level

Figure 4.39 Friction ridges flow in concert. When one ridge stops, other ridge paths are diverted to fill in the void. There are no empty areas under the skin surface. All blank areas are due to situations at the surface or are types of distortion.

detail unconsciously becomes part of the comparison at second level, whether the identification specialist realizes it or not. Identifications based mostly on the individualizing weights of third level details are considered an advanced identification technique. Novices should seek the advice of an experienced identification specialist when this type of print is encountered.

Third Level Details

Third level details are small shapes on the ridge, the relative location of pores, and the small details contained in accidental damage to the friction ridges. These shapes are created by differential growth or random damage at the ridge unit level. For example, the alignment or misalignment of individual ridge units, ridge unit shape, ridge unit thickness or thinness, and relative pore location is caused by differential growth. The twisting or puckering of the ridge units caused by a scar, or the formations found in dissociated ridges or dysplasia are caused by physical or genetic damage to the friction skin. All of these ridge formations can be used to individualize, but third level detail is always used in concert with second level detail.

The small intrinsic details of the friction ridges have tremendous individualizing power. The smaller the details progressively found in agreement, the more individualizing power they have. In other words, third level details have power if first and second level details have been found in agreement previously. In fact, it was likely third level detail, which was unconsciously observed in clear prints years ago, that prompted the International Association for Identification to change its philosophy of identification in 1973.

It is certain that third level detail is the stimulus to the brain when, on occasion, identification specialists find themselves in the predicament, "I know it is an identification, but I don't have enough to take it to court." Usually in these instances the brain is observing and comparing the volume of unique details within the ridge structures and forming an opinion.

The comparison is complete when all areas of the latent print which are available in the exemplar print have been compared. When the details present have been found to be in agreement, an evaluation as to whether there is sufficient uniqueness to individualize is the next area of consideration.

Friction Ridge Evaluation

There are times when the evaluation takes place at the same time as the comparison, especially if the comparison is terminated due to elimination. This type of comparison is especially common when the crime scene print is clear, needs little analysis, and there is an ample volume of unique details present to individualize or eliminate. However, it is a good practice to make an effort to separate the two steps. Even though comparisons of this nature are considered the easy ones, that does not mean the process is synonymous with carelessness.

At the other end of the spectrum are the poor quality prints that are not as easy to compare. They fall into what I call the *gray area*. Prints falling into this gray area may lack clarity, unique details, or contain one or more distortions. This type of print requires that the value of the unique details in the print be weighed. The gray area has parameters of its own. At one end is the obvious identification, agreement with more than a sufficient volume of unique details to individualize; at the other end is agreement, but too small a volume of details to eliminate all other possible donors or not enough unique details to individualize.

The size of the gray area and the number of prints that will fall into this area is dependent on one's training, knowledge, experience, ability, and the philosophy of identification employed. A poorly trained and inexperienced forensic identification specialist will have a larger gray area than a well-trained and experienced veteran. For example, the gray area of the novice is established and limited by personal knowledge, amount of training, ability, and experience. On the other hand, a veteran should be capable of addressing more complex prints and will have fewer prints fall within this zone. As one's knowledge and experience increases, the gray area should decrease if the identification specialist has received adequate training, regular updating, and is, of course, capable.

Identification specialists functioning under a static threshold, or a specific number of ridge characteristic identification philosophy, are at a distinct disadvantage as the gray area is a fine line. They are limited by doctrine to a black or white mentality. Knowledge and experience will not increase their ability to evaluate friction ridge formations and therefore form an opinion as to their worth. With the static threshold philosophy, all prints are basically compared at second level detail regardless of clarity or the volume of other unique formations present. The philosophy requires minimal training. The points are there in sufficient numbers and are the appropriate type or not. They are visible or not. Clarity plays a minor role and uniqueness is not really an issue.

Many countries outside of North America have not given their identification specialists the training or the mandate to work outside the static threshold philosophy. The conflict between the brain's ability to recognize and evaluate shape and the static threshold philosophy has created a collection of hybrid doctrines such as teasing out points, non-provable identifications, rules for making identifications under the threshold using two separate prints, a specific number of points in each print, and other dogmatic rules not based in science.

The human brain identifies things using a quantitative-qualitative analysis process. For example, imagine one is at a parade on a foggy day. A local group of youths is participating in the parade and one wishes to watch their performance. There are other similar groups in the parade, but one is aware that each group is wearing a similar but distinctive uniform. A group, marching in formation, is approaching, but due to the fog one cannot clearly see all the details of their uniforms. One notices one person wearing a hat consistent in shape with the local group. As the group passes, one also notices that their shoes are the type worn by the local group. Other parts of their uniforms, one item at a time, are observed and found to be consistent with the mental image one's brain has of the various uniform items worn by the local group.

After several different parts of uniform are found in agreement with the mental image one has of the local group, one forms the opinion that this is the local group. That opinion is based on a sufficient volume of information gathered from comparing the shapes worn by various individuals in the group to a mental image in the brain. When all the facts are considered in the aggregate an identification is made. Or, one may have formed the opinion that even though there were several similarities, one is not sure whether the similarities are unique enough to eliminate the fact that it may be one of the other groups. Therefore, one is unable to individualize them from the other groups in the parade. The lack of information was due to an inability to see clearly or a lack of clarity caused by the fog. Now, consider the same situation on a clear day. One glance at the group and the volume of information received by the brain would be overwhelming; either it is the local group or it is not. Clarity plays a major role in all types of identifications.

An evaluation of the results of comparison, can be broken down into two parts. The first part addresses the agreement of friction ridge formations. The second part addresses whether there is sufficient uniqueness to individualize. An evaluation of the data compiled during the comparison leads back to the philosophy of identification. The identification specialist must answer two questions unequivocally "yes" for an opinion of individualization to take place: "Is there an agreement of the friction ridge formations present in the latent and exemplar prints?" and "Is there sufficient uniqueness to individualize this one donor as the only possible source?"

As friction skin is unique in a very small area, an identification specialist must evaluate the clarity of the print and ascertain the quantity and the quality of the agreement. An opinion is then formed as to whether the prints are in agreement and if there is sufficient uniqueness to eliminate all possible donors except this one. The opinion of individualization is expressed in various terms which basically mean *elimination, individualization*, and *not sufficient uniqueness to individualize or eliminate*. The opinion of individualization is subjective as it is based on one's knowledge and ability.

Elimination

The elimination opinion is obvious: the specific details are not the same and therefore the donors are different. Elimination usually takes place at an earlier stage of the identification process. Identification specialists seldom have the opportunity to discuss or think about the thousands of people who are proven innocent of a crime based on a search of a crime scene print. This is certainly a topic to consider when ethics is an issue during cross-examination in court.

Individualization

An opinion of individualization is unambiguous. The details in both prints are in agreement and, in the opinion of the identification specialist, there is sufficient uniqueness present in the friction ridge detail to eliminate all other possible donors. This opinion is subjective and it is based on the knowledge and ability of the examiner.

Experienced identification specialists have learned through training and practice the limits of how much distortion or difference is still considered within the parameters of agreement. For the benefit of those who do not have much experience, if each area of friction ridge detail being compared requires justification for why the formation appears slightly different or why it is not spatially correct, be cautious, one may be talking oneself into agreement that is not really there. Small discrepancies appear in all prints. Most have a rational explanation based on a distortion during deposition, in the substrate, or in the development medium. However, when discrepancies appear at each turn in the ridge path, ensure the explanation for the differences is rational and based in physical fact. One should be able to point to something physical in the print, substrate, or crime scene to defend one's position, otherwise the explanation may be that the print is from another donor.

Insufficient Uniqueness to Individualize

At times the friction ridge details present in a latent print are in agreement with the exemplar print but there are few details present, or the details that are present lack quality, so an opinion on individualization cannot be formed. In these situations the identification specialist is admitting that he or she is unable to distinguish the origin of the print in question from others that could have left a print of similar appearance. It is unknown how many other people could leave such a print. The identification specialist is unable to individualize, and therefore any assessment of the value of this latent print has no scientific basis.

The value of latent prints with insufficient detail to individualize is simply unknown and will remain that way until a process of evaluation based on scientific study is found. The so-called probability identifications of friction ridge prints is extremely dangerous, especially in the hands of the unknowing. The insufficiently detailed print still has only one possible source of origin, but a reliable means of determining the probability as to whether the examiner would be correct or incorrect is, as yet, unavailable.

Other sciences and scientists express the results of some physical evidence comparisons on a graduating scale. This may appear rational, especially when peripheral investigational data such as circumstantial investigative information or culpable statements are permitted to seep into the identification process. The analysis, comparison, and evaluation of physical evidence must stand on its own. The peripheral issues are not part of the identification process. Others may enter this type of evidence in court and the judge may choose to weigh its value, but that duty belongs to the court and not the identification specialist.

When agreement is found, but there is not a sufficient volume of unique details present to individualize, the identification specialist has recognized that other prints may be indistinguishable from this one. At present we have no basis to establish how many other prints may be involved in this group. Extensive study is necessary before this type of probability opinion can be expressed with some degree of confidence and consistency within the friction ridge identification science. This is an advanced issue. The lack of a solution is only compounded by the need for basic training to ensure all experts are familiar and competent with the quantitative-qualitative friction ridge analysis philosophy as mandated by the International Association for Identification Standardization Committee.

Verification

Verification is a form of peer review and is a part of most sciences. Many organizations erroneously use verification in place of adequate training as a method of protecting against errors. While verification may prevent the occasional error, its purpose is to verify process and objectivity as opposed to only checking results. It is also an excellent vehicle for training. It can be a time for learning and an opportunity to discuss the various aspects of the friction ridge identification science. When adequately trained forensic identification specialists follow sanctioned scientific identification processes and procedures, a false identification is virtually impossible.

An issue which could have been mentioned in several areas in this book is the practice of consultation, which is a valuable part of the identification and scientific process. While some harbor a hidden fear that seeking consultation at any stage of the analysis, comparison, or evaluation is an admission of weakness, the reverse is actually the truth. No one person knows everything or has so much knowledge and experience that he or she is never in a position of requiring some form of consultation. Those having that opinion are demonstrating the very attitude that prevented this science from reaching its potential years ago. Experts must be free to discuss issues with their peers, confirm the presence of specific shapes or features that they see, and then form their own opinions. The comparison is objective, others must be capable of seeing the physical attributes that one sees. If one feels his or her objectiveness has been compromised due to the consultation, one should ask a third party to carry out the verification.

Poroscopy and Edgeoscopy

V

The relevancy and use of poroscopy and edgeoscopy have been addressed in earlier chapters. Both are third level detail that can be used during the identification process to assist with the individualization of friction ridge prints. This chapter may reexamine some of those issues, but the primary objective is to give the reader a historical overview of the background information relating to the development of each of these branches of science. While discussing the historical aspects, the reason for the success or failure of poroscopy and edgeoscopy at their initial time of introduction will become obvious. Having this knowledge will promote an understanding of the relevancy of poroscopy and edgeoscopy and how they correlate with the quantitative-qualitative friction ridge analysis process used today.

Poroscopy

The use of pores as the sole ridge formation used to individualize friction ridge prints is rare or perhaps nonexistent. Friction ridges must be present for pores to be visible, and those friction ridges would have individualizing value simply by being present and in agreement. Poroscopy will almost always be used in conjunction with other friction ridge formations.

In the past there was a general feeling that poroscopy had little practical value due to the minuteness of its detail and the failure of pore structure to be reproduced consistently in crime scene and inked friction ridge prints. When poroscopy was first introduced the identification philosophy of the day was the threshold ideology based on a specific number of ridge characteristics. The relevancy of friction ridge clarity, third level detail, and quantitative-qualitative analysis were not understood by the friction ridge identification discipline. As a result, poroscopy was relegated to the fringe of the identification sciences, accepted in theory but ignored in practice.

Over the last 20 years the friction ridge identification science and the methods of crime scene examination have progressed to such an extent that those earlier impediments are now nonissues. Today, experts within the friction ridge identification discipline have a solid understanding of the relevance of clarity, third level detail, and the evaluative identification process. Understanding the value of relative pore location, as well as other third level detail, will enhance the ability to narrate how an identification is carried out. When poroscopy is approached from a position of knowledge, a bonafide identification medium worthy of study is revealed. Forensic identification specialists should have a basic understanding of the various historical and functional aspects of poroscopy when presenting themselves to a court as experts in friction ridge identification.

Dr. Edmond Locard

Dr. Edmond Locard

The science of poroscopy was established by Dr. Edmond Locard of Lyons, France in 1912. He began to study poroscopy as the result of a break-in and theft at the apartment of M. Chardonnet at Number 6 Rue Centrale in Lyons. The thieves had stolen several pieces of jewelry and 400 francs in cash. There were no witnesses, but a rosewood jewelry box which had held the stolen jewelry was found to be covered with fingerprints. Several latent prints were developed with carbonate of lead and photographed.

The latents were searched through a local fingerprint collection and some were identified to a known thief by the name of Boudet. As Boudet was known to work with an accomplice named Simonin, both men were arrested and their prints taken. One of the crime scene latents, which turned out to be the left middle phalange of Boudet, had 78 ridge characteristics in agreement. Another palm print, left by Simonin, had 94 ridge characteristics in agreement. Neither man would confess to the crime and the case went to trial.

During this time friction ridge identification was in its infancy and, to a degree, still somewhat novel. One can only surmise that Locard wanted to present as much incriminating evidence as possible at the trial. As both prints clearly illustrated relative pore location, Locard decided to compare them. After the pore locations were compared, Boudet's phalange print was found to have 901 pores in the correct relative position (Figures 5.1A, 5.1B). Simonin's palm print had 2000 pores in agreement. This amount of third level detail when found in agreement has an enormous value toward individualization. Both men were convicted and sentenced to five years of hard labor.

Figure 5.1A and B Boudet's left middle phalange containing 78 ridge characteristics and 901 pores.

Locard believed that the comparison of the pores played a major role in the conviction of the two men due to the fact no evidence was available other than the friction ridge prints. Also, both prints lacked an overall pattern configuration, which played a major role in the identification process at that time. Today, considering the number of major ridge path deviations present and the area of friction skin compared, one may feel that Locard's opinion was self-serving or that the comparison of relative pore position was redundant. However, when one considers that the friction ridge science was relatively new and the scientific basis was empirical only, then Locard's opinion has merit.

Locard published his research into poroscipy in "Les pores et l'identification des criminals", *Biologica*, vol. 2, pp. 357-365, 1912. He concluded that:

1. The sweat pores present the triple characteristic of perpetuity, immutability and variety which establishes them as a means of identification of primary importance.
2. Identification by the comparison of pores in a striking manner confirms the evidence from finger prints, by adding to the determination of ridge details that of the visible sweat pores, the number of which is often many hundreds and in a good impression may exceed a thousand.
3. In most cases in which the digital or palmar impression is too fragmentary for an absolute identification by the dactyloscopic method, which requires a minimum of twelve characteristic points, the comparison of

pores, providing these are discernable, will permit the attainment of positive identification."

Locard felt that various aspects of the sweat pores could be examined and used for identification purposes. Wentworth and Wilder reported the following in their book *Personal Identification* in 1918:

According to Locard, the sweat pores vary in the following ways:

(1) *The size of the pores.* The size of the pores varies apparently without system, and pores of several sizes may be found near together. Locard measured the diameters of several, taken from developed impressions, which are much sharper than prints, employing the methods of microscopists, and using their unit, the micron, and found them to vary in diameter from 88 to 220 micra. The largest pores had thus three times the diameter and nine times the area of the smallest. *[A micron — plural micra — is 1/1000 of a millimeter or 1/25000 of an inch.- Auth.]*

(2) *The form of the individual pore.* In form a pore may be round, or it may be elliptical, oval, square, rhomboid, or triangular. In an ordinary inked print the pores are usually more or less filled with ink, so that their actual shape is not revealed, but in an accidental impression, developed by oxide of lead or an equally good substance, and then photographed to the proper enlargement, as in the illustration here given, the individual shapes are clearly seen.

(3) *The position of the pore on the ridge.* This is practically the most useful character, and is certainly the most conspicuous. The pores usually lie in a single row along the middle or crest of the ridge, parallel to the lateral furrows, but now and then a single pore, or a series of several of them, open on the side, occasionally almost into the furrow between the ridge and the next. Such a laterally placed pore is likely to appear in a print as an open notch, since the substance used in printing covers only the middle of the ridge, and does not include the outer margin of the lip of the pore. On this very account one must not expect to find two separate prints of the same pore to be exactly alike in this respect, as the pore may be open in one and closed in the other, in accordance with the breadth of the printed surface in the two.

Again, the position of the pores may differ with respect to the adjacent ones in the same row, a few being near together, followed along the same ridge by others further apart. Occasionally, too, at certain points, two pores may occur, running abreast or nearly so, across a ridge, or again three may crowd so closely together as to form a triangle. Such striking points, the form of which is easily held in the eye, form valuable characters in locating an area upon a complete print, and thus determining the identity of a fragment under consideration.

(4) *The number or frequency of the pores.* This feature is characteristic of an entire print, or indeed of all the prints of a given individual, and may be calculated in two ways: (1) The average number of pores that occur on a given length of ridge, or (2) the average number of pores found within a given area. For instance, Locard finds that the number of pores along a centimeter of ridge varies from 9 to 18, and as two and a half centimeters are almost the equivalent of an inch, this would mean 23 to 45 per inch. In the entire area shown in Figure 119, *[Boudet's developed phalange print — Auth]* which is enlarged 7.5 diameters, there are more than 900, but in this individual the pores were larger than usual and very numerous.

We have, then, in the sweat pores, with their great individual differences, and their persistence throughout life, an invaluable series of individual features, which can be employed to advantage in cases where the record is too incomplete to show a definite pattern or too fragmentary to make out even the ridge details with certainty. As compared with one case where definite finger patterns are left upon the premises there are dozens where only the marks of a few ridges can be obtained, and these often of other parts of the hand than the finger bulbs. Such fragments may be often identified by poroscopy, if we have for comparison the prints of the corresponding parts of the hands of suspected persons.

Nor is this search as great an undertaking or as arduous as one would think. In the first place a careful study of the objects handled will suggest the parts of the hand which would come most naturally into contact with those places where the impressions are left, perhaps the bulb or middle phalange of the index finger, or the outer, or ulnar, cushion of the palm. Such a preliminary diagnosis greatly assists the search, as it directs the attention to certain limited areas which are to be studied first. The investigator should naturally be in possession of prints, or still better, developed impressions, of these parts taken from the hands of the suspected party or parties, and enlarge both these and the traces found to about the magnification shown in Figure 122; that is, 40 diameters, for easy comparison.

In starting it is well to select a characteristic group of pores, not too many to remember readily, and then, with the picture of these in mind, to search over the likely places of the more complete print for a duplicate group. When noted, compare the surrounding pores, and eventually test the entire fragment under inspection. Mathematically the positive establishment of some 20 to 40 pores should establish a complete identity for the two duplicate areas, yet, where a much larger number of details is obtainable, one should use his full opportunities, and make the comparison cover some hundreds of pores, or, if so many are not available, all there are. *[20–40 pores was Wentworth's and Wilder's opinion and we do not know if Locard agreed — Auth]*

Such a proof, which, in the case of an ordinary chance impression may be based upon hundreds or even thousands of different points of identity, incalculably strengthens any proof brought forward by the use of the ridge details, and when shown up by the use of enlarged photographs, presents an overwhelming piece of evidence to any judge or jury.

In closing their chapter on poroscopy Wentworth and Wilder made the following comments:

Identification by the sweat pores has been used but little to the present time, perhaps mainly by Dr. Locard in France and by the present authors in the United States, but the suggestion that this field is still largely unexplored may induce others to experiment and investigate along these lines. Locard says, "If the jury or magistrate hesitate because it may seem to them audacious to believe that 12 — 15 points are sufficient to identify an impression, they will do so no longer when they are shown the perfect accord of hundreds of pores." As an illustration we may cite the Matern case, also from Lyons, where a fragmentary imprint without details contained 200 pores, and was thereby identified as coming from the right ring finger of the accused burglar, Matern.

The majority of fingerprint texts published after *Personal Identification* devoted little space to poroscopy. As a result there has been little further research in the field. The lack of interest in poroscopy has been blamed on its so-called shortcomings such as powder fill-in of crime scene fingerprints, poor inked impressions for comparison, inadequate visual aids to examine pore structure, difficulty locating the pores to be compared, the low percentage of fingerprints displaying pore structure in their developed or inked forms, the degree of study required to gain expertise in poroscopy, and the time required to make a comparison. The truth likely has more to do with the level of understanding the experts of the day had of the identification process rather than any of poroscopy's shortcomings.

To use poroscopy effectively, it must be incorporated into an evaluative identification process. In Locard's day and up to recent years, a threshold philosophy of identification was in use. This is likely the reason Wentworth and Wilder expressed a specific number of pores as a ballpark figure for individualization. The modern quantitative-qualitative analysis philosophy removes this impediment as pores become one more link in the chain of available ridge formations if clarity permits.

My studies and those of others have found that prints containing pore structure seldom record all of the parameters Locard suggested for pore comparison. However, the technology used today to develop friction ridge

 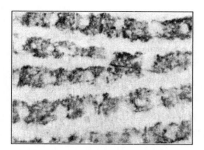

Figure 5.2A and B   These two bifurcations were in the same location on similar patterns. Normal examination would find them in agreement, but their relative pore locations differ. Pores on adjacent ridges can be compared by triangulation, which is not advised over more than one ridge.

prints at crime scenes has improved to the point where pore locations appear more frequently in ridge detail, hence the comparison of relative pore location is now a more feasible method of evaluating friction ridge prints. Even if pores are only visible in a small area, that can enhance the individualizing power of that area of friction ridges.

Also, the scientific information available today clearly establishes the immutability of pore location along the friction ridge. Fill-in, or failure to record, will likely always be a problem the examiner will need to address. In these instances Locard felt that a filled-in pore was simply overlooked as long as it was not obviously visible in another location. Pressure distortion is another factor encountered. As with pressure distortion involving major ridge path deviations, the pores will remain in the same relative position to one another during the flexion of the friction skin.

Comparison of Relative Pore Location

During ridgeology research two methods of pore comparison were used. The first method was used when pore locations were on and around major ridge path deviations. In this instance the relative positions of the pores became part of the visual evaluation of the friction ridge formation itself. The ridge characteristic was used as a focal point and the shapes of the surrounding ridges and distances between the pores were compared visually. The relative position of pores on any ridge were compared to pores on adjacent ridges. The comparison of pores on ridges separated by more than one friction ridge were subject to the flexibility of the skin and comparative measurements were not found to be accurate.

In situations where the relative pore locations of a large area of friction ridges is being examined, work notes can be used to record the progress of the comparison. A second, more visual method is using an overlay to record the agreement of pores in a small area, and to record the route followed as the comparison is taking place. This technique is especially useful if several open fields are encountered and the route the comparison follows is complex and difficult to remember.

The overlay method starts after the comparison of friction ridge formations at second level is found in agreement. Photographic enlargements of both the latent and exemplar prints are made. A sheet of clear plastic is placed over the exemplar print and one ridge characteristic is marked on its surface and numbered as a starting point. A written description of the location of the ridge characteristic is made. All the pores on the same ridge as the ridge characteristic are marked as well as the pores on the adjacent ridges. The furrow is then crossed and the location is marked. The relative pore locations on the adjacent ridge are then marked. If the pore locations in that area of the latent and exemplar are found in agreement, then the process is repeated in an adjacent area. Each area compared should be expanded enough to touch an adjacent area so all of the available pores are compared. A second ridge characteristic is then noted, marked, and numbered, and the pore locations marked in that area. Most experts will develop their own symbols for this process. A benefit of this method is that it can be repeated, as a demonstration to peers or in court, to show how the identification was carried out. A partial copy of a plastic worksheet is illustrated in Figure 5.3. A glossary has been added to identify each symbol.

The agreement of relative pore locations increases the individuality of an area of friction ridges. Poroscopy is a perfect example of the principle that the smaller the detail found progressively in agreement, the greater the individualizing value it has. This principle is the key to the quantitative-qualitative analysis philosophy. This axiom was understood by such experts as Wentworth and Wilder. It was also understood by Locard but he expressed it in a slightly different manner.

Locard refers to a philosophy very similar to ridgeology in a paper published in 1914. Locard's philosophy was reported by Christophe Champod in a guest editorial entitled, "Edmond Locard — Numerical Standards & Probable Identification," *JFI*, Vol. 45, No. 2, 1995, pp. 136-163.

Champod reports Locard's philosophy of identification in the following manner and refers to the philosophy as *Locard's Tripartite Rule*:

1. If more than 12 concurring points are present and the fingerprint is sharp, then the certainty of identity is beyond debate.
2. If 8 to 12 concurring points are involved, then the case is borderline and the certainty of identity will depend on:
   a) the sharpness of the fingerprint;
   b) the rarity of its type;

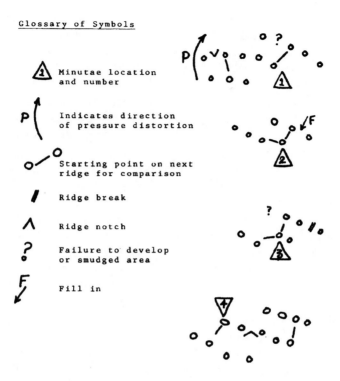

Figure 5.3 The ridge characteristics are numbered and marked with triangles. The pores are marked with circles. Some ridge shapes are marked as well as signs of pressure distortion and suspected pore fill-in.

c) the presence of the center of the figure (core) and the triangle (delta) in the exploitable part of the print;

d) the presence of pores (poroscopy);

e) the perfect and obvious identity regarding the width of the papillary ridges and valleys, the direction of the lines, and the angular value of the bifurcations. (ridgeology/edgeoscopy)

In these instances, certainty can only be established following discussion of the case by at least two competent and experienced specialists.

3. If a limited number of characteristic points are present, the fingerprint cannot provide certainty for an identification, but only a presumption proportional to the number of points available and their clarity.

The tripartite rule can be compared to the quantitative-qualitative analysis philosophy of today. Rule One tells us that in cases where several ridge characteristics are in agreement in a clear print, then individualization or identification is beyond any doubt.

Rule One refers to clear prints that contain a sufficient volume of unique details for comparison and identification, the easy ones. Rule Two describes a situation where second level detail is limited and, if third level detail is present, it can be used for comparison and identification. This print is moving into the gray area where various aspects must be evaluated, the success of which depends on the knowledge and ability of the examiner. Locard mentions sharpness or clarity, pores, ridge shapes, and the presence of a core and delta in the pattern. Also, Locard feels with this type of print, where third level detail has played a large role in the identification process, verification is required by two other competent and experienced specialists. An expert carrying out a comparison of this type of print would require considerable knowledge of the friction skin, the evaluative identification process, and ample empirical comparison experience.

Rule Three describes a situation where the friction ridge details present have been found in agreement but are not sufficient in quantity or quality to individualize. As one has no idea how many others may have a portion of friction skin that could appear similar in a small area due to a lack of clarity, one cannot identify or eliminate. Generally, those rules are followed today.

Locard did not have the luxury of the knowledge contained in papers published by modern scientists such as Hale, Okijima, or Cummins. Had that information been available earlier, an evaluative identification process may have developed. While ridgeology is taken in stride by most experts today, Locard was considered avant-garde in his day, a man truly ahead of his time.

Edgeoscopy

Edgeoscopy

Over the last few years edgeoscopy has been documented numerous times as having little practical value. If the worth of edgeoscopy is evaluated using the threshold identification philosophy, where number of points is the issue, then those statements have merit. However, when the value of edgeoscopy is considered as being part of a quantitative-qualitative analysis philosophy, those statements do not have merit.

Unknowingly, edgeoscopy has considerable value even to those who use a static threshold philosophy of identification. For example, when two bifurcations are found in the same location in latent and exemplar prints, as the examiner compares them the brain automatically compares their edges or

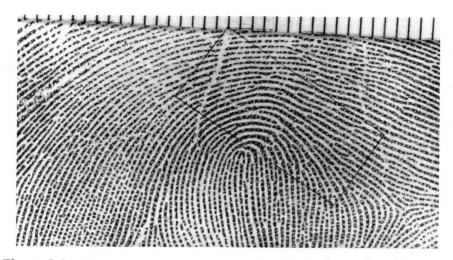

Figure 5.4 This area of a palm print was identified using friction ridges and poroscopy. Enlargements of the identified area of friction skin are reproduced in Figures 5.5 and 5.6.

Figure 5.5 This partial palm print was developed with cyanoacrylate on the plastic coating of a telephone extension wire approximately 5 mm wide. It was pulled from the wall by the culprit during a robbery.

Figure 5.6 This is the area blocked out in the palm print in Figure 5.5. It solved an armed robbery after an erroneous visual identification had been made of an innocent suspect. This identification was based on ridge characteristics, edges, and pores. (Poroscopy photos by Frank Barclay, Thunder Bay Police)

shapes whether or not the examiner wishes to do so. It is this natural ability that allows an examiner to differentiate among characteristics of the same type. Experts using the evaluative identification process are cognizant of this fact and use it to their advantage. Therefore, the value of edgeoscopy hinges on one's knowledge, the sophistication of the identification process, and the clarity of the print.

Salil K. Chatterjee

Salil Kumar Chatterjee

The term "edgeoscopy" was originally coined by Salil K. Chatterjee in a paper published in *Fingerprint and Identification*, September 1962 issue, and republished in the second printing of his book *Finger, Palm, and Sole Prints*, in 1967. Chatterjee's original idea was to use ridge edges in concert with other friction ridge formations to establish individualization.

Chatterjee encountered some shapes on the friction ridge edges that tended to reappear frequently, so he gave them specific names. He used the following terms to describe the various characteristics encountered: 1. Straight edge; 2. Convex edge; 3. Peak; 4. Table; 5. Pocket; 6. Concave edge; 7. Angle; and 8. Others (Figure 5.7). Subsequent research into edgeoscopy has found that all the characteristics encountered along the friction ridges can be placed into one of these categories. Very few of the edge characteristics look exactly as illustrated, but they generally are consistent with the basic designs put forward by Chatterjee. At times the difference between a narrow convex edge and a small peak edge was a judgment call.

In practice, the use of edge shapes during comparison does not require the shape to be classified. One shape is compared to another and found to be consistent or not. The value of Chatterjee's shapes is in their use when describing the specific shapes found along the friction ridge edges, especially when explaining the evaluative identification process.

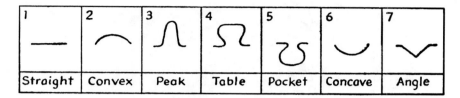

Figure 5.7

The source of Chatterjee's shapes are the shapes along the side of the ridge units. Some are caused by the effects of differential growth on the ridge itself, and sometimes a shape is caused by a pore being located near the edge of the friction ridge, such as with pockets and tables. The pocket is a single pore location recorded on the edge of the ridge while the table is the edge of the ridge between two pore locations opening into the furrow.

Considering that the average width of an epidermal ridge for a young adult male is approximately 0.48 mm and that ridge units are approximately as long as they are wide, every millimeter of ridge could theoretically contain four edge characteristics. In a perfect situation, with each ridge unit having a visible edge characteristic on each side, a ridge 5 mm long would contain approximately 10 ridge units and 20 edge characteristics. The theory is sound, but in practice the flexibility of the friction skin tends to mask all but the largest edge shapes. On occasion, if clarity permits, a series of Chatterjee shapes will be visible and can be compared.

Edgeoscopy has always been a part of friction ridge comparison, but its use as an independent identification science is not feasible. Having an understanding of the relevance of edge shapes as third level detail can only enhance comparison and improve one's ability to describe how an identification is carried out. The essence of friction ridge comparison is comparing shapes in sequence. Chatterjee recognized the importance of edge shapes and moved the science another step toward the establishment of an evaluative identification philosophy.

The two prints in Figures 5.8A and 5.8B display numerous edge characteristics. Figure 5.8A was deposited using mostly vertical pressure, while Figure 5.8B was rolled or has lateral pressure. Some edge shapes have been altered due to the differing deposition pressure. For example, the spur at 9 o'clock has more edge detail in figure 5.8B than it has in figure 5.8A. However, when the differing deposition pressure is taken into account these formations are consistent in shape. There are numerous other examples of edge shapes in agreement in these two prints. One obvious formation is the short ridge at the core. This short ridge has a specific overall shape, but is especially

Figure 5.8A This print was deposited using vertical pressure similar to the pressure used with plain impressions on fingerprint forms.

Figure 5.8B This print was deposited using lateral pressure similar to a rolled impression. (Both prints submitted by John R. Vanderkolk)

unique at its lower end. Also, the ridge to the left of the short ridge has a peak on its right side opposite the center of the short ridge. Thin ridges, thick ridges, pockets, peaks, and ridge breaks can be found in agreement throughout these two prints. When small characteristics are found in agreement, the volume of individualizing detail is greatly increased. However, edgeoscopy is only of value to the identification process when the examiner has the knowledge to understand the significance of the shapes encountered and the ability to compare the variety of very unique shapes available.

Friction Ridge Analysis Report

The rationale for using a friction ridge analysis report was discussed during the analysis of friction ridge prints. The following analysis was prepared for the verification of a very complex print. Photographic enlargements were used during the analysis. The report has been altered to ensure confidentiality of all people involved with the case. The prints compared are reproduced in Figures 6.1 and 6.2.

Friction Ridge Analysis and Comparison for Identification Verification Purposes

Completed by:	Submitted by:
Staff Sergeant David R. Ashbaugh,	Sergeant Ralph Smith,
Forensic Identification Specialist,	Forensic Identification Section
Caledonia Forensic Identification Services,	Hagersville Police Department,
Caledonia Police Department,	3 Harris Street, Hagersville Ontario
66 Argyle Street, Caledonia Ontario	

The analysis is of a latent fingerprint photographed on a plastic thermos with an approximate diameter of five inches. The latent fingerprint is then compared to the right little finger on an exemplar fingerprint form in the name of Peter Edward MURRAY BD:46-03-11, FPS 567830A. The analysis and comparison were carried out using enlarged photographs supplied by Sergeant Ralph Smith.

Analysis of Unknown Fingerprint

Substrate Distortion

The substrate in the photograph is relatively smooth but appears to have several scratches in its surface. The surface is reported to have been dusted with black powder, which appears to have accumulated in several of the surface scratches creating black lines within the substrate. The appearance of the

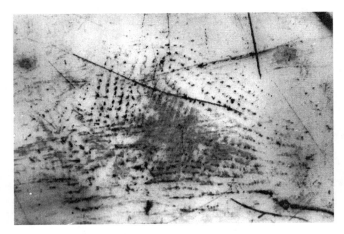

Figure 6.1 This latent fingerprint is a wet print developed on a concave plastic surface. It was developed with black powder and has varying deposition pressure, pressure distortion, and red flags.

Figure 6.2 The exemplar print used during the comparison is a rolled ink impression.

substrate is consistent with plastic that has been dusted with black fingerprint powder. The substrate shape or damage by scratches does not interfere with the continuity of the ridge paths in the developed latent fingerprint.

Matrix Particulars

The appearance of the print is consistent with a *wet print*, which has a flowing dot appearance and a narrowness of the ridges. The phenomenon occurs when a matrix is deposited mainly from the top surface of the friction ridges and is of thin viscosity. This type of matrix tends to pool in the pore openings. Each pore is relative to a ridge unit which is the biological building block of a friction ridge. Pores are more or less evenly spaced along the friction ridge surface. The flowing appearance of the dots is due to the thin viscosity of the matrix and the tendency of the matrix to adhere to the substrate as the digit is lifted.

The narrow ridges also cause the intervening furrows to appear wider than normal. The fingerprint matrix is likely sweat or a foreign material with a thin viscosity. These factors do not disrupt the course of the friction ridge paths in the print, but they eliminate almost all intrinsic ridge shapes from the comparison.

Development Medium

The appearance of the substrate and the development of the fingerprint matrix are consistent with a plastic substrate being dusted with black fingerprint powder as reported.

Deposition Pressure

The appearance of the fingerprint matrix leads me to believe that deposition pressure was normal to light. There is the possibility of a double tap caused by pressure distortion through a shifting of pressure from the core element in the center of the pattern to the triradius element in the lower left or in reverse order. This is indicated by a smearing of the ridges between the core and triradius areas.

Pressure Distortion

There is apparent pressure distortion in the latent print. Due to pressure distortion the print has three distinct areas or elements: the core element in the center of the print, the triradius element on the lower left side of the print, and the base ridges that run across the bottom of the print.

Slippage is evident between the core and triradius elements. The core element appears to be shifted away from the triradius element toward 2 o'clock. Or the triradius element could have moved down and away from the core element. The platform ridges are distorted in the same direction as the triradius element. The slippage distance of the ridges between the core and triradius elements is approximately the width of one friction ridge when measured center to center.

Clarity

First and second level detail are present. A very small amount of third level detail is evident in the platform ridges of the print. The ridge paths are evident in the core, triradius, and platform ridge elements.

Comparison of Unknown to Known

Ridge Path

The ridge paths in the core, triradius, and platform ridge elements of the latent print can be followed without much difficulty. When the latent print ridge paths were compared to the exemplar print they were found to be in agreement. The platform ridges of the latent print were affected by the shift of the core away from the triradius. This resulted in the platform ridges being slightly flexed downward on the left side, under the triradius. As these ridges were closely aligned with the direction of slippage, from 8 o'clock toward 2 o'clock, some ridges were longitudinally extended. This is evident in the lengthening of a major ridge path deviation, an enclosure, found in the platform ridges near the left of the base ridge element.

Deposition pressure and a lack of matrix also affected a major ridge path deviation two ridges up and to the right of the enclosure in the latent print. The ridge appears to end prematurely in the latent print when compared to the exemplar. However, upon examining the exemplar print in this ridge ending area, this section of friction ridge is very narrow. As a result, the ridges likely failed to deposit sufficient matrix for the development medium to adhere.

Furrows

The furrows in the core area of the latent print appear wider than the furrows in the exemplar print. However, comparative measurements from ridge center to ridge center in both prints were found to be consistent. The wide furrow appearance is caused by a narrow band of matrix from the top of the friction ridges being deposited on the substrate. This issue was also addressed during analysis.

Major Ridge Path Deviations

There are several major ridge path deviations, commonly called "ridge characteristics," within the ridge paths of the latent print. These major ridge path deviations were found to be in agreement in both prints.

Sequence

The ridge paths of the ridges in the base ridge element were found to be in sequence with the ridges in the core element. The core and triradius elements were also found to be in sequence. The core and triradius elements join together at the extreme top edge of the latent print above the triradius. There is a slight spatial misalignment in this area between the core and triradius elements due to slippage. When the core element is compared in juxtaposition with the triradius element, the major ridge path deviations are in spatial sequence. Therefore, this dissimilarity can be explained.

Area of Slippage

The smeared area between the core and triradius elements indicates that the core element has moved approximately one ridge width (center to center) away from the triradius element. The ridges in this area of the print flow at approximately 90 degrees to the direction of slippage. The direction of movement is recorded by the smearing of matrix on the ridges, which was revealed when the smears were dusted with fingerprint powder. The length of the smearing is consistent with the various movement distortions found throughout the latent print, such as the flattening of the platform ridges described earlier.

Due to slippage between the core and triradius elements, it is difficult to count ridges or observe ridge paths within the smeared area. Ridges can only be tracked part way through this area due to smudging. When the smudged area is isolated from the surrounding ridges it becomes evident that the correct number of ridges enter the top of the smeared area and exit the bottom. By carefully tracking the smeared ridge paths through this area and by examining adjacent ridges just outside the isolated area, there is no indication that there are any unknown major ridge path deviations within the smear. The friction ridges traveling through the smeared area of the latent print appear to be in agreement with the ridges found in the corresponding area of the exemplar print.

Amount of Slippage

The core element appears to have moved approximately one ridge width, measured center to center, toward 2 o'clock. This has increased the core/triradius distance. The length of the visible slippage in the smear area is consistent with the length of the extra distance found between the core and triradius elements, taking into consideration the flexibility of the friction skin. Although this factor makes comparison more difficult, it does not decrease the value of the comparison.

Evaluation

The area of friction ridge detail developed in the latent fingerprint contains a sufficient degree of uniqueness to individualize. During comparison the ridge paths of the latent and exemplar prints were found to be in agreement, taking into consideration the clarity of the print and various aspects of friction ridge distortion revealed during the analysis.

The referenced double tap is a common form of distortion frequently found on bottles or other drinking vessels. I am familiar with this type of distortion and in my opinion it does not diminish the evidential value of the latent fingerprint. The various major ridge path deviations present are in the correct relative position and are accurate in configuration, considering the double tap distortion and the flexibility of the skin. Therefore, the comparison has the two ingredients, agreement and sufficient volume of detail, necessary to form an opinion. Based on my knowledge and experience, it is my opinion that the latent fingerprint and the right little fingerprint on form C-216 in the name of Peter Edward MURRAY, FPS: 567830A, were made by the same finger.

Verification

The latent print and the exemplar prints were compared by Corporal Alain Richard of the Caledonia Forensic Identification Services. My opinion of individualization was independently verified by Corporal Richard. I therefore verify the identification made by Sergeant Ralph Smith to be accurate.

Original signed:
_____

David R. Ashbaugh, S/Sgt.,
Forensic Identification Specialist,
Caledonia Forensic Identification Services,
Caledonia Police Department,
Caledonia, Ontario.
_____

Ridgeology
Formula

VII

The ridgeology formula is an overview of the relationship between the scientific basis and the identification process. This chapter also has lists of key words taken from the contents of this book that can be used for study. The ridgeology formula identifies a topic and lists the key words that should trigger specific areas of knowledge in which the expert should have some degree of understanding. The three-dimensional aspects of the friction skin, which is the basis of the science, and the scientific procedural aspects involved in the comparison of two-dimensional prints are bridged together with an understanding of clarity. The amount of friction skin details reproduced in the friction ridge print and the fact that all deposited prints have some form of distortion are the underlying principles of clarity. Experts must have a clear understanding of these two separate issues to describe the scientific basis of friction ridge identification and to narrate the identification process. This is followed by lists of key words denoting the type of ridge formations used during the identification process, and the key words used to recall the various stages of the procedural aspects of the identification process. Each key word represents an area of knowledge that, when put together, tell a story. These key words tell a story about friction ridge development and the manner in which the various friction ridge formations are applied to the identification process.

Once the various aspects of the friction ridge identification science are fully understood, the key words should be enough to trigger the important issues necessary to describe the scientific basis of friction ridge identification and explain its procedural aspects. The tables in the ridgeology formula can be duplicated on wallet-sized cards and used as a reference, bookmark, or study guide. The ridgeology overview is an excellent tool for review just prior to giving evidence or for training purposes when there is a need to refresh one's memory.

The ridgeology formula is broken down into areas of knowledge where each word relates to the next. Review the topics and words in each column.

Table 7.1   Ridgeology Formula

Scientific Basis		Identification Process		
(Biology)		(Procedure)		
(Three-Dimensional)		(Two-Dimensional)		

Clarity Bridge
(Details/Distortions)
(3D-----------2D)

			Methodology	
Friction Skin	Protocol	Philosophy	A.C.E.	Verification
Formation ☞	Rationale	Formations	Analysis	Peer Review
Persistency	Brain	Sequence	Comparison	⇓
Uniqueness	⇓	Sufficient	Evaluate	Scientific
	Sight	Individual		Process
Found				
⇓				
Anatomy		←	←	←
Embryology				
Genetics	←		←	

Verification Starts at the Beginning

Tie them all together to tell the story of the friction ridge identification science.

1. **Scientific Basis:** The scientific basis is a biology issue. The knowledge learned about the friction skin can be applied to the identification process as it has been established through years of research by experts working in various related sciences such as biology, embryology, anatomy, and dermatoglyphics. The most important issues assimilated from these sciences are keynoted in the premises of friction ridge identification, which relate to and are descriptive of the three-dimensional friction skin.

2. **Identification Process:** The identification process represented in the ridgeology formula reflects a scientific procedure describing how friction ridge identification is accomplished. It consists of a protocol, philosophy, methodology, and verification. Protocol and verification are not part of the identification process but have been added to complete the picture. The identification process is applied to friction ridge prints which, unlike the friction skin, are two-dimensional and are found with varying degrees of clarity caused by distortions during deposition.

3. **Clarity:** Clarity is the bridge between the three-dimensional friction skin and the two-dimensional print. It describes how well the three-dimensional friction skin was recorded in the two-dimensional print. When there is little distortion in a print and a large volume of detail has been reproduced that is representative of the three-dimensional friction skin, the print is considered to have clarity. When details are not present due to a distortion, the print is considered not to have clarity.

4. **Protocol:** The identification process is inherent to the brain and is a natural cerebral procedure. The natural process is synonymous with sight. However, the brain has certain quirks to assist with the sight process which are counterproductive to forensic identification. Due to these factors a specific and structured protocol has been established to ensure the methodology of friction ridge identification is fully objective and unbiased. The difference between the sight process and the forensic identification process is in the systematic, structured, and scientific protocol of the latter.

5. **Philosophy:** The philosophy of friction ridge identification answers the question "How much does it take to individualize?" The formal philosophy statement is "Friction ridge identification is based on the agreement of friction ridge formations in sequence having sufficient uniqueness to individualize." All friction ridge formations are evaluated in the aggregate based on a quantitative-qualitative friction ridge analysis formula.

6. **Methodology:** The methodology describes the scientific procedure followed to carry out a friction ridge identification and answers the question "How do you make an identification?" The methodology consists of an analysis, a comparison, and an evaluation.

> **Analysis:** The analysis is a structured intelligence gathering process. All deposited prints suffer from some form of distortion. The analysis examines substrate distortion, matrix distortion, development medium distortion, deposition distortion, pressure distortion, anatomical aspects, clarity, level of detail available for comparison, and the presence of red flags.
>
> **Comparison:** The unknown or latent print is compared to the known or exemplar print. The comparison proceeds in sequence or systematically to compare all of the available friction ridges in the latent print to the friction ridges in the exemplar print.
>
> **Evaluation:** The evaluation consists of two parts, which can be expressed with two questions experts must ask themselves: 1. Is there agreement between the latent and exemplar? 2. Is the agree-

ment sufficient to eliminate all possible donors in the world except this one? If both answers are yes, the opinion of individualization has been established.

7. **Verification:** Verification is not part of the identification process but is part of the scientific process in the form of peer review. All sciences have peer review as part of their process whether as part of an experiment or during the publication of a paper. Peer review is a form of quality assurance. While it can help to ensure errors are not made, it is not a replacement for adequate training. Verification starts at the beginning with the verifier having a knowledge of the scientific basis and identification process. The verifier then repeats the steps taken by the initial expert to establish individualization.

Table 7.2   Friction Ridge Formations

Class	Unique	Accidental
Overall pattern	Spec path/ridge shape	Damage
Volar pads	Ridge unit	Path/shape
Heredity/stress	Differential growth	Random
Narrow group	Individualize	Individualize
1st level	2nd and 3rd level	2nd and 3rd level
Rarity	Degree of uniqueness	Degree of uniqueness

Table 7.3   Identification Process

Philosophy (how much)	Methodology (how done)
Ridge formations	Analysis unknown (bottom-up)
Sequence	Compare to known (top-down)
Sufficient uniqueness	Evaluation (agree — sufficient)
Individualize	Objective (others must see)
Subjective (opinion)	
(Knowledge-Experience)	

Analysis	Comparison
(Collect intelligence)	(Use intelligence)
Unknown	Unknown to known
Substrate distortion	Overall pattern
Matrix distortion	Specific ridge path
Development medium	Specific ridge shape
Deposition distortion	Relative pore position
Pressure distortion	
Anatomical aspects	**Evaluation**
Clarity 1st-2nd-3rd	
Tolerance	Agreement
	Sufficient to individualize

An Introduction to Palmar Flexion Crease Identification

Introduction

Palmar flexion crease identification has been on the periphery of forensic identification for years. However, a thorough search of the available literature found little information. No one within the forensic identification community has conducted a study of the suitability of the palmar flexion crease as an identification medium. In spite of this lack of research, palmar flexion creases have been assumed to be a viable personal identification medium by some. However, the lack of information has deterred most forensic identification specialists from using palmar flexion creases during the identification process.

Palmar flexion crease identification has the potential to parallel friction ridge identification in evidential value. The coveted direct link between criminal and crime scene is innate. As with friction ridges, culprits cannot throw away their flexion creases after committing an offense. The reluctance of identification specialists to pursue the use of the palmar flexion crease as an identification medium may be resolved by examining its nomenclature, morphological formation, uniqueness, and persistency, and reviewing the research that established the data. With that information the merits of the palmar flexion crease can be applied to the current identification process and assessed to ascertain its suitability as an identification medium.

In the past, research into the intrauterine formation of palmar flexion creases was limited. However, recent research into their embryonic formation has opened a door which has the potential to establish a new branch of forensic identification science. This chapter explores the available palmar flexion crease research data and identifies the established nomenclature for the various crease systems. It further documents the embryonic formation of palmar flexion creases, addresses the genetic influences of parents on crease shape, and discusses the persistency and uniqueness of the creases. Comparison tests are also reported where a twin palm print collection was used to evaluate the influences heredity has on palmar flexion crease path and configuration. Further comparisons assess uniqueness and persistency to ascertain if palmar flexion creases have sufficient uniqueness to be used to individualize and, therefore, qualify as suitable personal identification media.

Nomenclature

The palmar surface is divided into topographic areas. Each area is consistent with the early morphological development of the volar pads. It is believed that these pads were at one time walking pads but now only appear on the fetus and take a part in shaping friction ridge patterns and some flexion crease locations. Along the base of the digits are four interdigital areas numbered one to four, starting at the thumb side (Figure 8.1). At the base of the thumb is the thenar area, on the opposite side of the palm is the hypothenar area, and in the center of the palm is the central area. Each area except the central area signifies the location of an intrauterine volar pad of the same name.

Three main groups of flexion creases appear on the palms. The first group, the Major Flexion Creases (Figure 8.2), is also the most visible. These include the thenar crease, proximal transverse crease, and the distal transverse crease. The major flexion creases are the largest on the palm and often take on the shape of an uncompleted letter M. At times they also appear as if they are constructed of bundles of smaller creases similar to fiberoptic cables. Smaller creases frequently branch off a main crease or the main crease appears to separate into two or more smaller creases. These branches are referred to as "major accessory creases" and are part of the secondary crease group, the smallest of the creases.

The second group of palmar creases is the Minor Flexion Creases. They are more variable in presence, prominence, and length than the major flexion creases. There are four types of minor flexion creases: the Longitudinal or Finger Creases, Accessory Distal Transverse Crease, "E" Lines, and a Hypothenar Crease. (Figures 8.3 and 8.4)

1. Longitudinal or Finger Creases. The paths of these minor creases run longitudinally from the middle of the base of the fingers toward the center of the wrist (Figure 8.3). They are named after the finger they relate to, little finger crease, ring finger crease, middle finger crease, and sometimes an index finger crease. The configuration of the finger creases are made up of several short creases all following the same path, as opposed to one main crease.

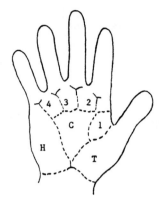

Figure 8.1 Palmar Topography.

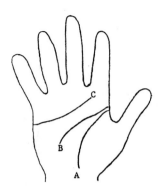

Figure 8.2 Major Flexion Creases **A.** Thenar Crease; **B.** Proximal Transverse Crease; **C.** Distal Transverse Crease

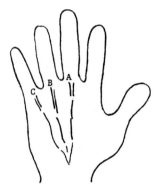

Figure 8.3 Minor Finger Creases **A.** Middle Finger Crease; **B.** Ring Finger Crease; **C.** Little Finger Crease

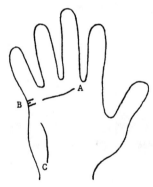

Figure 8.4 Minor Flexion Creases **A.** Accessory Distal Transverse Flexion Crease; **B.** "E" Lines; **C.** Hypothenar Crease

2. Accessory Distal Transverse Crease. The path of this minor crease is situated between the base of the fingers and the distal transverse crease. The accessory distal transverse crease may run under the third, fourth, and sometimes the fifth digit. It can be rather complex with several branches, or it can be a simple short crease. Some palms do not have an accessory distal transverse crease at all (Figure 8.4).

3. "E" Lines. These minor creases are found on the ulnar edge of the palm between the base of the little finger and the distal transverse

crease. There are usually three parallel short creases that take on the appearance of the letter E when viewed together in a print.

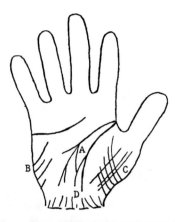

Figure 8.5 Secondary Creases **A.** Major Accessory Creases; **B.** Hatch Creases; **C.** Checker Creases; **D.** Wrist Hatch Creases

4. Hypothenar Crease. This minor crease appears in the hypothenar area of the palm. Its path is generally concave toward the ulnar side of the palm and, when present, is usually a single crease.

The third group of flexion creases are the Secondary Creases (Figure 8.5). Secondary flexion creases are all the remaining creases not classed as major or minor creases. Secondary creases may be found anywhere on the palmar surface. An example of secondary creases are the major accessory creases (branch type creases), but they are also prevalent along the edge of the hypothenar area (hatch creases), on the thenar eminence (checker creases), and along the edge of the palm just above the wrist (wrist hatch creases).

Embryology

Palmar flexion creases have a firmer attachment to underlying skin structures and are folding points of the skin and subcutaneous tissues during movement of the palm and fingers.

At one time movement of the joints was thought to be the only factor in the formation of all palmar flexion creases, but this theory was shown to be not completely correct. Spontaneous hand movements of the fetus usually do not start before 11.5 weeks' gestation. Some of the major creases were found to be visible during the eighth week. This does not rule out that flexion creases form in anticipation of joint movement, but it is now believed that genetic programming and physical movements both contribute to the formation of palmar flexion creases.

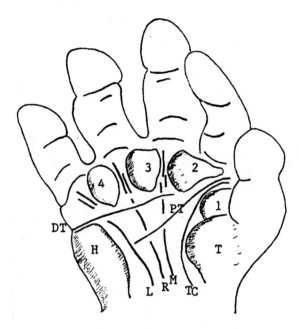

Figure 8.6 **T.** Thenar Pad; **H.** Hypothenar Pad; **1.** First Interdigital Pad; **2.** Second Interdigital Pad; **3.** Third Interdigital Pad; **4.** Fourth Interdigital Pad; **DT.** Distal Transverse Crease; **TC.** Thenar Crease; **PT.** Proximal Transverse Crease; **M.** Middle Finger Crease; **R.** Ring Finger Crease; **L.** Little Finger Crease

The morphological formation of the hand has been divided into three distinct stages. During the first 6 to 10 weeks the hand takes shape and the fingers are visible. From 6 to 12 weeks the volar pads appear along with the palmar flexion creases. From 12 weeks onward the friction ridges form.

The paths of the thenar crease, distal transverse crease, and the finger creases are either channeled in narrow grooves between volar pads at the base of the fingers or are formed between volar pads and nonvolar pad skin. The thenar flexion crease develops with the appearance of the thenar pad and the first interdigital pad. The distal transverse crease develops with the appearance of the remaining interdigital pads, hypothenar pad, and small integumentary thickenings that appear in the center of the palm. The proximal transverse crease is the only major crease that has not been linked to volar pad formation, even though its appearance coincides with the other major creases. The minor finger creases form between the second, third, and fourth interdigital pads in the distal area of the palm and converge between the thenar and hypothenar area near the wrist (Figure 8.6).

The fetus commences palmar grasping during the last part of the second stage of hand formation, around the 11th week and just prior to friction ridge formation. At this time the major creases and minor finger creases have formed and the volar pads are regressing. The fetus is usually grasping tightly between 16 and 20 weeks' gestation. This folding of the palmar skin before, during, and after friction ridge formation is believed responsible for the development of the E lines, accessory distal transverse crease, hypothenar crease, secondary creases, and all the small interconnecting accessory creases of the major crease systems.

The time when palmar flexion creases are forming is the time when various diseases attack the fetus. Several abnormal flexion crease configurations have been related to specific diseases and reported during dermatoglyphics studies. A general reference to these variations and related research can be found in "Dermatoglyphics in Medical Disorders" by Blanka Schaumann and Milton Alter, or other dermatoglyphics papers.

Chronology

In a 1986 experiment by Kimura and Kitagawa, the following sequence of events was observed:

Six weeks —The fetal hand plate has developed interdigital notches.

Seven weeks —Five thick areas show that the fingers are forming. The fingertips are separate and the thumb is moving away from the fingers. The central palm is bulged.

Eight weeks —The fingers begin to separate and the thenar, hypothenar, and interdigital pads begin to appear. The thenar flexion crease starts to appear between the thumb and index finger. The central palm area starts to regress.

Nine weeks —Finger separation is almost complete and the thumb rotates. The early stage of the thenar flexion crease is clearly visible. The palm has become depressed.

Ten weeks —All the volar pads are prominent and small papillary integumentary thickenings appear in the central palm area. The thenar crease has extended to the center of the palm along the thenar pad. Longitudinal grooves between the interdigital pads have formed.

Eleven weeks —The volar pads begin to regress. The longitudinal grooves, where the palmar finger creases form, are less pronounced but still remain. The distal transverse crease is visible between the second and third volar pad. Later in this same stage the distal transverse crease extends toward the ulnar side of the palm.

Twelve weeks —The volar pads continue to regress and the longitudinal grooves between the pads have disappeared.

Thirteen weeks —The volar pads have almost completely regressed and the distal transverse crease is visible to the ulnar edge of the palm. The proximal transverse crease is visible.

Fourteen weeks —After 14 weeks' gestation the major creases are clearly visible. At 15 weeks' gestation they are comparable to an adult's.

Table 8.1 Relationships of Fetal Hand Development

(Gestation Time is approximate)

Weeks' Gestation	6	7	8	9	10	11	12	13	14	15	16	17	18	19	20
Hand formation	>>>>>>>>>>>>>>														
Volar pad growth	>>>>>>>>>>>>>>>>>>>>>>														
Major and minor flexion creases				>>>>>>>>>>>>>>>>>>											
Volar pad regression							>>>>>>>>>>>>>>>>>>								
Friction ridges						>>>>>>>>>>>>>>>>>>									
Secondary flexion creases									>>>>>>>>>>>>>>>>>>>>>>						

Genetics and Uniqueness

The influences of heredity on the flexion creases is a relatively unexplored area except in the study of diseases. There are similarities between the formation of flexion creases and friction ridges. They both develop intrauterine and are in part shaped by the genetic programming that controls the appearance and regression of the volar pads. The correlation in genetic programming of volar pad activity in closely related people may cause the formation of similar friction ridge patterns. However, the random development of the ridge units that make up the friction ridges differentiates any similar-shaped patterns.

Major and minor finger flexion creases are also subject to volar pad influence during formation. The path of major and minor finger creases follow the outer edges of the volar pads. Therefore, major flexion crease and minor finger flexion crease paths may be affected by genetic influences through the size and shape of the volar pads. While the general path may be influenced, the multitude of major accessory creases, the small creases that branch off the main creases, and the many short creases that make up the longitudinal finger creases are not affected by heredity and appear at random. That factor differentiates these crease systems.

The greatest opportunity for duplication of flexion creases in two different people is in the case of monozygotic or identical twins. Monozygotic twins develop from the same egg and have the same DNA. Their volar pads are genetically programmed to develop to the same size and shape unless influenced by some external intrauterine physical force. If duplication is to occur, due to genetic influences it should occur with identical twins. To explore the influence heredity has on flexion crease configuration and to ascertain if duplication is possible, a twin palm print collection was used to make several comparisons. The collection consisted of 30 pairs of monozygotic male twin palm prints, 30 pairs of monozygotic female twin palm prints, 30 pairs of dizygotic (fraternal) same sex twin palm prints, and 30 pairs of dizygotic different sex twin palm prints.

The palmar flexion crease systems of one twin was compared to the other twin. The palmar flexion creases were compared in 12 areas: the three major flexion creases, three major accessory crease systems, three minor finger creases, the accessory distal transverse crease, the secondary crease system on the hypothenar area, and the secondary crease system in the thenar area. For this set of comparisons the "E" lines were considered part of the hypothenar area.

As the major creases are considered class characteristics or nonspecific details, they were compared first to ascertain the degree of similarity of overall path. If the flexion crease path in each twin was similar it was scored with an "S." If it was different it was scored with a "D." All the remaining flexion crease systems were then compared in order. As these flexion crease systems are considered to be unique characteristics or specific details, they were compared for agreement or not. If the crease system was in agreement it was scored with an "A," and if different it was scored with a "D."

The results were such that they could be reported in an abbreviated form in Table 8.2. The three major creases were scored as to being similar or not. That could be expressed in the table as a percentage of the total major creases compared that were found to be similar. Obviously the remaining ones were not similar. After the comparisons were complete, all crease systems in the remaining nine areas were found to be different, therefore they were not listed separately but were bulked together under the heading "Remaining". As all remaining flexion creases were found to be different, the percentage was 100%.

The overall results of the comparisons revealed that the path of the major creases of the monozygotic twins followed the same path more often than those of the dizygotic twins. However, when the smaller accessory creases were compared in both monozygotic and dizygotic twins they were different in both groups. When they were available for comparison, the minor flexion creases, even though they tended to follow paths through similar areas of the palm, were always different due to their fragmented configuration. When

Table 8.2   Uniqueness

Results	Crease	# Compared	Percentage
Monozygotic males	Thenar	60	S = 63.3
	Proximal	57	S = 70.1
	Distal T.	60	S = 81.7
	All remaining creases	373	D = 100
Monozygotic females	Thenar	59	S = 66.2
	Proximal	58	S = 55.2
	Distal T.	59	S = 86.4
	All remaining creases	395	D = 100
Dizygotic same sex	Thenar	60	S = 50.0
	Proximal	59	S = 52.5
	Distal T.	59	S = 72.8
	All remaining creases	439	D = 100
Dizygotic different sexes	Thenar	60	S = 46.7
	Proximal	59	S = 37.3
	Distal T.	60	S = 55.0
	All remaining creases	434	D = 100

available for comparison, the accessory distal transverse crease and the secondary creases of the thenar and hypothenar areas were also found to be different.

A second comparison test was carried out to ascertain if the percentage of similarity of major creases would continue to decrease when the comparisons were between unrelated people. Unlike twins, the palms of unrelated people are not always a similar size. Palms were selected from unrelated people for comparison based on their similarity in size. Therefore, by removing the different palm sizes from the comparison of unrelated people, the percentage results obtained were artificially high in favor of similarity. Thirty palms were selected of generally the same size from unrelated people. The palms were paired at random and their flexion creases were compared to each other in the same 12 areas as in Table 8.2.

Three other palms, also of similar size, were selected and the flexion creases from each were compared to a collection of ten randomly selected palms of similar size, again in the same 12 areas. The percentage of similarity in major flexion crease path dropped considerably. When the nine crease systems, other than the three major crease systems, were compared they were found to be different. Therefore, they were reported in bulk under the heading "Remaining." The remaining crease systems could always could be differentiated among the various palms.

From these comparisons it is safe to conclude that, as the genetic relationship of the subjects moves farther apart, the influence of heredity on the opportunity of major flexion crease paths to be similar decreases. The same

Table 8.3   Uniqueness

Results	Crease	# Compared	Percentage
Unrelated same size	Thenar	60	S = 36.7
	Proximal	58	S = 27.6
	Distal T.	60	S = 60.0
	All remaining creases	429	D = 100
Unrelated three pair	Thenar	60	S = 45.0
Compared to ten each	Proximal	60	S = 21.7
	Distal T.	60	S = 43.3
	All remaining creases	433	D = 100

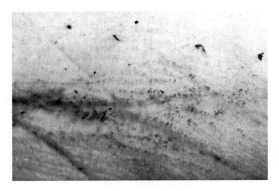

Figure 8.7   Flexion creases on the epidermal surface of the friction skin.

can be said for the path of the minor finger creases. The creases on unrelated people are subject to the restrictions of the anatomical body formation of the human hand. There is only a small area or window of opportunity in which major flexion creases may actually vary their path configurations. Therefore, major flexion creases may occasionally appear in the same location on unrelated people. However, during all these comparisons, even when the path of major creases and minor finger creases were similar the major accessory creases and the numerous segmented creases of the minor finger creases were never found to be the same. The presence of major accessory creases, minor crease configuration, and secondary creases were always available to differentiate between any palms with similar major flexion crease paths.

Persistency

As covered in earlier chapters, the overall structure of the palmar friction skin lends itself to the persistency of flexion creases. Flexion creases are areas of firmer attachment to underlying skin (Figure 8.7). This suggests a deliberate substructure, which is the case with flexion creases that form prior and during the early stages of friction ridge formation. At this time the basal layer of the epidermis is still forming and the presence of flexion creases disrupts the formations of these substructures (Figure 8.8) and causes a void in the

Figure 8.8   The dermal surface of the friction skin. Flexion creases disrupt the dermal surface.

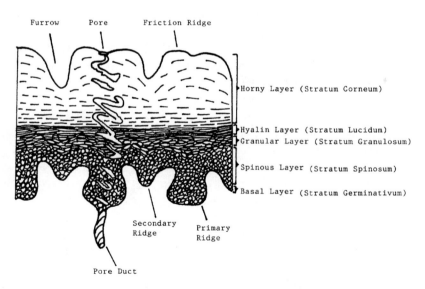

Figure 8.9   Understanding the formation and structure of the friction skin is as important with palmar flexion crease identification as it is with friction ridge identification. This knowledge is a prerequisite for understanding the uniqueness and persistency of palmar flexion creases.

primary and secondary ridges developing on the bottom of the epidermis.*
The result is that on the surface of the palm there are no friction ridges

* The disturbance of the basal layer has been observed by Schaumann, who related it to the author during discussions.

running through the furrows of the major flexion creases and minor finger creases.

All remaining creases, which also formed prior to differentiation of the friction ridges or before approximately 16 weeks' gestation, also disrupt the subcutaneous structure in the basal layer. It is a scientific fact that friction ridges do not change from before birth until after death. The only areas on the palm not covered with friction ridges are the flexion creases. Flexion creases are therefore bound within an unchanging sea of friction ridges. If these early forming flexion creases are capable of change, friction ridges must also be capable of change, which is not the case.

Creases forming after friction ridge differentiation, before or after birth, are skin folds commonly called "white lines." This name comes from their appearance on a white fingerprint or palm print form. On a histological section, skin folds show a disruption of subsurface skin cells down to the hyalin layer. These folds do not interfere with the ability of the basal layer to regenerate friction ridge cells as flexion creases do. The result of this, on the surface of the palm, is that the skin folds appear to have friction ridges running down into the furrow where they are interrupted by the fold in the skin.

Skin folds forming intrauterine are dependent on the anatomical shape of the hand and degree of grasping by the fetus for their configuration and location. They can be compared to creases forming in a new leather glove. Skin folds associated with a permanent crease, such as the major accessory creases, have a greater potential for permanence due to having one end anchored by a permanent crease.

The few skin creases that form after birth are also dependent on the anatomical formation of the hand, how the hand is used, and skin quality of the deep dermal and epidermal structures. Although not permanent to the degree of the earlier forming creases, they are described by Schaumann as being more or less stable. Montagna reports that, "Although the skin of infants and children is free of creases except over joints, it nonetheless has all the congenital markings and all the true congenital flexure lines." It is impossible to distinguish the smaller permanent flexion creases from more or less stable white lines except for the creases that appear in predetermined locations.

A major physiological change in shape or prehensile use of the palm would be required for skin folds to actually change. As the skin ages, its ability to remain moist and reproduce cells in the deeper layers diminishes, as does the subcutaneous layer of fat. The result is an increase in very fine skin folds accompanying aging, as well as an enhancement of folds already in place. In any event, any change to the palmar surface due to major physiological deformation of the palmar area would take several months before it would affect skin folds.

Table 8.4 Persistency

Results	Crease	# Compared	Percentage
	Thenar	50	A = 100
	Acc. thenar	48	A = 100
	Proximal	49	A = 100
	Acc. proximal	38	A = 100
	Distal T.	50	A = 100
	Acc. distal T.	48	A = 100
	Minor acc. distal T.	32	A = 100
	Acc. minor acc. distal	17	A = 100
	Middle finger crease	28	A = 100
	Ring finger crease	32	A = 100
	Little finger crease	39	A = 100
	Thenar secondary	48	A = 100
	Hypothenar secondary	36	A = 100

To examine the persistency of flexion creases, a comparison test was carried out. Fifty pairs of palm prints taken from the same people at different times were compared to each other. The time span between the first and second sets of palm prints ranged from 1 to 60 months, with the average time span approximately 32 months. The palms were compared in 13 areas: the three major creases, the accessory crease systems of the three major creases, accessory distal transverse crease, any accessory creases that branched off the accessory distal transverse crease, the three minor finger creases, the thenar secondary creases, and the hypothenar secondary creases which included the "E" lines. At times some crease systems were not available for comparison. That factor is reflected in the number of areas compared in Table 8.4. The results of these comparisons were scored as agreement "A" or different "D."

All flexion creases were found in agreement if they were available for comparison. As with fingerprints, pressure distortion and clarity of the flexion creases came into play. Each time there was a slight difference in the position of a crease or a change in the width of a crease, the palm print was evaluated to ascertain if it was explainable. Based upon experimentation, it was determined that small differences were caused by a variance in printing practices. For example, if the fingers are forced wide apart, the depth of the distal transverse crease is increased on the ulnar side of the palm, as are the "E" lines and any other crease in that area. The printed crease, therefore, appears wider. Closing the fingers tightly increases the depth of the finger creases, which in turn causes them to appear wider in the print.

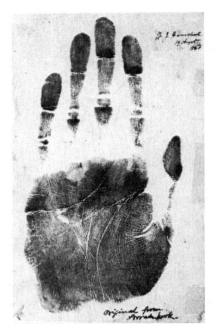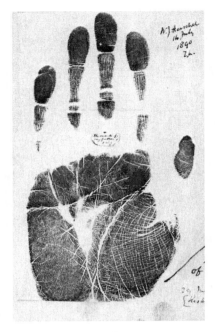

Figure 8.10A and B Sir William Herschel's left palm print taken 30 years apart, in 1860 (Left) and 1890 (Right).

Other tendencies were noticed during these experiments. Taking a palm print with the wrist shifted toward the ulnar side causes the creases along the hypothenar area to deepen, and some appeared more substantial than they really were. Bridging the palm slightly removes the central palm flexion area from the print and increases the depth of the major creases. Moving the thumb out from the palm shifts the thenar eminence ridge system on a bias in relation to the other palmar creases, while moving it in tight to the palm shifts it the opposite way. Moving the thumb closer to the palm may also increase the depth of the thenar crease, and sometimes the proximal transverse crease. Using a small circular object on which to roll palm prints, such as a bottle or roll of hand towels, tends to compress the length of the palm and flexion crease patterns.

The most famous palm prints ever used to demonstrate persistency were those of Sir William Herschel, a pioneer of fingerprint identification. He took prints of his palms in 1860 and again in 1890 (Figures 8.10A and 8.10B). These palms have been used as the classic example to demonstrate the persistency of friction ridges for years. The flexion creases recorded in Herschel's inked palm prints are in agreement when compared even though age has enhanced the creases in the later print.

Flexion Crease Comparison

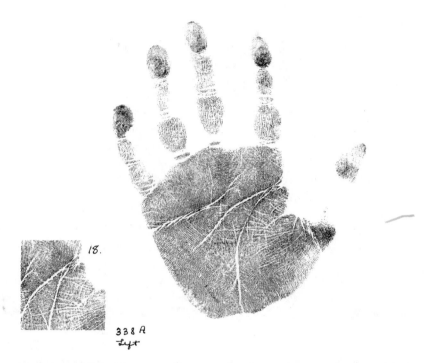

Figures 8.11A and B Example of unknown and known used during the blind search. Unknown (Left); Known (Right). Small areas of palm can be located and identified through palmar flexion creases.

The patterns created by flexion crease networks have been noticed by forensic identification specialists for years. These configurations have often been used as markers to locate palm prints with similar flexion crease patterns, or for locating a specific area of a palm print for the comparison of friction ridges. To test the practicality of searching palms by their flexion crease networks, a blind search was set up by a colleague. Twenty partial palm prints were cut from photocopied palm print forms and numbered. These partial palm prints were then searched against a bank of 132 palm prints. The comparison was based on the flexion crease patterns, but the flow of the palmar friction ridges was also used along with the flexion creases to identify palmar location (Figure 8.11).

In all 20 instances the correct palm and palmar locations were identified using this method. Just as important is the fact that other palms were quickly recognized as not being in agreement by comparing the flexion crease systems. It became rather apparent that a very small area of friction skin containing small but often complex flexion crease networks was all that was required to individualize during this search.

Conclusions

Permanent flexion creases are formed intrauterine. Heredity may influence the path followed by major flexion creases and minor finger flexion creases through genetic programming of the volar pads. The path of these creases are therefore class characteristics and not variable enough to individualize. They may, however, be of considerable value as the first breakdown in a palmar classification system or during the search of a palm print collection.

The configuration of accessory major creases, the short segmented sections of the minor finger creases, other minor creases, and secondary creases are not affected by heredity and form at random. This is due to intrauterine flexing of the palm, the anatomical shape of the part, and the genetic programing that mandates the formation of flexion areas in appropriate locations on the surface of the skin. These creases are unique in the aggregate and therefore qualify as a personal identification medium. They may be used to individualize. The clarity of the print and the uniqueness of the flexion crease network dictate the area of friction skin required for individualization.

The flexion creases most prevalent on the palm and most likely to be used for comparison have subcutaneous structure and do not change. The smaller skin folds are relatively stable and only change with considerable physiological rearrangement of the part. Some flexion creases may appear to change due to a variance in printing techniques such as improper inking or fill-in from the development medium. This type of pressure distortion is addressed by forensic identification specialists during friction skin comparison daily and should not be a problem. New skin folds may also form due to age, skin condition, or considerable physiological rearrangement of the part.

The palmar flexion creases, when applied to the identification process, are a suitable method of personal identification. They are persistent and variable enough to individualize. Skin folds are also variable enough for individualization and are persistent as long as deformation of the part has not taken place. An increase of small skin folds due to aging would take a minimum of several months to develop. If these small folds are being considered as a basis of comparison, the time span between collection of the crime scene print and printing of the suspect may be an issue that will need to be addressed during the comparison process.

Due to their persistence and uniqueness, palmar flexion creases are suitable for personal identification alone or when used in conjunction with friction ridges. Obviously, if friction ridges are present, using both together would be the recommended method. *Always!*

Postscript

New Scotland Yard has carried out several comparison tests of palmar flexion creases and their results agree with the author's findings. Deputy Head W. Evin, of Branch S03 — Identification Services, reported the following on November 11, 1991:

> I was appointed to conduct further investigation into the claim that palmar flexion creases are a suitable medium for identification, and that these creases persist and are recognizable. I have, when time permitted, conducted some one hundred searches against bundles in the Metropolitan Police Palm Collection. This comprised of searching a set of palmar impressions against approximately 300 sets of left and right palmar impressions, therefore making approximately 600 comparisons.
>
> My findings were as follows:
>   In a small proportion of cases major creases could appear similar in palmar impressions from different donors.
>   In all cases major accessory, minor and secondary creases would never agree in palmar impressions taken from different donors.
>
> I also conducted tests to the theory of persistency. This involved obtaining the palmar impressions of offenders who had been palm printed on at least two occasions, with a significant time lapse in between. In fact, all the comparisons were with at least three sets of palmar impressions, of the donor available, although the "Persistency Comparison" sheets, attached at 7A, show only the first and last set taken.*
>
> My findings were as follows:
>   All major, major accessory, minor and secondary creases, where available, were in agreement and had persisted without variation.
>   I consider that these comparisons fully support the findings of Sgt. Ashbaugh that palmar creases are variable enough to individualize and persist.
>   I am in agreement with all the points and comments made by Mr. Luff as 3A.
>   The area of palm needed to be available to satisfactorily identify the creases, invariably means that a good number of friction ridges will be available for comparison and I suggest that this will always remain our primary route for identification purposes.

---

* The author did not receive copies of the comparison sheets.

I consider that the main value of the paper presented by Sgt. Ashbaugh is to endorse the value of creases when positioning palmar impressions from scenes of crime for comparison purposes and for quick searches.

The individuality of the whole crease system and its persistence should be emphasized on SO3 Training Courses. It is important that all technical staff are aware of current developments. I fear that we will be unable to enter into identification of persons by means of their palmar flexion creases in an operational sense as we are sorely pressed to process the ever increasing amount of friction ridge surfaces submitted to this Branch and the identifications resulting from them.

Ken Luff F.F.S. (New Scotland Yard)
President of the Fingerprint Society

(Fingerprint Whorld, Vol. 19, No. 71, January, 1993)

The use of palmar flexion creases for positioning palmar impressions from Scenes of Crime for comparison with inked impressions is well known, but, when this article first reached New Scotland Yard, I suggested that Sgt. Ashbaugh's claim should be researched with the use of our large palm collection.

Mr. Ervin, F.F.S., Deputy Head of Branch, Identification Services at N.S.Y., undertook this project and made a total of 600 comparisons using palmar impressions taken with a significant time lapse in between. The "Persistency Comparison" was repeated. The conclusions were that "all major accessory, minor and secondary creases, where available, were in agreement and persisted without variation". This survey supported the conclusions of Sgt. Ashbaugh.

We could not however, envisage when this method would be of use for identification purposes. It was expected that where there were enough palmar flexion creases available for comparison, there would be sufficient ridge detail to prove identification by the long accepted and convenient use of ridge characteristics.

I wrote to Sgt. Ashbaugh earlier this year about another matter and his reply included comment on finding palmar crease impressions on cloth with no ridge detail visible. If such impressions were to be found, say, in blood then a valuable identification could ensue.

I hope to meet David Ashbaugh in October, 1992 at the I.A.I. Educational Seminar in Miami and discuss the method of presentation of this evidence at Court which will complete this research into this interesting and potentially important medium of identification.

Palmar Flexion Crease Identification Process

Before palmar flexion creases can be used to individualize, an expert must have an understanding of the formation, uniqueness, and persistency of

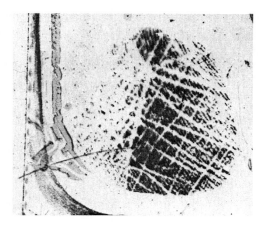

Figure 8.12A   Partial palm print found on the rear view mirror of a stolen car. There are not enough continuous friction ridges to identify this print, but by comparing the checker flexion creases it can be individualized(Photo by Deborah A. Fertgus)

Figure 8.12B   Inked suspect print for the partial palm print.

palmar flexion creases. The previous pages, coupled with the information on the friction skin presented in earlier chapters, have presented this information. The identification process followed during palmar flexion crease identification is basically the same as the identification process used during friction ridge identification, or any other physical evidence for that matter. The identification process consists of a philosophy and methodology.

Philosophy of Palmar Flexion Crease Identification

Identification by palmar flexion creases is based on a knowledgeable expert finding flexion crease formations in agreement during the comparison of a latent palm print to an exemplar palm print. There must be sufficient agreement present to individualize. A simple phrase to describe the philosophy of palmar flexion crease identification is "Palmar flexion crease identification is established through the agreement of flexion creases in sequence having sufficient uniqueness to individualize." Obviously, the creases compared must be the type of creases that form at random. The comparison is carried out systematically or sequentially. All flexion creases available for comparison must be found to be in agreement when the configuration and flexibility of the substrate and the flexibility of the friction skin is taken into consideration. The volume of flexion creases found in agreement must be sufficient for the expert to eliminate all other possible donors. The opinion of the expert that there is enough uniqueness to individualize is subjective. It is based on the expert's knowledge, experience, and ability.

Methodology of Palmar Flexion Crease Identification

The methodology of palmar flexion crease identification follows the A.C.E.V. formula, "Analysis, Comparison, Evaluation, and Verification." As these steps have been addressed in depth when dealing with friction ridges, the following is only a brief review.

Analysis

The analysis of the latent print proceeds from the bottom up. The substrate, matrix, development medium, deposition pressure, pressure distortion, and anatomical aspects are analyzed to ascertain if any could have caused some type of distortion. An analysis of clarity establishes the level of detail available to compare and one's tolerance for minor differences. The location and path of all creases are carefully established. After all possible intelligence has been gathered from the latent print, the comparison can begin.

Comparison

The comparison compares all the paths of the flexion creases available in the latent print to the exemplar print. At times this may include friction ridges that terminate at the crease edge. Some matrices, such as blood, may not record friction ridge configuration throughout the print but may clearly record the ridge ends as they terminate at a flexion crease. These ridge ends and their shapes are a type of third level detail that can be considered along with the flexion crease. The configuration created when the flexion crease interrupts friction ridge flow can be extremely unique. In most cases comparison will include both flexion creases and friction ridges. The comparison of flexion creases is objective. Flexion creases are a form of physical evidence. Others must be able to see what one sees.

Evaluation

During the evaluation part of the comparison experts must ask themselves two questions. The first is whether there is an agreement of flexion crease path and configuration. If the answer is yes, then the second question is whether, in the opinion of the expert, there is a sufficient volume of unique flexion crease details in agreement to eliminate all other possible donors. If the answer to the second question is yes, then an opinion of individualization or identification has been formed. This opinion of sufficient uniqueness to individualize is subjective as it is based on one's personal knowledge, experience, and ability.

Verification

As with friction ridges, verification is part of the scientific process, a form of peer review. It is also an excellent method for training others to recognize the value of palmar flexion creases as a medium suitable to individualize friction skin prints. Consultation with other experts is acceptable during the analysis, comparison, and evaluation stages of the comparison. One must remember, however, that the opinion of having a sufficient volume of unique detail present to individualize is a personal opinion, one that must be personally defended.

Flexion Crease Evidence Presented in Court

To date, I am aware of several incidents where palmar flexion crease identifications have solved murders and other investigations or eliminated suspects. In two major cases, palmar flexion crease identification evidence has been presented and accepted in court. In both cases the accused was convicted.

Sulphur Springs, Texas, 1995

In the spring of 1995 the body of a 19-year-old female was found in her apartment. Investigators described the body as having been butchered. The victim had been stabbed, mutilated, and dissected with several different weapons including knives, razor blades, and forks. Several organs and body parts had been removed, and some had been placed in the victim's throat. The suspect had also carved what appeared to be initials in the victim's back.

The attack had taken place on the victim's bed. The Sulphur Springs Police Department collected considerable physical evidence with the assistance of the Texas Rangers, Dallas County Sheriff's Department, the local medical examiner, and others. All evidence led to an ex-boyfriend of the victim. Her blood was found on the suspect's clothing, and hair consistent with the suspect was found on the victim. A latent fingerprint in blood was found on a window blind adjustment rod, and a palm print in blood was found on a bed sheet where the victim had been lying. The bloody palm print did not have any visible friction ridges but displayed a considerable number of palmar flexion creases (Figure 8.13).

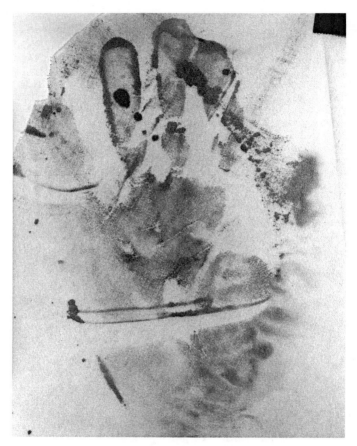

Figure 8.13 Flexion Crease Ident, Sulphur Springs, Texas (Photo by J. Cron)

The Dallas County Sheriff's Department sought outside expertise to examine the bloody palm print. While the author was originally contacted, a local expert was found who was qualified to handle the case. James Cron, a retired Dallas area identification expert with 40 years police service, was requested to examine the bloody palm print in his current capacity as a forensic identification consultant. Cron identified the palm print to the suspect through the comparison of the palmar flexion creases and presented his findings to the Hopkins County District Attorney's Office.

District Attorney Frank Long presented the case to the court. Cron took the witness stand and conducted a brief training session for the jury on the scientific basis of palmar flexion crease identification. Cron then presented his evidence and opinion to the court. At the end of the trial the jury deliberated approximately 15 minutes before finding the defendant guilty. The judge sentenced the defendant to life. The defense appealed but was unsuccessful.

While there may or may not have been enough evidence to convict the defendant without the palmar flexion crease evidence, the fact that this was the first case to be accepted by the courts in North America is a milestone for this branch of forensic science.

St. John's, Newfoundland, 1996

In late fall 1996 the body of a 51-year-old female was found in a downtown boardinghouse. The victim had been brutally beaten about the head and upper torso and left in her bedroom wrapped in a blanket. Blood was evident in several places in the scene, including two bloody palm prints on the bedroom wall.

The section of the wall where the bloody palm prints were located was seized by the Royal Newfoundland Constabulary. Examination of the prints revealed that one print had some friction ridge detail present but was considered insufficient to individualize. This print also had several palmar flexion creases (Figure 8.14). Constable Bradley J. Butler, a Forensic Identification Specialist with the Royal Newfoundland Constabulary, examined the print and compared them to a suspect. Using both the friction ridges and the palmar flexion creases, Constable Butler identified the print to the suspect.

On June 4, 1998, Constable Butler presented this evidence to the Supreme Court of Newfoundland, Trial Division. His evidence was accepted by the court and the defendant was convicted. This case is the first instance where palmar flexion crease evidence has been tendered and accepted by the courts in Canada.

There have been numerous other palm prints found at crime scenes that have led to arrests. Just prior to the original "Palmar Flexion Crease Identification" paper being published in 1991, the Connecticut State Laboratory found a bloody palm print on the fabric of a chesterfield at a murder scene. The victim had been stabbed several times. The print revealed several palmar flexion creases but did not display any friction ridges (Figure 8.15). Members of the Connecticut State Laboratory identified the palm print to the suspect and, while the case did not go to trial, the evidence was instrumental in the suspect's entering a plea of guilty to manslaughter.

Many scenes of crime officers would leave the unknown palm print in Figure 8.16A at the crime scene unaware of the unique detail it contains. While this print displays some pressure distortion, which tends to shorten

Figure 8.14 Flexion Crease Ident, St. John's, Newfoundland (Photo by B.J. Butler)

the vertical distances between some of the flexion creases, there are ample unique details present for comparison and individualization. The known print in Figure 8.16B was taken in the normal fashion on a flat surface. Taking palm prints on a flat or rounded surface tends to elongate the palm, especially in the hypothenar area. If there is an opportunity to take custom-inked impressions for court purposes, the forensic identification specialist should attempt to duplicate the same pressure that was used when the crime scene print was deposited.

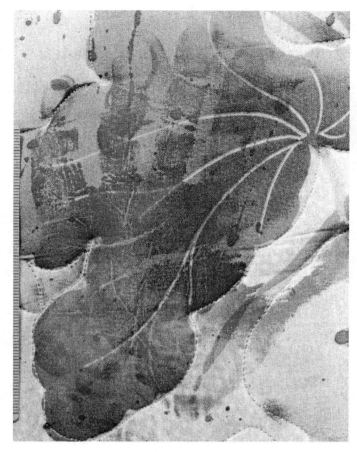

Figure 8.15 Photograph of a bloody palm print on fabric submitted by Lead Fingerprint Examiner Bob Finkle of the Connecticut State Police Laboratory.

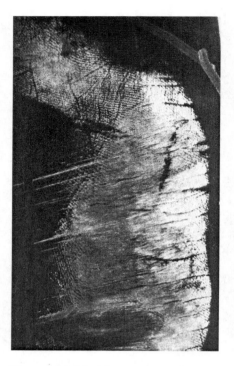

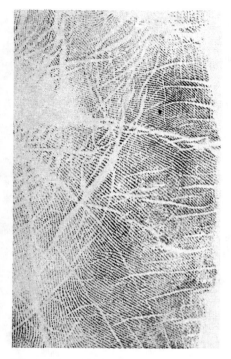

Figure 8.16A Cover this unknown print with a document protector and mark on the plastic all visible flexion creases.

Figure 8.16B Place the document protector on this known print and compare the various flexion crease locations.

The Beginning

This book has addressed the concepts of basic ridgeology and has introduced the reader to several advanced ridgeology and palmar flexion crease identification techniques. There are many other areas of friction ridge identification open to exploration such as more advanced ridgeology techniques, poroscopy, palmar flexion crease identification, the analysis of complex and problem prints, and the techniques used to carry out and present these types of comparisons in court. If this book assists anyone in reaching the level where they are prepared to study any of the more advanced techniques, or if it encourages them to seek further information, it will have served its purpose.

At this point in a book most authors have a conclusion. I think it is obvious to all who work within the friction skin identification science that this is not the end, but the beginning. In 1973 the International Association for Identification Standardization Committee set the stage whereby the science would mature and eventually come together as a true international entity. There is little doubt that we have been struggling to understand the ramifications of their resolution on a science that many truly believe in. Over the years, many have given a great part of themselves to demonstrate that this science has substance, credibility, and extreme forensic value. One has only to look to the members of organizations such as the International Association for Identification, the Fingerprint Society, and the Canadian Identification Society for verification of that.

The friction ridge identification science is being challenged more and more as the days pass. These challenges are not due to a failure within the science, but are due to success. Friction skin identification is a physical evidence science that is, as the saying goes, "in your face," when presented in court. It is straightforward and cost effective when compared to other sciences. It frequently puts the suspect within arm's length of a specific location, a location which is often right in the middle of a crime scene.

Many sciences require years of study to master just the paraphernalia used to perform the tasks required within their respective disciplines. In the friction ridge identification science most can master a fingerprint glass and ridge pointers after minimal training, and the natural ability of the human brain to compare and identify shapes does the rest. However, recent court cases have shown the future. The ability to compare and identify is not enough. The expert must have an understanding of the process and the ability to defend, describe, or narrate that process. The knowledge and understanding expected of an expert in the future will greatly surpass that which has been accepted thus far. We can never go back; we can only go forward. This is the beginning.

Bibliography

Ashbaugh, David R., Edgeology, *RCMP Gazette,* 44(2) 1982.

-----. Poroscopy, *Identification Canada,* 9(1), 3, January 1986.

-----. Fingerprint Identification Today, *Identification News,* XXXIII(9), September 1983.

-----. Ridgeoscopy — The Time Is Now, *Fingerprint Whorld,* 8(30), October 1982.

-----. The Key to Fingerprint Identification, *Fingerprint Whorld,* 10(40), April 1985.

-----. Identification Specialist and Trainer, *RCMP Gazette,* 44(6), 1982.

-----. Ridgeology: Our Next Evaluative Step, *RCMP Gazette,* 45(3), 1983.

-----. Ridgeology, *J. For. Ident.,* 41, 16, 1991.

-----. Palmar flexion crease identification, *J. For. Ident.,* 41, 255, 1991.

-----. Incipient ridges and the clarity spectrum, *J. For. Ident.,* 42, 106, 1992.

-----. Defined pattern, overall pattern and unique pattern, *J. For. Ident.,* 42, 503, 1992.

-----. The premises of friction ridge identification, clarity and the identification process, *J. For. Ident.,* 44, 499, 1994.

Babler, William J., Embryologic development of epidermal ridges and their configurations, *Birth Defects, Orig. Artic. Ser.,* 27(2), 95, 1991.

-----. Prenatal Communalities in Epidermal Ridge Development, *Trends in Dermatoglyphic Research,* Kluwer Academic Publishers, Norwell, MA, 1990.

-----. Prenatal development of dermatoglyphic patterns: associations with epidermal ridge, volar pad, and bone morphology, *Coll. Anthropol.,* 11(2), 297, 1987.

-----. How Is Epidermal Ridge Configuration Determined?, *Newsletter of the American Dermatoglyphics Association,* 2(1), 3, 1983.

-----. Quantitative differences in morphogenesis of human epidermal ridge, *Birth Defects, Orig. Artic. Ser.,* 15(6), 199, 1979.

-----. Prenatal selection and dermatoglyphic patterns, *Am. J. Phys. Anthrop.,* 48(1), 21, 1978.

Bade, William F. Fingerprints on Pottery Aid in Tracing Past, *Science Newsletter,* 261, October 27, 1934.

-----: *A Manual of Excavation in the Near East,* University of California Press, Berkeley, 1934.

Bansal, I.J.S, Shobha Rani Dhiam, and Harminder Kaur. A study of the inheritance of palmar mainlines, *Ind. J. Phys. Anthrop. & Hum. Genet.,* 13, 201, Lucknow, 1987.

Bassett, C. Andrew L. Biologic Significance of Piezoelectricity, *Calcif. Tissue Res.,* 1, 252, 1968.

Blake, James W. Identification of the Newborn by Flexure Creases, *Identification News,* 9(9), September 1952.

Blank, Joseph P. The Fingerprint That Lied, *Reader's Digest,* September 1975, 81.

Bridgewater, B.R. *Fingerprints: the Basic Facts,* Unpublished.

Brodie, J.M. *Skin Creases and Their Value in Personal Identification,* Canadian Police College, Unpublished.

Burdi, Alphonse R., William J. Babler, and Stanley M. Garn, Monitoring patterns of prenatal skeletal development, *Birth Defects: Orig. Artic. Ser.,* 15(5A), 25, 1979.

Butler, Bradley. Palmisty Refined — Flexion Crease Identification Accepted by Our Judicial System, *Identification Canada,* 21(3), 1998.

Califana, Anthony L. and Jerome S. Levkov. *Criminalistics for the Law Enforcement Officer,* McGraw-Hill, New York, 1978.

Canadian Police College, *Fingerprints,* 1977, Unpublished, Ottawa, 1977.

Carlson, Bruce M., ed. *Human Embryology and Developmental Biology,* C.V. Mosby,, St. Louis, 1994, 153.

Cassidy, Michael J., *Footwear Identification,* RCMP Pub., 1980.

Castellanos, Israel M.D. New Techiques of Skin Impressions, *Identification News,* Jan 1970, 13.

Caton, H.E. Physical and Chemical Aspects of Latent Print Development, *F.B.I. Pub.*

Champod, C. Edmond Locard — numerical standards and probable identifications, *J. For. Ident.,* 45(2), 136, 1995.

Champod, C., C. Lennard, and P. Margot. Alphonse Bertillon and dactyloscopy, *J. For. Ident.,* 43(6), 604, 1993.

Chapman, Carey L. Alphonse M. Bertillon — his life and the science of fingerprints, *J. For. Ident.,* 43(6), 585, 1993.

-----. Dr. Juan Vucetich — his contribution to the science of fingerprints, *J. For. Ident.,* 42(4), 286, 1992.

Chatterjee, Salil K. and Richard V. Hague. *Fingerprints or Dactyloscopy and Ridgeoscopy,* Srijib Chatterjee, Calcutta, 1988.

Chatterjee, Salil K. *Finger, Palm, and Sole Prints,* KOSA Publishers, Calcutta, 1967.

-----. *Speculation in Fingerprint Identification,* Srijib Chatterjee, Calcutta, 1983.

Cherrill, Frederick R. *The Fingerprint System at Scotland Yard,* Her Majesty's Stationery Office, London, 1954.

Clements, Wendell W. *The Study of Latent Fingerprints,* Thomas, Springfield, IL, 1987.

Cohen, Stanley A. B.A., LL.B, LL.M. The Role of the Forensic Expert in a Criminal Trial, *Criminal Reports,* (3rd Series), 1.

Cooke, T.G. Hands of Mystery, *Fingerprint,* 31(7), 4, 1959.

-----. Famed French Criminologist Throws Some Light on Bertillon's Use of Fingerprints, *Fingerprint and Identification,* May 1950.

Cowger, James F. *Friction Ridge Skin,* Elsevier, New York, 1983.

Cron, James G. Palmar Flexion Crease Identification Precedent Trial Testimony, *The Print,* 13(6), 1997.

Cummins, Harold. Fingerprints — Normal and Abnormal Patterns, *Fingerprint and Identification,* 49(5), 3, 1967.

-----. Epidermal-ridge configurations in developmental defects, with particular reference to the ontogenetic factors which condition ridge direction, *Am. J. Anat.,* 38(1), 89.

-----. The Fingerprint Carvings of Stone Age Men in Brittany, *Science Monthly,* 31, 273, 1930.

-----. Ancient Fingerprints in Clay, *Science Monthly,* 52, 389, 1941.

-----. Fingerprints of Phantoms, *Fingerprint and Identification,* December 1960.

-----. Dermatoglyphics: an Introductory Review, *The Interne,* November 1949.

-----. The configurations of epidermal ridges in a human acephalic monster, *Anat. Rec.,* 26(1), 1923.

-----. The Skin and Mammary Glands, *Morris Human Anatomy,* 10th ed., The Blakiston Co., New York, 1942.

-----. Some Members of N.Y. Family Lack Usual Ridge Patterns, *Fingerprint and Identification,* March 1970.

-----. Why Takeshita Lacks Patterned Friction Skin, *Fingerprint and Identification,* May 1950.

-----. Loss of Ridged Skin before Birth, *Cummins Collection,* Tulane University, New Orleans.

-----. Skin, *Cummins Collection,* Tulane University, New Orleans.

-----. Underneath the Fingerprint, *Cummins Collection,* Tulane University, New Orleans.

-----. The Anatomy of Research, *Cummins Collection,* Tulane University, New Orleans.

-----. The topographic history of the volar pads (walking pads; tastballen) in the human embryo, *Contrib. Embryol.,* Carnegie Institute, Washington, D.C., 394, 103, 1929.

-----. Harold Cummins Explains Some Mighty Curious Ridge Patterns, *Fingerprint and Identification,* Oct 1960.

-----. *Dermatoglyphics: a Brief Review,* Academic Press, New York, 1964, Chap. 10.

-----. Harold Cummins Describes Dissociated Ridges in a Letter to a Colleague, *Cummins Collection,* Tulane University, New Orleans.

Cummins, Harold and R.V. Platou. Mongolism: an objective early sign, *South. Med. J.,* 39(12), 1946.

Cummins, Harold, E.E. Dudley, Hereward Carrington, Arthur Goadby, andWalter Franklin Price, The Walter-Kerwin Thumbprints, *Boston Soc. Psychic Res.,* XXII, 1934.

Cummins, Harold and Charles Midlo. *Fingerprints, Palms, and Soles,* Research Publishers, South Berlin, MA, 1976.

Cummins, Harold and Charles Midlo. Palmer and plantar epidermal ridge configurations (dermatoglyphics) in European-Americans, *Am. J. Phys. Anthrop.,* 1X(4), 1926.

Cummins, Harold, Walter J. Waits, and James T. McQuitty. The breadths of epidermal ridges on the fingertips and palms: a study of variation, *Am. J. Anat.,* 68(1), 1941.

Cummins, Harold and Edwin A. Ohler. Sexual differences in breadths of epidermal ridges on fingertips and palms, *Am. J. Phys. Anthropol.,* XXIX(3), 1942.

Cummins, Harold and Rebecca Wright Kennedy, Purkinje's observations (1823) on fingerprints and other skin features, *Am. J. Police Sci.* incorporated into *J. Crim. Law and Crimonol.,* XXXI(3), 1940.

Cummins, Harold. The Structure and Development of Skin, *Dermatology in General Medicine,* McGraw-Hill Book, New York, 1971.

David, T.J., A.B. Ajdukiewicz, and A.E. Read. Fingerprint Changes In Coeliac Disease, *Br. Med. J.,* 4, 459, 1970.

Davis, John E. Further Thoughts on Fingerprint Comparisons, *Fingerprint,* July 1955.

Deutscher, D., H. Leonoff, *Identification Evidence,* Carswell Publishing, Calgary, 1991.

De Varigny, Henry. Anthropology — The fingerprints according to M.F. Galton, *Rev. Sci.,* May 1891.

Edzhubov, Leo G. National Standards of Fingerprint Identification, *Fingerprint Whorld,* 153, Oct, 1996.

Evett, I.W.Expert Evidence and Forensic Misconceptions of the Nature of Exact Science, *Science and Justice,* 36(2), 118, 1996.

Evett, I.W., R.L. Williams. A review of the sixteen points fingerprint standard in england and Wales, *J. For. Ident.,* 46(1), 49, 1996.

Federal Bureau of Investigation. *The Science of Fingerprints,* U.S. Department of Justice, 1974.

-----. An Analysis of Standards in Fingerprint Identification, *FBI Law Enforcement Bulletin,* June 1972.

-----. *Fingerprints,* U.S. Government Printing Office, Washington, D.C., 1937.

Feng, Xu, Huang Li, and Guo Renqiang. On the development of dermal papillae and epidermal ridges of human skin, *Acta Zool. Sin.,* 34(3), Nanking, 1988.

Forbes, Anne P. M.D. Fingerprints and Palmprints (dermatoglyphics) and palmar-flexion creases in gonadal dysgenesis, pseudohypoparathyroidism and Klinefelter's syndrome, *N. Eng. J. Med.,* June 1964.

Fraser, F. Clarke Ph.D and James J. Nora M.D. *Dermatoglyphics, Genetics of Man,* 2nd ed.,Lea & Febiger, Philadelphia, 1986.

Galton, Sir Francis RS: *Fingerprints,* Macmillan and Co., New York, 1892.

Gregory, R.L. Eye and Brain, The Psychology of Seeing, *World University Library,* McGraw-Hill, New York and Toronto, 1981.

Grieve, David L.The identification process: attitude and approach, *J. For. Ident.,* 39(5), 211, 1988.

-----. Reflections on Quality Standards — an American Viewpoint, *Fingerprint Whorld,* 110, April 1990.

-----. The identification process — traditions in training, *J. For. Ident.,* 40(4), 195, 1990.

-----. The identification process — the quest for quality, *J. For. Ident.,* 40(3), 109, 1990.

-----. 100 years and counting, *J. For. Ident.,* 42(4), 278, 1992.

-----. Ed., Faulds, faults and forensic fundamentals, *J. For. Ident.,* 44(4), 353, 1994.

-----. Ed., Still keep the passion fresh, *J. For. Ident.,* 44(2), 127, 1994.

-----. Tilting at treadmills, *J. For. Ident.,* 46(2), 144, 1996.

Gupta, Sia Ram. Statistical survery of ridge characteristics, *Int. Police Rev.,* May 1968.

Hale, Alfred R. Morphogenesis of Volar Skin in the Human Fetus, *Am. J. Anat.,* 91(1), 1952.

Harrison, D.E. *Finger-Growth Effects on Auto-Class Searches,* RCMP Pub., 1993.

Hasty, Danny. President's Message, *J. For. Ident.,* 46(4), 459, 1996.

Headrick, A.M. *The Vulnerability of Scientific Evidence,* RCMP Pub.

Heindl, Dr. Robert. Sir Edward Henry, *Arch. Kriminol.,* 88, 1931.

------. Sir William Herschel, *Arch. Kriminol.,* 70, 1918.

Henry, E.R. *Classification and Uses of Fingerprints,* Geo. Zoutledge and Sons, London, 1900.

Hepburn, David. The papillary ridges on the hands and feet of monkeys and men, *Sci. Trans. R. Dublin Soc.,* 5(2), 1895.

Hill, S. Casey. *The Right to Fingerprint,* Unpublished.

Hirsch, W. and J.U. Schweichel. Morphological evidence concerning the problem of skin ridge formation, *J. Ment. Defic. Res.,* 17, 58, 1973.

Holt, Sara B. *The Genetics of Dermal Ridges,* Charles C. Thomas, Springfield, IL, 1968.

-----. The morphogenisis of volar skin, *Dev. Med. Child Neurol.,* 12, 369, 1979.

-----. Polydactyly and brachymetapody in two English families, *J. Med. Genet.,* 12, 355, 1975.

-----. Dermatoglyphics In Mongolism, *Ann. N.y. Acad. Sci.,* 171(2), 602, 1970.

-----. Palmprints and Their Uses in Medical Biology, *Cereb. Palsy Bull.*, 3(4), 333, 1961.

Hough, Walter. Thumb Marks, *Science*, VIII(185), 166.

Huber R.A. The Philosophy of Identification, *RCMP Gazette*, July/August 1972.

-----. Expert Witness, *Criminal Law Quarterly*, 2, 1959-60.

Huberman, Marvin J. Anatomy of a Problem: Proving the Identity of Fingerprints in Limiting Situations, *The Advocate*, 41(2), 1983.

International Association for Identification. Report of the Standardization Committee, 1973.

Interpol Symposium Report of First Meeting. Fingerprinting problems, *Int. Crim. Police Rev.*, Mar 1968.

Jevons, W. Stanley and Ernest Nagel. The Principles of Science — a Treatise on Logic and Scientific Method, Dover Publications, New York, 1958.

Jungbluth, William O. Knuckle print identification, *J. For. Ident.*, 39(6) 375, 1989.

Kikuchi, Syozo. Concerning the Appearance of Linear Dots in Fingerprints, *Fingerprint and Identification*, January 1977.

Kimura, Sumiko and Blanka Schaumann. Embryological development and prevalence of thumb flexion creases, *Anat. Rec.*, 222, 83, 1988.

Kimura, Sumiko, Blanka Schaumann, Chris C. Plato, and Tadashi Kitagawa. Embryological development and prevalence of digital flexion creases, *Anat. Rec.*, 226, 249, 1990.

Kimura, Sumiko and Tadashi Kitagawa. Embryological development of human palmar, plantar, and digital flexion creases, *Anat. Rec.*, 216, 191, 1986.

King, Reg. The Independent Fingerprint Consultant, *Fingerprint Whorld*, 144, October 1996.

Kingston, Charles R. and Paul L. Kirk. Historical development and evaluation of the "12 point rule" in fingerprint identification, *Int. Crim. Police Rev.*, March 1965.

-----. The Use of Statistics in Criminalistics, *J. Crim. Law. Criminol. Police Sci.*, 55, 1964.

Klen, Rudolf Dr. Purkinje — a Man of Science, *Fingerprint*, March 1950.

Kloepfer, H. Warner. *Kloepfer Collection*, Louisiana State University, New Orleans.

Kutz, Larry D. ed. A millstone, not a mile stone, *J. For. Ident.*, 43(1), 1, 1993.

Krush, Anne J., Blanka A. Schaumann, and Hagop Youssoufian. Arachnodactyly and unusual dermatoglyphics: study of a case, *Am. J. Med. Genet.*, 31, 57, Alan R. Liss, New York, 1988.

Lacroix, Brigitte, Marie-Josephe Wolff-Quenot, and Katy Haffen. Early Human Hand Morphology: an Estimation of Fetal Age, *Early Human Development*, Vol. 9, 127, Elsevier, New York, 1984.

Lambourne, Gerald. *The Fingerprint Story*, Harrop, London, 1984.

Laufer, Berthold. The history of the fingerprint system, *Smithson. Inst. Annu. Rep.*, 1912.

-----. Concerning the History of Fingerprints, *Science,* XLV(1169), May 25, 1917.

Lee, Henry C. and R.E. Gaensslen. *Advances in Fingerprint Technology,* Elsevier, New York, 1991.

Loesch, Danuta. The contributions of L.S. Penrose to dermatoglyphics, *J. Ment. Defic. Res.,* 17(1), 1973.

-----. *Quantitative Dermatoglyphics-Classification, Genetics, and Pathology,* Oxford University Press, Great Britain, 1983.

Lohnes, R.C. Infant footprint identification by flexure creases, *Int. For. Symp.,* Quantico, VA, July 7–10, 1987.

Ludy, John B. Congenital absence of Fingerprints, *Trans. Atlantic Dermatol. Conf.,* Philadelphia, March 1943.

MacArthur, J.W. and Ernest McCullough. Apical Dystrophy an Inherited Defect of Hands and Feet, *Human Biology,* 4(2), May 1932.

MacArthur, J.W. Reliability of Dermatoglyphics in Twin Diagnosis, *Human Biology,* 10(1), February 1938.

MacArthur, J.W., and O.T. MacArthur. Finger, palm, and sole prints of monozygotic quadruplets, *J. Hered.,* Washington, D.C., XXVIII(4), April 1937.

Macauley, Roderick. A Crown Prosecution Service Point of View, *Fingerprint Whorld,* 76, April, 1996.

Mairs, G. Tyler. A Study of the Henry Accidentals with an Analysis of the Distinction between Deltas and Triradii, *Fingerprint and Identification,* 25(2), August 1943.

-----. Identification of Individuals by Means of Fingerprints, Palmprints, and Soleprints, *The Scientific Monthly,* October 1918.

-----. Supplement to "Digi-Print" Evolution Chart.

-----. Can Two Identical Ridge Patterns Actually Occur — Either on Different Persons or on the Same Person? *Fingerprint and Identification,* 27(5), November 1945.

Manners, John. Time for Change, *Fingerprint Whorld,* 57, April, 1996.

McDougall, Patrick S. Different Fingerprint Types Provide a Clue to Mentality, *Cummins Collection,* Tulane University, New Orleans.

-----. Expert Asserts Fingerprints Can Be Forged Successfully, *Cummins Collection,* Tulane University, New Orleans.

-----. Dionnes Cause New Problem, *Cummins Collection,* Tulane University, New Orleans.

Mavalwala, Jamshed. Dermatoglyphics: looking forward to the 21st century, *Prog. Dermatog. Res.,* Alan R. Liss, New York, 1982.

McLauglin, Glen H. The Case of Robert James Pitts, *Texas Department of Public Safety,* Austin, 1941.

Meier, Robert J. Anthropological Dermatoglyphics: A Review, *Yearb. Phys. Anthropol.,* 23, 147, 1980.

Midlo, Charles. Form of hand and foot in primates, *Am. J. Phys. Anthropol.*, XIX(3), 1934.

-----. A comparative study of volar epidermal ridge configurations in primates, *La. Acad. Sci.*, IV(1), 136, 1938.

-----. Dermatoglyphics in tupaia lacernata lacernata, *J. Mammal.*, 16(1), 1935.

Midlo, Charles and Harold Cummins. Dermatoglyphics in Eskimos, *Am. J. Phys. Anthropol.*, XVI(1), 1931.

Miller, J.R. Dermatoglyphics, *J. Invest. Dermatol.*, 60, 435, 1973.

-----. Dermal ridge patterns techinique for their study in human fetuses, *J. Pediatr.*, 73, 614, 1968.

Miller, James R. PhD. and Joan Giroux B.Sc. Dermatoglyphics in pediatric practice, *Am. J. Hum. Genet.*, 69, 1966.

Mishoe, David C. Identification of a suspect by skin fragment — comparison of shape, size, and ridge flow, *J. For. Ident.*, 43(3), 234, 1993.

Misumi, Yuko and Toshio Akiyoshi. Scanning electron microscopic strucure of the fingerprint as related to the dermal surface, *Anat. Rec.*, 208:49, 1984.

Moenssens, Andre A. Poroscopy — Identification by Pore Structure, *Fingerprint and Identification,* July 1970.

Moenssens, A. A., F.E. Inbau, and J.E. Starrs. *Scientific Evidence in Criminal Cases,* 3rd ed., Foundation Press, Mineola, NY, 1986, 421.

Montagna, William, Albert M. Kligman, and Kay S. Carlisle. *Atland of Normal Human Skin,* Springer-Verlag, New York, 1992.

Montagna, William, and Paul F. Parakkal. *The Structure and Function of Skin,* Academic Press, Orlando, 1974.

Montgomery, Geoffrey. Seeing with the Brain, *Discover,* December 1988.

Montgomery, Robert B. Sole patterns — a study of the footprints of two thousand individuals, *Anat. Rec.*, 33(2), 1926.

-----. Sole prints of newborn babies, *Am. J. Med. Sci.*, CLXIX(6), 830, 1925.

-----. Sole patterns of twins, *Biol. Bull.*, L(4), 1926.

-----. Classification of footprints, *J. Crim. Law Criminol.*, XVIII(1), 1927.

Moore, Susan J. and Bryce L. Munger, The early ontogeny of the afferent nerves and papillary rides in human digital glabrous skin, *Devel. Brain Res.*, 48, 119, 1989.

Morohunfola, Kehinde A., Terrel E. Jones, and Bryce L. Munger. The differentiation of the skin and its appendages — altered development of papillary ridges following neuralectomy, *Anat. Rec.*, 232, 599, Wiley-Liss, New York, 1992.

-----. The differentiation of the skin and its appendages — normal development of papillary ridge, *Anat. Rec.*, 232, 587, Wiley-Liss, New York, 1992.

Mukherjee, Deba Prasad. A Brief note on use of dermatoglyphics in medical genetics, *Appl. Phys. Anthropol.*, India, 1963.

Mulvihill, John J. The genesis of dermatoglyphics, *J. Pediatr.*, 75(4), 579, 1969.

Myers, Harry J., II. The First Complete and Authentic History of Identification in the United States, *Fingerprint and Identification*, 20(4), October 1938.

-----. Supplemental History of Identification in the United States, *Fingerprint and Identification*, 25(6), December 1942.

-----. A Third History of Identification in the United States, *Fingerprint and Identification*, 29(10), April 1948.

-----. The Henry System Semi-Centennial, *Fingerprint and Identification*, 31(12), June 1950.

-----. Psychic Fingerprints, *Fingerprint and Identification*, 15(13), July 1934.

-----. A Note On Tabor, *Fingerprint and Identification*, 46(10), April 1965.

Ne'urim Declaration. Symposium Report, *J. For. Ident.*, 45(5), 489, 578, 1995.

Newman, H.H. Palmar dermatoglyphics of twins, *Am. J. Phys. Anthropol.*, XIV(3), 1930.

-----. Aspects of twin research, *Sci. Mon.*, LII, 99, 1941.

-----. Methods of diagnosing monozygotic and dizygotic twins, *Biol. Bull.*, LV(4), 1928.

-----. Asymmetry reversal or mirror imaging in identical twins, *Biol. Bull.*, LV(4), 1928.

-----. Differences between conjoined twins, *J. Hered.*, XXII(7), 1931.

-----. The fingerprints of twins, *J. Genet.*, XXIII(3), 1930.

-----. Dermatoglyphics and the problem of handedness, *Am. J. Anat.*, 55(2), 1934.

-----. Palm print patterns in twins, *J. Hered.*, XXII(2), 1931.

Okajima, Michio. Frequency of forks in epidermal ridge minutiae in the fingerprint, *Am. J. Phys. Anthropol.*, 32(1), 1970.

-----. Development of dermal ridges in the fetus, *J. Med. Genet.*, 12, 243, 1975.

-----. Dermal and Epidermal Structures of the Volar Skin, *March of Dimes Birth Defects Foundation*, XV(6), 179, 1979.

-----. A methodological approach to the development of epidermal ridges viewed on the dermal surface of fetuses, *Prog. Dermatog. Res.*, 175, 1982.

O'Hara, Charles E. and James W. Osterberg. *An Introduction to Criminalistics*, Macmillan, New York, 1949.

Ortelle, M. An Evaluation of Infant Footprinting, *Identification News*, 14(7), 4, 1964.

Osterburg, James W. Fingerprint Probability Calculations Based on the Number of Individual Characteristics Present, *Identification News*, October 1974.

-----. An inquiry into the nature of proof, *J. For. Sci.*, 9(4), 1964.

Olsen, Robert D., Sr. *Scott's Fingerprint Mechanics*, Thomas, Springfield, IL, 1978.

-----. Friction ridge characteristics and points of identity — an unresolved dichotomy of terms, *J. For. Ident.*, 41(3), 195, 1991.

Ontario Police College. *The History of Fingerprinting*, Aylmer, Ontario, 1987.

-----. *Fingerprint Identification,* Aylmer, Ontario, 1982.

-----. *Seeing and Perception — the Psychology of Seeing,* Aylmer, Ontario, 1987.

Penrose, L.S. Dermatoglyphics, *Scientific American,* 72, 1969.

Penrose, L.S. and P.T. O'Hara. The development of the epidermal ridges, *J. Med. Genet.,* 10, 201, 1973.

Plato, C., J.L. Cereghino, and F.S. Steinberg. Palmar dermatoglyphics of down's syndrome revisited, *J. Pediatr.,* 7, 111, 1973.

Plato, Chris C. and Wladimir Wertelecki. Changing trends in dermatoglyphic research, *Prog. Dermatog. Res.,* Alan R. Liss, New York, 1982.

Polakowski, Renata R., M. Piacentini, R. Bartlett, L.A. Goldsmith, and A.R. Haake. Apoptosis In Human Skin Development: Morphogenesis, Periderm and Stem Cells, *Dev. Dynam.,* 199, Wiley-Liss, New York, 1994, 199.

Puri, Dewan K. Further thoughts on fingerprinting, *Int. Crim. Police Rev.,* 178, 130, 1967.

-----. Thoughts on fingerprinting, *Int. Crim. Police Rev.,* 160, 225, 1962.

RCMP. *Fingerprint Textbook,* RCMP Pub., 1966.

-----. *Scenes of Crime,* RCMP Pub., 1966.

Rice, Karen Anne. Printing of the underside of the epidermal surface of decomposed fingers, *J. For. Ident.,* 38(3), 98, 1988.

Robinson, Dr. Victor. Johannes Evangelista Purkinje, *Sci. Mon.,* XXXIX(3), 217, 1929.

Saviers, Kathleen D. Friction skin characteristics — a study and comparison of proposed standards, *J. For. Ident.,* 39(3), 157, 1989.

.-----. The reliability of linear measurement methods in friction ridge skin comparisons, *J. For. Ident.,* 39(1), 33, 1989.

Schaumann, Blanka and Milton Alter. *Dermatoglyphics in Medical Disorders,* Springer-Verlag, New York, 1976.

Scientific Sleuthing Review. Fingerprint Identifications Rocked to the Core — Seeing Is Not Observing, 17(2), 7, 1993.

Singh, Parduman. Is This a Contribution to the Science of Fingerprints?, *Identification News,* March, 1975.

Singh R.D. Digital Ridge-Count Variations in Some Castes of India, *Progress in Dermatoglyphic Research,* Alan R. Liss, New York, 1982.

Slatis, Herman M., Mariassa Bat-Miriam Katznelson, and Batsheva Bonne-Tamir, The inheritance of fingerprint patterns, *Am. J. Hum. Genet.,* 28(3), 1976.

Soderman, Harry and John J. O'Connell. *Modern Criminal Investigation,* 5th edition, Funk and Wagnalls, New York, 1962.

Steinwender, Ernst. Dactyloscopic Identification, *Fingerprint and Identification,* 41(10), 1960.

Stevens, Cathy A., John C. Carey, Madhuri Shah, and Grant P. Bagley. Development of human palmar and digital flexion creases, *J. Pediatr.,* 128, July 1988.

Stoney, David A. and John I. Thornton, A systematic study of epidermal ridge minutiae, *J. For. Sci.*, Sept, 1987.

-----. A method for the description of minutia pairs in epidermal ridge patterns, *J. For. Sci.*, October 1986.

-----. A critical analysis of quantitative fingerprint individuality models, *J. For. Sci.*, October 1986.

Svensson, Arne and Otto Wendel. *Crime Scene Investigation*, Elsevier, New York, 1972.

Swensson, O., L. Langb ein, J.R. McMillan, H.P. Stevens, I.M. Leigh, W.H.I. McLean, E.B. Lane, and R.A. Eady, Specialized keratin expression pattern in human ridged skin as an adaptation to high physical stress, *Br. J. Dermatol.*, 139, 767, 1998.

Swensson, O. and R.A.J. Eady, Morphology of the keratin filament network in palm and sole skin: evidence for site-dependent features based on stereological analysis, *Arch. Dermatol. Res.*, 288, 55, 1996.

Temtamy, Samia A. Diagnostic Significance of Dermatoglyphics in Certain Birth Defects, *Prog. Dermatoglyphic Res.*, Alan R. Liss, New York, 1982.

Taylor, Richard A. Flexure Creases — Alternative Method For Infant Footprint Identification, *Identification News*, September 1979.

Thompson, James S. M.D. and Margaret W. Thompson, Ph.D. *Genetics in Medicine*, W.B. Saunders, Philadelphia 1989.

Thornewill, S. The Sixteen-Point Standard — Implications for Training, *Fingerprint Whorld*, April 1996.

Thornton, John I. The one-disssimilarity doctrine in fingerprint identification, *Int. Crim. Police Rev.*, 306, 89, 1977.

Thorwald, Jurgen. *The Century of the Detective*, Harcourt, Brace and World, New York, 1965.

Tiller, C.D. Identification of Fingerprints — How Many Points Are Required?, *RCMP Gazette*, 39(11), 1977.

-----. That's Him But, *Identification Newsletter*, 2(4), 1979.

-----. Are You A Professinal? *Identification Newsletter*, 3(4), 1980.

-----. Identification by Fingerprints — The Real Anatomy, *Advocate*, 41(4), July 1983.

Tsuchihashi, Yasuo. Studies on Personal Identification by Means of Lip Prints, *Forensic Science*, 3, 233, 1974.

Tuthill, Harold. Individualization — Principles and Procedures in Criminalistics, Lightning Powder Co., Salem, Oregon, 1994.

Updegraff, Howard L., Changing of fingerprints, *Am. J. Surg.*, XXVI(3), 533, 1934.

Vanderkolk, John R. Ridgeology — animal muzzle prints and human fingerprints, *J. For. Ident.*, 41(4), 274, 1991.

-----. Class characteristics and could be results, *J. For. Ident.*, 43(2), 119, 1993.

Van der Meulen, Louis J. False fingerprints — a new aspect, *J. Crim. Law Criminol. Police Sci.*, 40(1), 1955.

Verbov, Julian, Dermatoglyphics in congenital absence of phalanges of the right hand, *Clin. Exp. Dermatol.*, 19, 412, 1994.

-----. Hypohidrotic (or anhidrotic) ectodermal dysplasia - an appraisal of diagnostic methods, *Brit. J. Dermatol.*, 83, 341, 1970.

-----. Palmar ridge appearances in normal newborn infants and ridge appearance in relation to eccrine sweating, *Brit. J. Dermatol.*, 93, 645, 1975.

Walker, Norma Ford. The use of dermal configurations in the diagnosis of Mongolism, *Pediatr. Clin. North Am.*, May 1958.

Wentworth B. and H.H. Wilder. *Personal Identification,* 2nd ed., T.G. Cooke, Chicago, 1932.

Werrett, David J. and Joan E. Lygo. *The Role of DNA Profiling in the Courts,* Home Office, London, 1988.

Wertheim, Kasey. An extreme case of fingerprint mutilation, *J. For. Ident.*, 48(4), 466, 1998.

Wertheim, Pat A. Qualifying as an expert fingerprint witness — designing a set of questions to assist in court testimony, *J. For. Ident.*, 40(2), 60, 1990.

-----. Detection of forged and fabricated latent prints — historical review and ethical implications of the falsification of latent fingerprint evidence, *J. For. Ident.*, 44(6), 652, 1994.

-----. Ed. The Ability Equation, *J. For. Ident.*, 46(2), 149, 1996.

Whipple, Inez L. The ventral surface of the mammalian chiridium, *Z. Morphol. Anthropol.*, 7, 261, 1904.

Willis, William W. The expert witness, *J. For. Ident.*, 43(2), 166, 1993.

Wilton, George. *Fingerprints,* Wm Hodge and Co., London, 1938.

Wilton, George Wilton. *Fingerprints: Home Office and Henry Faulds,* Tantallon Press, North Berwick, Scotland, 1960.

Xiang-Xin, Zhao, Liu Chun-Ge. The historical application of hand prints in chinese litigation, *J. For. Ident.*, 38(6), 277, 1988.

Xu, Feng, Huang, Li, and Guo Renqiang. On the development of dermal papillae and epidermal ridges of human skin, *Acta Zool. Sin.*, 34(3), 1988.

Glossary

Aberrant	Deviating from what is regular, normal, or right.
AFIS	Automatic Fingerprint Identification System.
Aggregate	Total amount; a mass of separate things joined together.
Analysis	Separate anything into its parts; to find out what a thing is made of.
Anatomical	Connected with the practice or study of anatomy.
Anatomical Aspects	The correlation between the anatomical capability of depositing a latent print and the location of the latent print on an item.
Anatomy	The science of the structure of plants and animals.
Anastomosis	Interlacing of veins, nerves, or canals of animal bodies.
Ancestral	From our ancestors.
Anlage (-gen *pl.*)	The first clustering cells constituting the beginning traces of an organ.
Anterior	Before or in front of.
Anthropoids	Man-like in shape only.
Anthropological	Having to do with anthropology.
Anthropology	The science of man.
Anthropometry	Dealing with measurement of the human body.
Apical	At the apex; situated at the tip of a conical figure; at the tip of a finger.
Apocrine Gland	Sweat gland opening into the hair follicle.

Appendages   Any one of various external attached parts, i.e., arms, legs, tails, fins.

Archaeology   The scientific study of the people, customs, and life of ancient times.

Basal   Pertaining to the base.

Basal Lamina   Basement lamina or membrane.

Bertillonage   Bertillon's method of anthropometry.

Bifurcate   Divide into two branches.

Biological   Of plant and animal life.

Branchings   Friction ridge bifurcation; divergence of a friction ridge path.

Capillary   Minute blood vessel; capillaries connect the smallest arteries and veins.

Chiridia   Hands and feet.

Chiridium   Hand or foot.

Clarity   Clearness, i.e., how well friction skin ridge detail is recorded in a print.

Clone   Any group of individuals produced asexually from a single ancestor; duplicate.

Class   Characteristics used to put things in groups or classes;
  Characteristics   nonspecific details.

Classify   To arrange in groups or classes.

Clones   Identical twins from the same zygote having identical DNA.

Collagen   A fibrous insoluble protein found in connective tissue.

Columnar Cells   Shaped like a column.

Comparison   The act of comparing or finding likenesses or differences.

Concavity   Concave condition or quality.

Concentrically   Having the same center.

Concomitant   Being together; existing or occurring together.

Convexity   A convex quality or condition.

Corium	Dermis; often referred to as the true skin.
Cornified	Changed into horny tissue.
C.R. Length	Crown-rump length; distance from top of head to base of spine.
Cuboidal Cells	Shaped like a cube.
Cuneiform	Wedge-shaped characters used in ancient Babylonian writing.
Cutaneous	Pertaining to the skin; dermal.
-cyte	Suffix denoting cell.
Cyto-, Cyt-	Prefix denoting cell.
Defined Pattern	Pattern used in classification; has a definition.
Delta	Classification term for triradius.
Deposition Pressure	The amount of downward pressure during the deposition of a print.
Dermal	Relative to the skin or derma.
Dermatoglyphics	Study of the surface markings of the skin; friction ridges.
Dermis	The layer of skin under the epidermis; the true skin.
Desmosome	A small thickening that is an intercellular bridge or joining.
Desquamate	To shed or slough off surface cells.
Development Medium	The substance used to develop friction ridge prints, i.e., powder.
Differential Growth	Develops at random without plan.
Differentiation	Becoming different, i.e., the cells of an embryo differentiate into organs and parts as it grows; specific friction ridge patterns become unique.
Digitigrade	Walking on the toes and not on the heel.
Dissociated Ridges	An area of ridge units that did not form into friction ridges.
Distal	Away from the center or point of origin.
Doctrine	Belief, what is taught as a group's belief.

Down's Syndrome	A genetic disease that results from an extra Number 21 chromosome.
Dysplasia	Ridge units that did not form friction ridges due to a genetic cause.
Dizygotic	Development from two fertilized zygotes.
Eccrine Gland	A sweat gland that opens on all surfaces of the skin.
Eczema	Inflamation of the skin that causes scaly patches and pimples.
Elliptical	An oval having both ends alike, shaped like an ellipse.
Embryology	A branch of biology that deals with the formation and development of embryos.
Embryonic	Of the embryo.
Eminence	A prominence, projection, or elevation.
Empirical	Relating to or based upon direct experience or observation.
Epidermis	Cuticle or outer layer of the skin.
Epithelium	The layer of cells forming the epidermis of the skin.
Epitome	A typical example or representation.
Etching	Engraving on metal, glass, or wood.
Evolution	Any process of formation or growth.
Expert	Person with much skill who knows a great deal about some special thing; has an in-depth understanding of a subject.
Fetus	An embryo during latter stages of development in the womb, after three months.
Fiber	Thread-like or film-like element, such as a nerve fiber.
First Level Detail	General overall pattern shape, i.e., circular, looping, arching, or straight.
Fraternal Twins	Dizygotic twins; produced from more than one ovum.
Friction Skin	Corrugated skin on the volar areas that enhances friction of the surface.
Granule	A small grain-like body; a minute mass in a cell that has outline but no apparent structure.
Genetics	Having to do with origin and natural growth or the genes.

Gestation	The act or process of having young developing in the uterus; the period of pregnancy.
Hallux	Big toe.
Heterogeneous	Of unlike natures or composed of unlike substances.
Histology	A branch of biology dealing with the microscopic structure of tissues.
Homogeneous	Uniform in structure or composed of like substances.
Hypothenar	Ulnar side of the palm between the little finger and wrist.
Hypertrophy	Enlargement.
Identical Twins	Twins developed from a single egg; monozygotic.
Identification	The act or process of identifying; prove to be the same.
Idiosyncrasy	A personal peculiarity as behavior or opinion.
Imbricated	Arranged in a regular pattern with overlapping edges like a shingled roof.
Incipient	Beginning; coming into existence; immature.
Individualization	The state of being individualized.
Individualize	Differentiate from other individuals; distinctive.
In situ	In position or localized.
Integument	A covering, i.e., the skin.
Integumentary System	The skin and appendages, including hair and nails.
Interdigital	Between the digits; an area at the base of the digits.
Interstitial	Lying between.
Intrauterine	Within the uterus.
Intrinsic	Belonging to a thing by its nature.
Islands	Friction ridges of varying lengths.
Juxtaposition	Put close together; side by side.
Keratin	An extremely tough protein substance in hair, nails, and horny tissue.
Keynote	Main idea, guiding principle.

Lamellar	Arranged in plates or scales.
Lamina	A thin, flat layer or membrane.
Lipids	Fats or fat-like substances that are insoluble in water.
Lymph	An alkaline fluid found in the lymphatic vessels.
Mammalian	Of or belonging to the mammals.
Manufactured	Made by hand or machine.
Matrix	The formative part of a fingerprint; the substance that is actually deposited by the finger and eventually developed, i.e., sweat, foreign material, sebaceous oils, blood, etc.
Meissner Corpuscles	Skin nerves that respond to pressure, i.e., sense of touch.
Melanin	Pigment that gives color to the hair and skin.
Methodology	A system of methods or procedures used in any field.
Minutiae	Small details.
Mitosis	Type of cell division.
Mitotic	Of cell division.
Monozygotic	Produced by the splitting of a single fertilized ovum.
Morphology	Science of structure and form without regard to function.
Morphogenesis	The structural changes in the evolution and development of an organism.
Mosaic	Something made of several small pieces.
Nascent	Just born; incipient or beginning; immature.
Neural	Pertaining to nerves or connected with the nervous system.
Neurology	Study of the nervous system and its diseases.
Nonvascular	Does not contain vessels that carry blood, lymph, or other fluids.
Nucleus	The vital body in the protoplasm of a cell.
Objective	Something real and observable.
Opposability	Capable of being opposed, i.e., the thumb and fingers when grasping.

Os calcis	A bone in the foot.
Osmosis	The passage of a solvent through a semipermeable membrane.
Overall Pattern	Overall pattern shape used during identification; first level detail.
Palmar	Concerning the palm of the hand.
Papilla	A small nipple-like protuberance or elevation.
Papillae	Plural of papilla.
Pedagogy	The act or practice of teaching; explaining.
Pentadactylous	Having five fingers on each limb.
Peripheral	Having to do with; situated in or forming an outside edge.
Persistent	Having lasting qualities; remaining the same; nonchanging.
Pervading	Spreading through every part.
Petroglyph	Rock carving.
Phalangeal	Of the bones in the fingers and toes.
Phalanx	Any bone in the fingers or toes.
Philosophy	The principles of a particular subject or field.
Phylogenetic	History of the genes of a species.
Plantar	Concerning the sole of the foot.
Plethora	Superabundance.
Points	(Fingerprints) Ridge characteristics.
Posterior	Opposed to anterior; toward the back; dorsal.
Prehension	The act of grasping.
Pressure Distortion	Lateral pressure during deposition of a fingerprint.
Primary Ridges	Ridges on the bottom of the epidermis under the surface friction ridges; the root system of the surface ridges.
Primates	Any of the highest order of mammals; human beings, apes, monkeys, and lemurs.

Primordium	The first cells in the early stages of the development of an organ.
Propagate	To cause to multiply by natural reproduction.
Prosimians	A subgroup of early primates, i.e., lemurs.
Postembryonic	Period following the embryonic stage of life or growth.
Proximal	Nearest the central portion of the body or point of origin.
Qualitative	Concerned with quality or fundamental form and construction.
Quandary	A state of hesitation, uncertainty, or a predicament.
Quantitative	Concerned with quantity or quantities.
Rarity	Fewness or scarcity of an item, thing, or shape.
Red Flags	Danger signs, common in latent fingerprints, that may indicate a distortion in the ridge path.
Regress	To go back or move in a backward direction.
Ridge Unit	Small section of a friction ridge containing one pore.
Ridgeology	The study of the uniqueness of the friction skin and its use for personal identification.
Rhomboid	A parallelogram with equal opposite sides, unequal adjacent sides, and oblique angles.
Rugae	Wrinkle, fold, or ridge.
Sebaceous Gland	Oil-secreting gland of the skin, most of which open into hair follicles.
Sebum	A fatty secretion of the sebaceous glands.
Second Level Detail	Ridge path, major ridge path deviations, and paths caused by damage such as scars.
Secondary Ridges	Ridges on the bottom of the epidermis under the surface furrows.
SEM	Scanning electron microscope.
Simian Crease	Single crease that crosses the palm in place of the distal and proximal creases.
Spacial	Having to do with space.

Specific Pattern	Pattern or path of the friction ridges used during identification; second level detail.
Squamous	Scale-like.
Stratum	A layer.
Subcutaneous	Beneath or introduced beneath the skin.
Subjective	Influenced by a person's knowledge, state of mind, or ability.
Substrate	The surface upon which a latent fingerprint is deposited or placed.
Synonymous	Having the same or nearly the same meaning.
Tactile	Having to do with the sense of touch.
Tangentially	Having the nature of a tangent; touching the surface in one spot.
Technician	A person skilled in the details of a subject or task, especially a mechanical one.
Thenar	Area of the palm beside the thumb.
Trabeculae	A structure in an animal or plant similar to a beam or a bar.
Third Level Detail	Ridge shape, relative pore location, and some accidental details.
Triradius	Area on the friction ridges where three ridge systems meet.
Topology	Study of the details of the surface and arrangements of parts.
Typical Arrangement	Usual placement.
Unique	Having no equal; one.
Unique Characteristics	Characteristics used to individualize; specific details.
Uniqueness	Very uncommon, unusual, atypical, or remarkable; a degree of distinguishing distinctiveness.
Vein	Vessel carrying dark red blood to the heart, except for the pulmonary vein.

Ventral	The front.
Verification	Proof; confirmation of a process.
Vestiges	Erratic local disarrangements of ridges not conforming to surrounding ridge formations.
Volar	To do with the palms of the hands or the soles of the feet.
White Lines	Fold in the friction skin that appear in prints as white lines.
Zygote	A fertile egg.

Index

a

Absent matrix, 119
Accessory distal transverse crease, 179, 182
Accidental characteristics, 98, 99
A.C.E.V. formula, 196
AFIS search, 115, 137
Amino acids, 121
Anatomy, 8, 172
Anthropometry, 26, 34

b

Basal cell layer, ability of to proliferate, 57
Belper Committee, 33
Bertillon, Alphonse, 26
Bertillonage, 26, 28, 29
Bertillon Signaletic System, 36
Bewick, Thomas, 20
Bidloo, Govard, 39
Bifurcation, 82, 139
Biology, 172
Birth defects, 52
Blind search, 191
Blood stamping, 18
Blood vessel-nerve pairs, 81
Brain
    ability of to reason, 105
    functioning of human, 104
    identification process inherent to, 173
    natural ability of human, 106
    quantitative-qualitative analysis process
        of, 145
    stimulus to, 143
Branchings, 54, 55
Break-and-enter, 129

British Association for the Advancement of
    Science, 33
Burglary, 130
Burial chamber, 12

c

Catalyst, 120
Chatterjee, Salil Kumar, 160
Check-off sheet, 113
Chief Constable Council, 7
Chinese clay finger seal, 16
Chinese Deed of Hand mark, 17
Chinese hand prints, 15
Cigarette package, latent prints on, 136
Clarity, 93, 131, 158, 167
    aspects of, 93
    definition of, 87
    factor, 3
    role of in identification, 145
    understanding of, 171
Classification methods, in South American
    countries, 31
Clay
    fingerprint trademarks in, 14
    finger seal, Chinese, 16
Cloud-watching, 106
Cluster identifications, 134
Connecticut State Police Laboratory, 201
Consultation, 148
Contract disputes, 22
Corrosive matrix, 119
Crease
    genetic influences of parents on, 177
    paths, major flexion, 186

systems, major, 185
Crime officer, evidence collected by, 5
Crime scene(s)
    fingerprints, powder fill-in, 154
    palm prints found at, 200
    photographs, 113
Criminals
    data bank on, 27
    distinguishing, 27
    fingerprinting, 28
Crossover ridges, 124
Cummins, Harold, 51
Cyanoacrylate, 93, 122

d

Darwin, Charles, 25
Deed of Hand mark, 15, 17
Degrees of rarity, 95
Degrees of uniqueness, 96
Deposition pressure(s), 123, 126, 131, 167
    differing, 124
    distortion, 109
    extreme, 123
    pressure distortion vs., 125
Dermal papillae, 54, 70
Dermatoglyphics, 43, 79, 172
Dermis, 70
Desmosome, 68, 69, 91
Development medium, 120, 167, 175
Differential growth, 57, 90
Digit determination, 129
Dirty substrates, 116
Disease, effects of, 72
Distal transverse crease, path of, 181
Dolmen, 12
Double tap, 114, 170
Down's syndrome, 79
Drinking vessels, form of distortion found
    on, 170
Drug bag, latent print on, 115
Dysplasia, 83, 84

e

East Indian monkey, 48
Eczema, 83
Edgeoscopy, see Poroscopy and edgeoscopy
Elimination, 146

E lines, 179, 182
Embryology, 8, 172, 180
Enclosure, 139
Epidermal cells, 68
Epidermal ridges, 38
    definitive character of, 52
    primary, 69
    secondary, 70
Epidermic wart, 57
Epidermis, 74
Exemplar print(s), 107, 166
    photographic enlargements of, 156
    ridge paths of, 169
Extreme deposition pressure, 123
Eye-brain combination, shortcomings of, 87

f

False identification, 148
False impersonation, 22
Faulds, Dr. Henry, 24, 25
Feline embryo, 47
Ferrier, John Kenneth, 36
Fetus, palmar grasping commenced by, 181
Field mouse, sketch of forefoot of, 45
Fight or flight scenario, 65
Fill-in, 155
Finger(s)
    creases, 179, 181, 186
    friction skin on, 62
    histologic sections of, 60
Fingerprint(s)
    analysis of unknown, 165
    bureau, latent prints submitted to, 112,
        113
    classification system, 30
    collection
        filing of, 33
        search, 129
    first murders solved by, 31
    glass, 137
    identification, 28
        pioneer of, 190
        reference, 17
    landmark court case, 37
    latent, 166
    lifters, 117
    matrix, 167
    oldest to date, 15
    in pottery, 14

powder, 121
stamp, carved in wood, 20
texts, 154
trademarks, in clay, 14
Fingerprinting
Chinese plan of, 28
experiments with, 32
in North America, 1877-1900, 34
Fingerprint Society, 194
First level detail, 95, 137
Flexible substrates, 114, 115
Flexion crease(s), 73, 189
comparison, 190
evidence, presented in court, 197
indent, 198
main groups of, 178
most prevalent, 192
Flexure lines, congenital, 188
Forensic identification specialists, 101, 102, 103
Forensic science, historical aspect of, 11
Foster, Edward, 36
Friction ridge(s), 62, 183, 196
aberrant formation of, 79, 83
anatomical formation of, 50
breadth, 63
clusters, 134
comparison, 106, 136, 161
configuration, uniqueness of, 82
cross section of, 71
detail, clarity and, 94
development, evolutionary process of, 47
differential growth of, 53
evaluation, 144
evolutionary process of, 44
flow of, 143
formation, disjointed, 100
growth process of, 85
identification, see also Friction ridge identification, history of
doctrine, 1
experts, observations of, 60
first premises of, 89
methodology of, 108
philosophy, 97, 173
pioneers of, 38
science, 6, 20, 149, 203
second premise of, 90
specialists, 61

imbrication, 67
immutability, 73
incipient, 66
individuality, early knowledge of, 19
pattern(s)
formation, 75
overall, 67
primate, 49
uniqueness of, 91
print(s)
clarity of, 3
matrix of, 118
photographing, 111
probability identifications of, 147
uniqueness of, 21
science, 151
substructure, 69
Friction ridge analysis report, 165–170
analysis of unknown fingerprint, 165–167
clarity, 167
deposition pressure, 167
development medium, 167
matrix particulars, 166–167
pressure distortion, 167
substrate distortion, 165–166
comparison of unknown to known, 168–169
area of slippage, 169
amount of slippage, 169
furrows, 168
major ridge path deviations, 168
ridge path, 168
sequence, 168–169
evaluation, 169–170
Friction ridge identification, history of, 11–60
early pioneers, 20–34
Alphonse Bertillon, 26–28
anthropometry in North America, 1897-1898, 34
Dr. Henry Faulds, 24–26
Dr. J.C.A. Mayer, 24
Juan Vucetich, 30
Rojas murders, 30–32
Sir Edward Henry, 32–34
Sir Francis Galton, 28–29
Sir William J. Herschel, 21–24
Thomas Bewick, 20

Thomas Taylor, 26
Troup Committee, 29–30
fingerprinting in North America, 1877-
    1900, 34–38
Edward Foster, 36–37
fingerprinting in Canada, 36
Gilbert Thompson, 35
I. West Taber, 35
Mark Twain, 35
New York State, 35
primitive knowledge, 11–19
Chinese clay finger seals, 15
Chinese hand prints, 15
Deed of Hand Mark, 15–17
early knowledge of friction ridge
    individuality, 19
fingerprint identification reference,
    17
fingerprint trademarks in clay,
    14–15
identification methods, 17
Japanese customs adopted from
    China, 17–19
Kejimkujik Lake petroglyph, 11–12
L'ille de Gavrinis stone carvings,
    12–13
Middle East clay pottery, 13–14
scientific researchers, 38–60
Alfred Hale, 53–56
Arthur Kollmann, 41
David Hepburn, 42–43
Govard Bidloo, 39
Harold Cummins, 51–53
Harris Hawthorne Wilder, 49–51
H. Klaatsch, 42
Inez Whipple, 43–49
J.C.A. Mayer, 40
Johannes Evangelista Purkinje,
    40–41
L. Reh, 42
Marcello Malphighi, 40
Nehemiah Grew, 38–39
Friction ridge medium, 61–85
friction skin histology, 67–73
dermal papillae, 70–71
dermis, 70
effects of injury or disease, 72
epidermal cells, 68–69
epidermis, 67
flexion creases, 73

friction ridge immutability, 73.
generating layer, 68
primary epidermal ridges, 69
secondary epidermal ridges, 70
growth of friction skin, 74–85
aberrant formation of friction
    ridges, 83–85
blood vessel-nerve pairs, 81–82
epidermis, 74
localized pattern configuration,
    76–77
localized pattern trend, 78–79
major ridge path deviations, 82
overall pattern flow, 75–76
primary ridges, 79
secondary ridges, 80–81
uniqueness of friction ridge
    configuration, 82–83
volar pads, 74–75
structure of friction skin, 61–67
friction ridge breadth, 63–64
friction ridge imbrication, 67
friction ridges, 62–63
incipient friction ridges, 66–67
overall friction ridge pattern, 67
ridge units and pores, 64–65
specific ridge path, 65–66
Friction skin, 93
damage, 97
embryonic studies of, 89
flexibility of, 126
formation, 88
growth of, 74
histology, 67
infrastructure, 63
physical trauma to, 99
sketch of, 41
structure of, 61, 187
three-dimensional aspects of, 171
Frostbite, 83

g

Galton, Sir Francis, 27, 28
Galton details, 82
Generating layer, 68
Genetics, 8, 43
Glossary, 217–226
Grew, Nehemiah, 38
Guillard, Archille, 26

h

Hair, 62
Hale, Alfred, 53
Hale's islands, 90, 138
Hammurabi, references dating from rule of,
    15
Hand
    areas of human, 51
    average ridge breadth of, 64
    external shape of, 59
    formation, 183
Heavy touch, 123
Henry, Sir Edward Richard, 32
Hepburn, David, 42
Heredity, influence of on similarity of major
    flexion crease paths, 185
Herschel, Sir William, 18, 21, 190
Hooghly Letter, 22, 25
Human species, evolutionary process of, 44
Hybrid doctrines, 145
Hypothenar crease, 180, 182

i

I.A.I., see International Association for
    Identification
Identification
    false, 148
    medium, palmar flexion crease as, 177
    philosophy, 8, 149
    specialist, 4, 100, 147
    verification, 165
Identification process, 87–148
    clarity and levels of friction ridge detail,
        94–95
    first level detail, 95
    first premises of friction ridge
        identification, 89–90
    friction ridge analysis, 109–136
        anatomical aspects, 129–131
        clarity, 131
        cluster identifications, 134–135
        deposition pressure, 123–125
        development media, 120–122
        intrinsic ridge formations, 133–134
        matrix particulars, 118–120
        pressure distortion, 125–126
        ridge path configuration, 131–133
        substrate distortion, 114–118

    friction ridge comparison, 136–144
        first level detail, 137–138
        second level detail, 138–143
        third level details, 143–144
    friction ridge evaluation, 144–148
        elimination, 146
        individualization, 146–147
        insufficient uniqueness to
            individualize, 147–148
    human sight, 103–108
    methodology of friction ridge
        identification, 108–109
    philosophy of friction ridge
        identification, 97–103
        friction ridge formations, 97–99
        having sufficient uniqueness,
            100–102
        how much is enough, 103
        individualization, 103
        sequence, 99–100
    premises of friction ridge identification,
        87–89
    second level detail, 95–96
    second premise of friction ridge
        identification, 90–91
    summary of first premise, 90
    summary of second premise, 91
    summary of third premise, 92
    third level detail, 96
    third premise of friction ridge
        identification, 91–92
    two aspects of clarity, 93–94
    verification, 148
Identification Standardization Committee,
    203
Imbrication, 67
Incipient ridge, immature, 58
Index print, 134
Individualization, 146
Injury(ies)
    deep, 72
    effects of, 72
Intelligence gathering process, 173
International Association of Chiefs of Police,
    34, 36
International Association for Identification
    (I.A.I.), 51, 148
International Health Exhibition, 28
Interpapillary capillary networks, 81
Intrinsic ridge formations, 109

Iodine fumes, 121, 122

j

Japanese customs, adopted from China, 17
Japanese Domestic Laws, 19
Jennings, Thomas, 37

k

Katsurakwawa, Churyo, 19
Kejimkujik Lake petroglyph, 11–12
Keretin development, 80
Kia Kung-Yen, 17
Klaatsch, H., 42
Kollmann, Arthur, 41
Konai
    contract, 21
    palm print of, 22

l

Latent print(s), 166
    analysis of, 196
    on cigarette package, 136
    on drug bag, 115
    furrows in core area of, 168
    photograph showing, 111, 112
    treated with cyanoacrylate, 122
Legal counsel, 4
Lens/mirror-type comparators, 110
Light touch, 123
L'ille de Gacrinis stone carvings, 12–13
Locard, Dr. Edmond, 150, 151
Longitudinal creases, 179

m

Major Creases, 73
Malphigi, Marcello, 40
Mammalian walking pads, primary, 47
Matrix distortion, 109, 175
Mayer, Dr. J.C.A., 24, 40
Medium touch, 123
Meissner corpuscles, 71
Metropolitan Police Palm Collection, 193
Middle East clay pottery, 13–14
Minakata, Kamagusu, 18
Minor Creases, 73
Minor Flexion Creases, 179

Mud-type matrix, 119

n

National Bureau of Criminal Investigation, 34
Natural identification process, 1
Necker cube, 104
Neolithic carving, 13
New Scotland Yard, 192, 194
New York City Civil Service Commission, 35
Ninhydrin, 121
Number of points philosophy, 2

o

Orient
    friction ridge identification originating in, 11
    previous uses of fingerprints in, 29
Overlaps, 140

p

Paint/blood matrix, 119
Palm print(s), 55, 114, 159, 160, 188
    found at crime scenes, 200
    inked suspect print for, 195
    of Konai, 22
    on rear view mirror, 195
    twin, 184
Palmar flexion crease identification, 177–202, 203
    analysis, 196
    chronology, 182–183
    comparison, 196
    embryology, 180–182
    evaluation, 196–197
    flexion crease comparison, 190–191
    flexion crease evidence presented in court, 197
    genetics and uniqueness, 183–186
    methodology of palmar flexion crease identification, 196
    nomenclature, 178–180
    palmar flexion crease identification process, 194
    persistency, 186–190
    philosophy of palmar flexion crease identification, 194–196

process, 194
St. John's Newfoundland, 199–200
Sulphur Springs, Texas, 197–198
verification, 197
Palmar topography, 178
Papillary ridges, 71
Pattern
    configuration, localized, 76
    flow, overall, 75
    trend, localized, 78
Permanent flexion creases, formation of, 191
Persistency comparison sheets, 193
Personal identification media, 178
Platform ridges, flattening of, 169
Points of comparison, 3
Police
    community, friction ridge identification
        science under control of, 4
    organizations, scientific training of, 5
Pore(s)
    ducts, 58, 64
    frequency of, 153
    glands, 55
    location
        comparison of relative, 155
        value of relative, 150
    opening, 65
    structure, 133
Poroscopy and edgeoscopy, 149–163
    edgeoscopy, 158–163
    poroscopy, 9, 149–158, 203
        comparison of relative pore
            location, 155–158
        Dr. Edmond Locard, 150–155
Pottery fingerprints in, 14
Pressure distortion, 109, 125, 131, 167, 189
Primary ridges, 54, 79, 80
Primate(s)
    friction ridge patterns, 49
    line of development leading to, 46
Prints, falling into gray area, 144
Procedural flaws, 1
Prosimians, evolution of, 45
Purkinje, Johannes Evangelista, 40, 41

q

Quantitative-qualitative analysis
    first step toward, 1–7
    philosophy, 158

r

RCMP, see Royal Canadian Mounted Police
Reasoning, subjective, 105
Red flags, 114, 128
Reh, L., 42
Relative pore locations, 155, 156
Ridge
    breaks, 132
    characteristics, 82, 139, 168
        identification philosophy, 144
        poorly-recorded, 142
    ending, 139
    formation(s)
        indicators, 137
        intrinsic, 133
        in sequence, 135
    length, 92, 141
    path(s)
        configuration, 109, 131
        deviation, 82, 94, 132, 168
        unique, 92
    position of pore on, 152
    shapes, 158
    unit(s), 64, 65, 83
        alignment, 133
        sketch of, 50
    width, fluctuations in, 92
Ridgeology
    formula, 171–175
    landmark survey in, 43
    revolution, 7–9
Rojas murders, 30
Rolled impression, 162
Royal Canadian Mounted Police (RCMP),
    37
Royal Newfoundland Constabulary, 199, 200

s

Scar(s)
    path of, 101
    permanent, 98
    ridge unit caused by, 143
Scotland Yard, 29
Sebaceous glands, 62
Secondary creases, 180
Secondary epidermal ridges, 70
Secondary ridges, 54, 80

Second level detail, 95, 96, 138

SEM observations, 59

Short ridges, 82, 139

Sight
    human, 108
    identification process synonymous with, 103

Signature, 120

Skin folds, 188, 192

Slippage, area of, 169

Smooth skin, 62

Soft substrates, 117

Standardization Committee, 2, 3, 6, 7

Static threshold philosophy, 145

Stratum Malpighii, 67

Stress lines, 57

Subjective reasoning, 105

Substrate
    distortion, 109, 114, 165
    shape, 115

Sweat
    glands, 56, 62, 65
    pores, 38, 152, 154
    -sebaceous matrix, 118

t

Taber, I West, 35

Taylor, Thomas, 26

Thenar crease, path of, 181

Thinking process, stimuli affecting, 107

Third level details, 96, 143

Thompson, Gilbert, 35

Threshold philosophy, 2

Tip Sahib, 21

Trifurcation, 140

Tripartite rule, 156, 157

Troup Committee, 29

True skin, 70

Twain, Mark, 35

Twin palm prints, 184

Typical arrangement, 46

u

Unique characteristics, 99

v

Verification, 174

Volar pad(s), 52, 74
    correlation between friction ridge patterns and shape of, 89
    disruption of development of, 78
    genetic relationship of, 78
    growth, 183
    in normal fetuses, 75
    physiology, 47
    tension and pressure created by, 77

Volar skin, morphogenesis of, 56

Vucetich, Juan, 30

w

Wart, 72

Wet prints, 118, 166

Whipple, Inez, 43

Whipple survey, 46

White lines, 73, 188

Whorl-type patterns, formation of, 77

Wilder, Harris Hawthorne, 49